Praise for *Transoceanic Lights*

"Tolstoy begins *Anna Karenina* with 'Happy families are all alike; every unhappy family is unhappy in its own way.' Fast forward 100 years to the humble origins of an immigrant Chinese family...and you'll be in the territory of *Transoceanic Lights*. Li has written an intense work that provides a rarely seen aspect of the Asian-American experience. Li infuses his narrator with a sophisticated voice balanced by childhood fears and whimsies. [The novel] moves through time effortlessly, painting vivid flashbacks to poignant moments of a life left behind...juxtaposed with a present that is rife with discontent and chaotic relationships. *Transoceanic Lights* is a singular contribution to the immigrant narrative and a necessary new voice."

—*SAMPAN*

"A strong autobiographical flavor."

—*Kirkus*

"Labels do not adequately describe the high quality of writing, subtlety of construction, or fresh look at the subject. The writing is remarkable for its lack of self-pity. The style is fluent. It surprises, in the way a reader likes to be surprised, takes chances, and fits the story the way a seasoned novelist suits the word to the action. The shifting points of view move the story effectively. The sense of place is marvelous. I doubt there will be many better published this year. Let me be the first to welcome a serious new talent to the room."

—Boston Area Small Press and Poetry Scene

"Li creates tension with such conflicting imagery [and] examines the heart of the American experiment from an outsider's point of view. The rapidly deteriorating inter-family relationship mirrors the evermore fragile relationship between the narrator's iron-willed mother and shady father. Li's writing style is dense...great detail given to mundane objects and sights...this rush of imagery and imagination mimics the onslaught and confusion of a child in a strange land."

—The Broadkill Review

"Ma's childbirth scene is a killer. The full account...should be enough to make any of us swear off having sex, much less fabricating babies, forever and forever, amen."

—The Review of Arts, Literature, Philosophy and the Humanities

"When Li focuses his narrative on the several tensions that threaten to tear the narrator's family apart, the novel makes for absorbing reading. Li also has an admirable linguistic command, an ability to spin out lovely descriptions and fresh, memorable metaphors. The precision and beauty of this description work on both sensory and emotional levels. Readers who stay the course...will be rewarded with a tender and persuasive portrait of Chinese-American immigration in the post-Mao era."

—*Pleiades Book Review*

"What Li accomplishes, as Lahiri and others have done before, is to put in stark relief the continuing social, emotional, and psychological consequences of the Faustian bargain struck when making the decision to leave one's country to come to another. Li is not afraid to say that such bargains are not only fraught with difficulty, but also sometimes doomed to failure. Nor is any failure the result of some simplified notion of a lack of will to succeed (a quintessentially Western notion). Sometimes, the cognitive dissonance is simply too great to overcome – but, sometimes, the details are simply in the journey."

—*Portland Book Review*

TRANSOCEANIC LIGHTS

A Novel

S. Li

Harvard Square Editions
www.harvardsquareeditions.org
New York
2015

Transoceanic Lights, S. Li

Copyright © 2014 by S. Li

ISBN 978-1-941861-33-2
Printed in the United States of America

Cover photograph © Moe Chen

Published in the United States by
Harvard Square Editions
www.harvardsquareeditions.org

THE CLOUDS BELOW drifted in the wind and swelled into rain-laden anvils the size of mountains before dispersing into wisps of cobweb.

My mother was sitting upright, looking straight at the underside of the tray table with an intensity in her eyes that seemed in search of some detail, some microscopic truth camouflaged on that nondescript plastic surface. She squinted at the collage of her thoughts projected upon that gray slab, scrutinizing as if through a faded window all the burdens of her heart, all that she would vent nightly through the telephone into a distant ear. For the duration of that flight, she could not find comfort in her seat, could not conform to its cramped angles, so she compromised, the first of many, by locking her body into a posture devoid of movement such that she appeared not merely inert but paralyzed, as if suspended in time.

Beside her, my father was slumped in slight recline with the stillness of avid daydreamers. The overhead light shone on the apex of his nose and on the arrowed point of his upper lip; his face, with its layer of ashen stubble, appeared deceptively calm. The rest of his body was cloaked in shadow, his head appeared to be floating above the collar of his shirt, and his hair, once parted to the side, was now messily matted, having lost its sheen of mousse applied many hours ago.

I was there in the window seat next to them, entirely unaware of the turbulence of their thoughts. I lifted the shade to look down at the clouds passing at the pace of snails and thought to myself that I could walk faster. We were confined inside that aerial juggernaut for what felt like months, crammed amidst rows of seats between which attendants clad in ocean blue vests served compartmented meals from rectangular carts on yo-yo wheels. For several nights in a row before boarding that flight, I had lain in bed wondering what it would be like to fly—how my heart would seize as on the first slope of a roller coaster, how the wind would rush against my face, how the passengers would be flung about—yet I did not imagine this, no, not so slow, not so still.

Ma and Ba stood in the aisle on occasion for me to sprawl across all three seats and doze off. In those semiconscious states between sleeping and waking, I sailed through a kaleidoscope of memories. I thought back to what had been our home: the second floor unit of an ailing tenement now thousands of miles away with its sagging wooden steps and termite-infested walls, a space once filled with our furniture now abandoned for the dust to settle and the vermin to feast and copulate without fear of human disturbance. I chuckled at the memory of my enraged mother hurling the cat from our balcony after it urinated on our bed; it scampered back up, limbs intact, not a single bruise or cut, and meowed to be let back in. I thought back to Grandfather whose burly calves resembled knotted rope as he sauntered down the road with a cigarette behind his ear and his belly bouncing in stride; whenever he came by to play mahjong, he always brought apples from the market, meticulously picking through heaps in search of the perfect shade of red which, he told me once, was somewhere between an audacious woman's lipstick and a glass of port wine. The argyle stitching on the coarse fabric of the airplane seats reminded me of the floral wallpaper in our living room peeling off in descending curls; the faint squeak of music leaking out of someone's headphones sounded almost like the creak of our balcony during typhoon season; the sour aftertaste from a cup of orange juice brought to mind, despite no similarities, the scent of fried dough soaked until soggy in white rice congee. The present and the past seemed to intertwine as if they were rooms demarcated by a billowing veil and one could pass between them with a mere swipe of the hand.

My mental wanderings were interrupted by an occasional noise from my two cousins or a snippet of conversation between their parents. They sounded far away, though they sat in the row in front and the one behind. We were three families embarking toward new lives, in transit over an ocean between two continents. We were all leaving our land of birth with no expectation of return for a promise of something better. Our fathers appeared rather solemn, in stark contrast to their excitement leading up to the departure. Perhaps they were bracing themselves for the inevitable discord between anticipation and reality. Our mothers were also submerged in thought, but each was musing over different things for different reasons. And we the children, their vessels of hope and the driving force of their collective sacrifice, had not the vaguest idea of the gravity of this journey. We drifted in and out of fragmented sleep as cabin fever blurred what was immediate and what was imagined. Despite being clustered together in nine seats, we could barely hear each other as the constant whir of engines diluted all the sounds within and suppressed everything in a hushed, almost heavy kind of silence.

When the descent started, the whole of my body clenched in the moments that mimicked free fall. I gripped the armrests, knuckles white, stomach churning, but still I shook with widespread jitters. The mounting fear escaped from my mouth in gasps; it was not the idea of a crash that terrified me, but the visceral sensation of rocking back and forth...Higher! Higher! I had once screamed for Ba to push the swing with all his strength so I could touch the low-hanging leaves with my outstretched feet. An irrational fear spawned overnight. The next day, the mere sight of the swinging dragon boat at the park left me sweaty and shaking.

The plane hiccupped its way down into the city that resembled a giant circuit board like the one in our video cassette recorder. Framed in the window with rounded corners, the city assumed its true immensity and threatened to make us a part of itself. A pressure swelled within my ears, made them itchy, bloated, and wanting to pop. Ma handed me two sticks of gum, their green wrappers printed with OK! (a false reassurance) in bold letters. The flavor of artificial mint quickly dissipated. I was left with achy ears and a nauseating aftertaste. I saved the second piece, closed my eyes, and tried to sleep, wondering how I slept through our first descent on the West Coast and why I could not sleep now. The sudden jagged drops separated the seat a few fingers' breadth from me and the metal buckle of the seatbelt jingled as I fell back onto the cushion. Tears coalesced in my eyes and flowed cheek-ward. Ma uttered soothing prospects of arriving at our new home where I could take a hot bath, eat dinner, and sleep in a warm bed. I thought back to a show that Ma watched on rented tapes about a family living in the decadent style of Westerners. They had an entire house to themselves with seemingly infinite rooms. There were rooms for the children, rooms for guests, rooms for studying, rooms for storage, rooms for eating, rooms full of books, rooms for cars, even rooms for dogs. They had lawns of immaculate grass kept lush by sprinklers, a swimming pool in the backyard, and every night they sat together and dined on a banquet fit for royalty under a perpetually shimmering crystal chandelier while they gossiped about other families living in equally extravagant circumstances. I recalled as many details as I could from that show. I was sure that it existed, this utopia, and that we were on our way there. It made perfect sense to me that one could leave everything behind and go live in such a luxurious setting; all one had to do was endure the agony of a plane ride. I curled up in the seat, knees bent, drilling both index fingers deep into my ears until my nails were sticky with wax. I clenched my jaws so tight that they went numb. I held on to Ma's promise: hot bath, dinner, warm bed. Time felt like it was racing and frozen at the same time. After touching down onto the runway with a quaking jolt, ailerons sprouted to slow the charging behemoth. The moment I stepped off the plane, I felt a gush from my nose; I raised a hand to my chin and blood pooled in the concavity of my cupped palm.

It's the change in pressure, Ba said, as tissue after tissue was crumpled red. We're here. He smiled. We're finally here.

Ma strapped my wrist to hers with a neon pink leash. Unlike her stainless steel pots, sewing machine, mahjong tiles, and uneven-footed stools, unlike the company of her friends and family, she could not part with me, no. She had even sold for a hefty sum that pissing cat, having convinced another woman of superstitious inclination that its rare golden hue would bring a flurry of luck, and for a much cheaper sum relative to its original cost, Ba's motorcycle. She kept her other hand firmly over her purse as we made our way to baggage claim. I jerked on the leash several times, eliciting that look of hers, her harbinger eyes warning of punishment in the privacy of home if I did not put an immediate stop to my misdemeanors.

Mei Lan, the oldest of the children by seven months, who took every opportunity to display her precocity, walked in stride between her parents and announced in a voice of intentional broadcast that she wanted to help carry something. Denied at first, she pleaded with gentle persistence until her father, Wei Jian, obliged and handed her a small backpack which rattled with things that were plundered from the airplane in an act of extreme frugality and prudence. Having just left a country so rampant with poverty and suddenly coming across such unheard-of abundance, their behavior was merely instinctual, almost outside of volition. The bag had been filled with plastic cups with ear-shaped handles, utensils still shrink-wrapped, small basins emptied of salad and wiped dry, bread rolls, bottled water, and orange juice. We used the cups as cups, the forks as forks, the knives as knives, and the salad basins we placed beside our telephone to hold loose change until the white plastic aged yellow and its surface was scratched shine-free. The backpack was cumbersome for her and, after a short distance, the pep in her six-year-old step was gone, replaced with a dragging of feet and slumping of shoulders, yet she trudged on with her head slightly lowered to hide any hint of struggle that might have been evident in her face. It's too heavy for you, just give it back to me, her father said. Only after the third offer did Mei Lan turn it over.

Why can't you be more like Mei Lan? She's so well-behaved. She always tries to help out, Lone Eye said to his son. You could learn so much from her.

Jia Ming paid not a speck of attention and sprinted ahead without looking back. Everything was new to him so everything piqued his interest. He stood on his tiptoes and stuck his finger into the gravel of an ashtray, he splashed his hands in a jet of water spewing from a fountain, and he

6

tapped the snout of a seeing-eye dog.

Stop that! his father yelled.

Just let him be, said Ah San. He's just curious about the new surroundings.

Lone Eye frowned at his wife. Exhausted from the trip, the last thing he needed was misbehavior from his son and lax discipline from his wife. He had some words ready for her but thought better of it and held them in.

I watched Jia Ming with envy; how I yearned for that kind of freedom! I tugged at the leash and said, I don't want...to be tied. The force of my statement paled midway as Ma looked me straight in the face with a glare that silenced the cowardly rebel within me.

We waited at the baggage claim for our three suitcases marked with a knot of white cloth upon which was written in black marker the names of my parents and our future address. What if our bags got lost? I thought, Then all of our clothes would go missing—Grandfather's last gift to me was a waxy turquoise one-piece jumpsuit with bulbous arm- and leg-sleeves that were capped with contractile bands of elastic. We were warned of the harsh winters and, having never known snow, came prepared for frostbite, blizzards, cars frozen onto pavement, crystal stalactites hanging from flower-void balconies....

When our belongings tumbled down the incline onto the slithering belt, my father pulled them off the rotating platform and piled them onto a cart, an action mirrored by his brothers. Freed from the anxiety of missing luggage, we all went to meet Uncle Hu, the oldest of Ba's brothers. He had settled in the United States some years earlier to open two Chinese fast-food restaurants in the suburbs and had accumulated enough wealth to convince both the American and Chinese governments that he was capable of sponsoring three families for immigration. After an exchange of greetings, handshakes, and inquiries into health, we packed into two vans which were used to commute workers from Chinatown to his restaurants to answer phones, take orders, cook, clean, and deliver—they were the same vans that our fathers would board in a few days as newly-hired chefs. Jia Ming yanked me by the collar as I shifted over to the window seat. Before my utterance of protest, Ma gave me her look again. Though she spoke not a word, I knew what she wanted me to do and begrudgingly backed away for Jia Ming to climb over my lap. The physical pain of his knees digging into my thighs paled in comparison to the fear I felt under my mother's piercing eyes, that look she always assumed to remind me in case I had forgotten (though she knew I could never forget) of the proper behavior, which in this case meant giving up an unobstructed view, an unsullied first impression of the streets leading to our new home. No need to start conflict over such a triviality was probably what she was thinking.

A rumble of sliding doors followed by thumps of closure and we were off, weaving through a network of roads down into a tunnel bathed in cough syrup orange and emerging under the full splendor of the sun on an elevated highway straight into the heart of the city. Mei Lan and her family were in the van behind us with Uncle Hu's wife and daughter. Uncle Hu kept one hand on the steering wheel and pointed out landmarks with his other hand while Lone Eye, in the passenger seat, interjected with questions of an intellectual nature.

Jia Ming spouted on repeat, Where are we? Where are we going? What's that? What about those? What are they doing? Who are those people? His father's efforts at calming him down merely roused him up more.

We made our way into Chinatown, passing a seven-storied garage with a monotonous facade of thousands of square holes.

What are those holes for? I asked.

They're nests for pigeons, Ba answered.

It was early afternoon when we parked on T— Street below an apartment complex of jaundiced bricks, rusted pipes, dust-coated windows, and torn screens. The air smelled cleaner and felt cooler than back home, the sky bluer, and the streets were less littered and free of mosquitoes. The buildings seemed sturdier, and there was a notable absence of disgruntled shopkeepers lazing in plastic chairs with legs splayed or one leg dangling limply over the other while fanning themselves with straw hats. The trashcan beside us was filled past the brim, and a manhole in the middle of the crosswalk emitted a constant plume of steam. Two and a half blocks down the street stood the Chinatown gate: two white pillars flanked by foo lions under a green-shingled roof with the proverb '*tian xia wei gong*' facing outward and the four Confucian virtues facing in. To the left of the gate on the side of a building was a mural of a ship sailing against the tide toward a cityscape of lights.

While Uncle Hu's wife and Mei Lan's parents went to buy lunch from the corner bakery, and Uncle Hu went to pick up keys to the building, Mei Lan started a game of rock-paper-scissors to pass the time. We congregated on the sidewalk brandishing our wrists: one, two, three, then one of three possibilities. Four way rock-paper-scissors: if all three symbols were present, a draw, and if not, then losers obviously lost. One by one, sometimes by two, and once by three, we were eliminated until there was one winner and a new round commenced. I felt for the last piece of gum in my pocket and timed out of the game to unwrap it. I watched as Uncle Hu's daughter, perhaps

9

failing to make a decision, flung her arm out with her thumb and index finger curled like rock and the other three fingers outstretched like paper, her hand resembling an OK sign.

What's that? Jia Ming asked.

I don't know.

She wins! She wins! Mei Lan shouted, stating that the OK symbol was now a new possibility that could beat rock, paper, *and* scissors. Jia Ming was eliminated. I timed back in, and we both flicked our wrists vigorously—OK, OK, OK, OK—for a long time. While the two of them looked on with stupid anticipating faces, I grew frustrated at the prospect that this would go on forever. I hated Mei Lan at that moment for rendering the game pointless. OK, OK, OK...rock could smash scissors, paper could swallow rock, scissors could cut paper, but what could OK do? OK was the logo on my stick of gum. Rock could pound gum into dust, scissors could snip it to pieces, paper could suffocate it...I wanted out, so a rock I flashed.

You lose! She's our winner again, declared Mei Lan.

Jia Ming joined in clapping, Did you think she was going to show scissors? You're a dummy!

Mei Lan's parents returned with pineapple-crusted buns, glazed rolls with ham and egg, spongy cupcakes, soy milk, and bottled water. We ate to the delight of nearby pigeons, one of which Jia Ming tried to kick as it ventured closer to peck at fallen crumbs. When Uncle Hu came back with the keys, he gave copies to each of his brothers. We opened the main doors and moved our luggage into a musty hallway where the walls were lined with discolored mailboxes, padlocked circuit boxes, and some broken lights. The lift accommodated only two people and one suitcase at a time, so we had to take it in turns to the third floor. It jolted and stuttered its way up like an old man coughing.

Ba, more than used to shoddy technology, asked with a nervous smile how safe it was.

When the elevator doors parted, we were greeted with an odor that wafted up from the rubbish chute at the end of the hall. It was not strong enough to induce nausea, but it made our nostrils crimp. It lingered with a presence more substantial than mere olfactory stimulus, occupying the corridor like a malevolent poltergeist, clinging to the air with invisible tendrils. At various times, it felt as if one could reach out and touch the smell. There was also a constant buzz either of lights on the verge of burning out or of insects trapped inside dead bulbs. Shorty, Mei Lan's mother, strained to move her bags out of the lift. She was the shortest of the three women; her nickname, contrary to its hint of insult, was actually a term of endearment. She was glad that everyone felt comfortable enough around her to address her in such an informal manner. She had been known by that name for as long as I could remember; in fact, I never knew what her real name was. Shorty was the kind of woman who every kid wanted for a mother. Her demeanor was gentle and her nature easygoing, she was always calm no matter the circumstances, and she seemed incapable of expressing anger or raising her voice. Perhaps that was why Mei Lan was so well-behaved. Under such tender care, the impulse to disobey simply did not exist; there was no reason for it. One would only feel ashamed at having disappointed a mother who showed so much kindness.

Ma and I stood before the door of our new home. Here we were—after so many grueling hours on that airplane breathing its filtered air and eating its preservative-laden food—we had finally arrived. Uncle Hu turned the key, the lock snapped, and a prolonged squeak of the hinges announced our arrival. The floor of the apartment was scattered with plastic bags, elastic bands, sheets of yellowed newspaper, rat-bitten slabs of cardboard, stray nails, screws, and dunes of dust, hair, spider web, and dead bugs. There was a broom next to the empty refrigerator that preserved behind its door the odor of sour milk and salted fish. There were three pieces of furniture in the house: a sagging mattress in each of the two bedrooms and one lumpy couch in the living room with torn fabric exposing its yellow stuffing that looked like scrambled eggs. The kitchen cabinets were filled with old bottles of soy sauce and other condiments that Ma set aside to discard.

My two cousins came in with their mothers. Shorty lifted the shades to reveal windows so caked with grime as to look frosted over. After some sweat and strain, the windows were opened to let the stale air circulate. Our mothers collectively swept, mopped, wiped, and scrubbed the whole place with cleansers purchased from the market across the street while Uncle Hu took his brothers on a tour of Chinatown. We spent the afternoon in the closets pretending they were elevators, time machines, and prisons. There was a flushing toilet in the bathroom—so fascinated were we by its slow swirling gurgle at the push of a lever that we harvested pinches of polystyrene foam from the packaging of a portable stereo that Mei Lan's father had unwrapped and took turns feeding it.

All afternoon we felt sleep-deprived and jet-lagged, but rest was held at bay by the novelty and immediacy of the new surroundings. While our parents busily settled in, we embarked on the most exciting of adventures in the various crooks and corners of our new home. Lone Eye and Wei Jian returned in the early evening with more cleaning supplies and household items. Surprised to find that my father was not with them, Ma asked his whereabouts and was told that he and Uncle Hu went to order food from a local restaurant and would soon return with dinner. The flow of steady commotion was suddenly interrupted after a whispered exchange between Lone Eye and his wife. He then called all the adults present into the living room and declared in a voice of seniority and authority, There are three families and only two bedrooms.

Someone will have to take the living room, said Ah San. I would like a bedroom, so if one family wants the living room, then it's settled.

Ah San was a pale woman with a face that was almost fleshless. The skin over her cheeks and jaws was stretched taut, there were two shallow concavities at her temples, and her eyes always seemed in perpetual daydream. Her hair was midnight black...I felt it once; a stray strand was stuck in the couch as if growing from a pore in the stitching. It was stiff and coarse and recoiled like a weak spring after I pulled it out. If it was thicker, upon closed eyes, it would have been indistinguishable from the bristles of my toothbrush.

Ah San, let's be honest, I think we all want a bedroom, Ma said.

I suppose we can take turns, said Wei Jian. Every few months, we switch. That way everyone gets a bedroom for some time. That would be most fair.

That's ridiculous, said Lone Eye. Have you thought about how much moving that would entail? I oppose.

How should we divide up the rooms?

Whoever doesn't mind the living room should just take it and—

Ah San, we all want a bedroom, Ma repeated.

Her eyes darted to her husband, who immediately said, We'll draw for it. He produced a deck of cards from his coat pocket and added, Lowest number gets the living

13

room. That's fair enough.

Shouldn't we wait until everyone is here?

Brother, we're doing it this way, and we're doing it now. He shuffled the cards, the backs of which were printed with the airline logo, and fanned them out face down. Go ahead and pick.

Shorty stepped forth and drew the nine of hearts.

A nine. Your turn.

Ma pulled the ace of diamonds.

Ah San's eyes flared open. Her face crawled with hundreds of subtle contortions.

Go ahead, Lone Eye told his wife.

She took two cards, one in each hand.

Why do you get two?! Shorty shouted in a tone surprising even herself.

Calm down. I'm picking between these two...which one? Left or right?

I don't know. Just pick one, her husband said.

She turned over a seven of hearts.

All settled now, said Shorty with a smile on her face that even she could not suppress. We'll take...we'll take this bedroom, she added. The inclination to never fully express her emotions was overwhelmed by the sheer magnitude of relief. Her husband remained quiet; his initial skepticism had vanished, now having secured some semblance of privacy. His face betrayed none of the elation that he felt.

Ah San pulled her husband aside and muttered something into his ear.

I can't do anything about it now, he said.

It was your idea so you better fix it, she stated.

I pulled your father aside when he came back and told him what happened, Ma told me years later. That bastard told me to keep my mouth shut. Your one-eyed uncle walked into the second bedroom and moved our bags out.

He said an ace was a one...and one was the lowest number. I argued and argued, but they ignored me. What could I do? He and his wife came into the room and scattered all their clothes on the bed. I complained to your father, and he just ignored me. He said that he was the youngest so he had no say, that if they had already made up their mind, he would not go and mess things up. I told him the whole thing was calculated and that Ah San and Lone Eye took advantage of the fact that he was out with Uncle Hu to weasel their way into claiming a bedroom. Do you know how your father responded? He berated me and told me to mind my own business. I wasn't so much upset that he didn't stand up for himself, but that he was clearly frustrated and directed his anger at me, as if somehow it was my fault.

After Ba's return, we bade Uncle Hu and his wife and daughter a quick farewell. We arranged ourselves into an irregular circle facing each other and portioned out the contents of the takeout boxes. Ma said nothing for the duration of the meal. She ate her food robotically, staring through the linoleum tiles on the floor, her body again in a stiffened posture. With the bowl close to her face, she hid perfectly well her seething fury. While the others unburdened themselves and spoke of immediate hopes and concerns, Ma receded into the chasm of her own mind, coming to a profounder understanding of the implications of having to live with these two families for the foreseeable future. Shorty attempted to engage Ma by offering her more food, but she refused each time with a mock smile and gentle shake of the head. Ah San also shot several glances at Ma with eyes of smug satisfaction.

He said he'd come out tomorrow for dim sum and bring us some furniture, collapsible tables, stools, pails for garbage, stuff like that, Ba said.

Why didn't he open his restaurants here in the city? Shorty asked.

Business must be better out in the suburbs where most of the people are white. There's higher demand. Supply and demand, that's the basic law of American economics, said Wei Jian. That's how things work here, that's why there are so many jobs, it's because Americans always want something.

Chinese people want things too, said Ah San. How come our economy's in the gutters?

Let's not talk about that now. Let's be thankful that we're here safe, and tomorrow...tomorrow we start anew, Ba said.

Well said! It's like they say, the youngest sibling is always the most optimistic.

The disposable plates and utensils were stuffed into plastic bags along with the rest of the trash and thrown down the rubbish chute. The other two families retired to their rooms and finished unpacking, a final burst of activity before succumbing to a deep dreamless slumber. Muffled snippets of their conversations could be overheard through the walls, and there sounded in their voices a comfort that had not been there a few hours prior, the kind of comfort one felt when the ground beneath one's feet became firm again. Ba sprawled over the couch with his eyes closed but in such a way that I could not tell whether he was asleep or awake. Ma huddled over our suitcases and devised a system to keep all of our clothes in neat and easily accessible piles. She smoothed out the corners of Ba's cookbooks, a three-volume set with laminated pages detailing classic Chinese recipes printed in calligraphy. I asked if I could help with her organization. She said no and gave me a kiss on the forehead. I felt a trickle run down my scalp and wondered why my mother was crying, but when I looked up, her eyes were completely dry. She wiped away the wet spot on my hair and squinted at the ceiling, trying to discern if there was a leak.

We slept that night on the blanket-covered floor of the living room. Ba stayed on the couch because his back was aching. He slept with his forearm over his eyes, as if shielding them from a bright light, and sounded intermittent snores from his labyrinthine nostrils. I stared at the ceiling in anticipation of sunrise and of all the escapades I would have with Jia Ming and Mei Lan in the days to come. I never thought living in such crowded quarters would hold so much appeal for me. Unaware was I of Ma lying next to me with tear-swollen eyes and sleepless due neither to difference in time zones nor to thoughts of having left the motherland for good.

What did it matter? she said to me years later. I had already been through the worst of it. We were all victims. He destroyed the institution of education so no one could overthrow him. I was taken from the second grade, given a false middle school diploma, and rushed to the countryside to labor on farms and learn from the working class. She remembered treading barefoot on soil fermented with animal droppings that seeded pustules in the webbing of her toes, painful yellow blisters that oozed and crusted over and kept her awake at night in the creaking bunks where rape was a common happenstance. She recalled the farmer who sneaked in one night, cut an opening in a girl's underwear with scissors, and after finishing the carnal act with minimal rocking, leaped off, tying his pants, and ran out into the darkness. How that girl slept through it, I have no idea, Ma said.

No, she was not sleepless over the prospect of having to find a job that required no English or over those last words of the Old Man or the sight of her sister waving

17

goodbye as the train pulled away or the memory of the floral wallpaper fast yellowing on our decrepit walls or the sewing machine packed away in its original box or the mahjong tiles rinsed in a sieve when they became sticky from use or the sale of the television bought secondhand with a contorted antenna that received only two black-and-white channels or the taking down of the altar nailed on the wall where the merciful Guanyin Pusa draped in white was flanked by pictures of our dead ancestors—no, not sleepless over such things, for Ma was never quite that sentimental.

I too was sleepless; my mind raced with questions and curiosities: What would I do tomorrow? The day after? And after? What would breakfast be?...I dreamt of my favorite hot chocolate malt drink, a perfect proportion of three teaspoons of condensed milk per glass (four made it too sweet and two was not enough), I thought of Ma's fingers turning the can opener, its little circle of teeth gnawing through the metal leaving two slits that were pried wider with a knife into two puckered never-kissing lips out of which poured a thin column of thick cream like a stream of syrupy moonlight into the concave teaspoon forming miniature dunes collapsing upon each other, down it went into the glass, thrice, swirling, clinking, and there it was, warming my hands, a cocoa whirlpool to be sipped with lip-smacking sighs...I dreamt of the walks along Pearl River, its canal-like shoreline barricaded by metal bars and lined with trees, hedges, shrubs, and a concrete walkway with crevices caked full of cigarette butts traversed by cyclists with baskets rattling full of groceries...I dreamt of all the old men who brought their caged birds out to the river each morning, little chirping treasures of lime green heads, sun yellow beaks, cobalt purple plumes, fire orange crests, pearl white underbellies, and onyx black eyes, the men who whistled out of tune, clicked their tongues, and sucked their teeth at the birds while feeding them translucent worms that smelled like molding almonds...I dreamt of the tickets printed on cheap rice paper to riverside amusements, rides in enclosed lots on cars shaped like animals and scooters flashing like fire engines and the small merry-go-round that sung catchy songs and the ten-car train on the elliptical track lined with ferns that brushed one's neck as one passed...I dreamt of old folks sitting on stone seats playing chess on stone tables, old folks practicing tai chi, old folks cutting hedges into the shapes of lions, tigers, cranes, elephants, and Buddhas...I dreamt of the big white bridge, almost phosphorescent in the sun, hazily shrouded by fumes of motorcars and motorcycles...I thought about the family that lived underneath us—the old man, the old woman, and the young child—visible in the space between each step of the wooden staircase so that every time I returned from some excursion, I could spy on them through that slotted view for the duration of the walk up...I remembered how we drummed our ceramic bowls with chopsticks each evening so that the cat knew when it was time to eat....

I was awake before the sun had risen the next morning. In preparation for meeting Uncle Hu for dim sum, we donned new outfits, heavily creased, appropriate for the weather, pulled fresh from the suitcase. It took over two hours to get ready as the bathroom was shared by all nine of us. Ah San herself spent over half an hour in there. Her husband knocked twice, politely at first and then with impatience. Ba led us to the appointed restaurant adjacent to the butcher shop with a window hung full of close-eyed ducks, headless chickens, crackling sides of pork, and neon yellow cuttlefish; the butcher in a grease-stained apron, neither smiling nor frowning, executed (like he had always done before and would continue to do with no end in sight) the same up-down swipe of a weighty meat cleaver with no margin of error as evidenced by ten intact fingers, cutting and packaging the displayed proteins into takeout boxes delivered into reaching hands.

Uncle Hu and his wife waved at us from across the street. After quick greetings, we walked through the double glass doors up three sets of carpeted steps under three chandeliers flanked by mirrored walls toward a woman in a faux Chinese silk dress with a walkie-talkie in hand, who led us to a table covered by a tea-stained tablecloth. At the back of the restaurant, nailed to the wall, was a dragon with golden scales and a phoenix with golden feathers.

How's the dim sum here compared to China? Uncle Hu asked.

I think it tastes better! proclaimed Mei Lan, setting off riotous laughter amongst all the fathers; she could not have uttered a more untrue statement.

We've already got a believer.

Your daughter is quite a sweetheart. She says things that kids twice her age would say, said Uncle Hu's wife. That's adorable.

Kids always say silly things, Shorty replied.

She's only six, and she already knows how to win people over. She'd make a great businesswoman or politician when she grows up.

I can say things like that! shouted Jia Ming from across the table.

But it's all about timing; knowing *when* to say something is just as important as *what* to say, Uncle Hu said, smirking.

I can talk like I'm twice my age, retorted Jia Ming who then spouted off some gibberish.

You're funny. If you want to talk like you're older,

you'll have to sound more intelligent, joked Uncle Hu's wife.

Mei Lan doesn't sound intelligent. She's not a genius! He continued to ramble off nonsense and included a few curse words.

Jia Ming, that's enough! shouted Lone Eye, his raised hand ready to smack.

Just let him be, said Ah San. He's just having fun.

Ma glared at me, a warning of what would come if I were to imitate such behavior.

I have things in the car for you all, Uncle Hu said. I brought a telephone that I'll help you set up.

They talked for the rest of the time about immediate and long-term goals. They reminisced about the past and spoke optimistically of the future. They conversed about the nature of work and money, the beauty of capitalism, and the differences between the American and Chinese way of life.

The vans came a few days later and drove our fathers to work at dawn. Those same vans brought our fathers back every night with calloused fingers and sore arms, their clothes stained with soy sauce and congealed oils, to collapse from merciless exhaustion and wake up the next morning to resume the perpetual cycle.

* * *

—Hello...hello? Can you hear me?...we have the telephone set up...we're all here in the same house...I didn't know we'd all be living together in so small a space...all of us...one living room and two bedrooms, it's smaller than the Old Man's place...I wasn't told...I thought...no, anticipation misleads, it's never the same as you imagine it to be...how's the Old Man doing? Is he still asleep?...don't wake him, I can always call back later...when he wakes up, tell him we've arrived safely, tell him we're doing well, and

21

tell him to stop smoking and stay healthy, I know he won't listen but you have to remind him...it's six o' clock here at night...what?...twelve hours?...I see...what?...I don't know, I haven't thought that far yet, they'll be in school for sure, sometime in the fall...it's comfortable now, not too hot, not too cold, and far less humid than China, the air's very crisp...we're in Chinatown, you can walk from one end to the other in less than ten minutes...the flight was fine...there's nothing up there...just clouds, no gods, no temples, no heaven, not like the movies...just the blue sky...

♦

Three weeks after our arrival, Ma found her first job. She sat in a large room of wooden flooring aerated with high ceiling fans before one of a hundred sewing machines with one of a hundred pedals to be stepped on for the creation of seams that bound pieces of fabric once separate. Not wanting to leave me home, she brought me to work. My first job in China was in a textile factory, she told me later, recalling the haggard man who inspired her after she returned from the countryside, the man who sat outside his shop on the street corner feeding fabric— measured, cut, and marked with blue chalk—toward the jackhammer-needle of the sewing machine to make pants. She reminisced about the numerous sun-parched afternoons when hundreds of thousands of exhaled breaths (both human and industrial, from the recesses of stuttering engines to those of plaque-covered gums) were accentuated by the humidity of oncoming typhoons, afternoons during which she watched the old, gray-haired man manipulate strips of cloth, the ends of which draped over the table and flapped in the breeze to be united under the needle. He brushed away stray shreds that on wet days were carried off in the gushing rain to dangle over the metal grid of the manhole for a few moments before falling.

I brought along my English books—yellow-paged, corner-furled, tea-stained—and studied on a desk that seemed to float on a sea of thread while Ma shouted conversation with the woman beside her, an employee of three years. I had endless hours to daydream. The whir of a hundred motors became white noise; whatever came to my imagination assumed a life of its own until an interruption—a tap on the shoulder, the hour for lunch, a vocal reminder to resume studying, an excursion to the restroom, a loud sound—brought me back to the present. I spent time at work with Ma and time at home with my cousins. The clarity of those days have long gone; they appear now as if viewed through myopic eyes. All the memories have vanished, replaced by figments, cobwebs, and ghosts. That first summer passed, as do all childhood summers, like an ephemeral dream of a midday nap.

* * *

—I've got great news, I'm hired...textiles...I couldn't have hoped for better...mostly immigrants, all women...I met with the manager, and he said he'd let me work for a week and if I was any good, he'd hire me...remember how I learned it? Self-taught, that's right...I showed the manager what I had done after the first day, he didn't say anything but the next morning, he came up to me and said I was hired...just a few streets over near downtown...eight to three, a half hour for lunch...I'm taking him to work with me...not yet...I know Shorty has been looking as well, but Ah San, I don't know what she's thinking, it doesn't seem like...I got lucky, very lucky, I ran into the woman next door in the elevator, she works there, she's the one who helped me get the job...is the Old Man there?...put him on...hello...we're all settled...he's at the restaurant...they have

23

to drive for almost an hour each morning, I thought I told you all this last time...I knew you'd ask, no, she's not working yet, I don't know if she's tried to find anything...I knew you'd ask that too...it's out of my control...she's been very difficult, she exaggerates every little thing and gets upset easily...her son is out of control...there are things that...I understand...he's doing fine, I bring him to work with me...it's amazing how he concentrates despite all the noise...he's meant for studies...he misses you, I can tell...what?...there's no television here, Jia Ming's been asking for one...if they get one, I don't think they will, but if they do, it's not going in the living room, that's for sure, I don't even want to think about how many conflicts that'll start...

* * *

Come in, have a seat...sorry the place is a mess. What can you expect with three families living here?

You're too welcoming, it's fine, I can sit here.

Ah San opened a crack in her door and peeked out. Ma and her friend looked over, and she closed it immediately.

Who was that?

My sister-in-law. Ma made some movements with her eyes and hands but said nothing more.

I understand, the neighbor said, tucking a lock of hair behind her ear.

Ma saw the circle of jade around her wrist. That's really nice, I'm a jade fanatic myself, I have a few Buddha pendants and bracelets...but yours...I love the shade of purple. You've worn it for some time, I can tell, it's got that luster.

Twenty-five years, I've worn this for twenty-five years. My husband couldn't afford a ring when we married so he bought me this instead.

Ma smiled. It's very beautiful.

They talked over tea about work, family, life, whatever came up. Shorty came out and joined the conversation. The neighbor talked about her time here, about her experience amidst these immigrants whose faces sagged year by year, weighed down by ever-elusive dreams. She told them how she had come with her husband five years ago and how he had struggled with odd jobs here and there and how he would go unemployed for months at a time. Now he was a janitor for an office building downtown. When Ma asked if she had any children, the woman shook her head.

I was playing in Mei Lan's room. Her father had bought her a baking set from a toy store. She pretended to be a pastry chef while Jia Ming and I took turns being cashier and customer. Mei Lan's bakery was open for business with a selection of cookies made from colored play-dough, the initial sight of which made me salivate. Each cookie was cut into a star, circle, triangle, or heart, then baked in an oven that, despite constant begging and pleading, we were not allowed to touch.

The hour passed unnoticed until Ah San opened her door and screamed, Jia Ming, get over here now!

The conversation outside abruptly ceased. The neighbor apologized for her inconvenient visit and got up to leave. Ma shook her head and offered her own apologies instead. After she left, Ah San came out and said, I hope you'll clean everything up and not leave the cups and chairs out of place. You know, it *is* a common area.

Ma ignored her and started preparing a vegetable soup in the kitchen.

Who was here earlier? Ah San asked during dinner.

The neighbor.

Why didn't you introduce me to her?

Ma paused, having spotted the invitation to argue.

You were in your room, said Shorty. It's not like we stopped you from introducing yourself.

I don't ever want to feel that way again.

Feel what way? Ma asked.

Like I'm not welcomed in my own house.

What are you talking about?

I don't want to walk into the living room and see a complete stranger sitting there.

She's our neighbor. I invited her over for a chat.

She's a stranger to me.

We certainly had no problems...in fact, it was very pleasant until you slammed the door.

Don't I have a right to slam my own door? It *is* my room.

Let's just calm down, said Shorty.

Next time I see a stranger in the house, I won't say a word, and if anything bad happens—

Whatever you say, Ma said.

Whatever I say? I'd like to say this then: Let's keep the floors clean and the refrigerator organized, let's make this place a home, the doorway is so cluttered with shoes I almost tripped the other day coming in—

As if you do any housework to be talking.

It was the continuation of that which began with the ace. Ah San had become confrontational toward Ma to the point of obsession, picking fights over issues of living room space, bathroom and kitchen privileges, and reimbursements for shared groceries. There was no shortage of exaggerated grievances for Lone Eye's ears: She's in the bathroom too long...she leaves dirty plates in the sink...she doesn't empty the dustpan...she keeps the windows open...she leaves the lights on and wastes electricity...she didn't wipe up a spill this morning and I could've slipped and fallen...

Ma's determined silence over these contrived outbursts solved nothing. She tried to talk it over with Ba, but he remained quiet and brooding until one night he burst out with: Ten hours! Ten fucking hours I've been standing in front of that wok, frying, sautéing, stirring...ten fucking hours, so don't talk to me about this. If she wants the broom behind the fridge, then put the damn thing behind the fridge. If she wants the windows closed, close them. If she wants to be difficult, stay out of her way. It's simple!

Ah San's complaints persisted, triviality after triviality. All part of her plan to force us out, Ma said later. That scheming bitch took it upon herself to make everything a little harder for all of us.

* * *

You won't believe what happened! I was buying some new utensils and asked the lady if she knew of any places hiring, and she said the store was looking for a part-time cashier. They gave me the job! said Shorty.

When do you start? asked her husband.

Next week. She told me to go in tomorrow morning and watch her for a few hours. She said I'll learn everything in no time.

That's great news. I'm very happy for you, said Lone Eye, looking over at Ah San who stared back defiantly.

This brings up...I wanted to ask you...Ah San, I don't think you have any commitments in the afternoon. I was hoping to leave Mei Lan at home with Jia Ming. Could you keep an eye on her also?

Ah San smiled but said nothing.

I can pay you of course.

Don't say such silly things! she shouted suddenly. We're one big family here, you don't need to pay me, I'll be glad to look after Mei Lan, she'll keep Jia Ming company so

27

he won't get so bored.

Thank you.

I'm just glad I can help. Ah San turned to Ma and said, You can leave your son here with me, too. You don't have to bring him to work.

Thanks for offering, but he likes it there.

What's there to do besides watching you sew? How could he like it?

He brings his books to study—

With all that noise? Well, the offer stands.

Ma did eventually leave me at home, spurred by the necessity to work some late nights. I remained under Ah San's supervision until the day Ah San came home to find a gaping wound on her son's forehead. It was Shorty's day off, and she had taken Mei Lan out for a haircut. Ah San went out on one of her usual shopping sprees. Left home alone, Jia Ming and I stumbled hysterically through the house. We howled before the fan, its spinning blades chopped our voices into machine-like reverberations. In a frenzied game of tag, we jumped off furniture, slammed doors, and crawled under beds.

You're it!

No, you're it.

I touched you first.

I touched you right back.

You can't do that.

Yes I can.

No you can't.

I can do whatever I want, he said. I can beat you up because I'm older, I'll squash your head like a bug. He threw a soft punch and cackled, Are you scared? He threw a few more punches and shoved me in the shoulder. Come on, you chicken.

I charged at him with outstretched arms, pushed him

onto the couch, and clamped a sliver of his skin between my teeth until he screamed and screamed, his voice cracking into a cough, and I did not let go. He thrashed his arms and legs trying to turn over and, unable to push me off, started to bawl wildly. I leapt off, leaving a bright red slit on his forehead like an eviscerated third eye. The taste of his blood in my mouth was salty and metallic.

Ah San was frantic when she came back. What happened? I knew I shouldn't have left you two alone!

He bit me, Jia Ming said.

The wound on his head was fresh; the scab had yet to form.

Look at this! screamed Ah San when Ma came home from work. Look what your son did. What if that leaves a scar?

Come over here! Ma yelled. Did you do this?

I looked her straight in the face, surprised at my own calm. No, I said with a cool confidence.

He's lying!

Do you know what happened? Ma asked.

He was running and bumped his head against the shelf.

Did you see it?

Yes.

Are you telling the truth?

I nodded. Jia Ming was amazed by my lie, as was I, perhaps even more so. An inspection of the teeth marks on his forehead would have exposed my dishonesty, but no one thought to look closely. Each mother was convinced of her own child's claim; neither sought further proof or refutation. The whole ordeal felt like a spectacle, a show, and I was watching myself from a distance immune to all consequences.

He's lying, Jia Ming protested. He pushed me down

and bit me.

Why would Jia Ming blame him for something he didn't do? Ah San asked.

Let's be serious here. Jia Ming is a full head taller and weighs almost ten pounds more. It's not even physically possible, Ma said.

He pushed me onto the couch and bit me! Jia Ming shouted.

I don't believe it. I'm sorry but that's absurd.

Your son is responsible! Ah San said.

I don't think so.

If that's the case, I'm not looking after—

Don't worry, he'll be coming back to work with me from now on.

* * *

We strolled one day through the city park flocked with pigeons, sparrows, and squirrels.

If this was China, they'd all be caught and eaten already, Ba jested.

The encounter with the squirrel was a first for me, for all of us. Its gray bushy tail reminded me of the feathered duster, the wooden end of which Ma used on occasion in the name of discipline. My cousins chased the critter up a tree and pranced around the trunk, laughing and tracing the animal through the rustling foliage with their index fingers.

What exactly is it? asked Shorty.

It's a kind of rodent. We don't have them back in China.

I remained cuffed in Ma's grip. The harder I tried to wriggle free, the tighter she squeezed. You're not getting close to that thing. What if it bites? Who knows what diseases it carries? We don't know any doctors here.

Envious of their freedom, envious of their lax

30

mothers, I stood at a distance watching them chase squirrels through the park, their figures receding on the green. I kept my frustrations to myself because there was no other alternative. Throngs of pigeons and sparrows pecked at crumbs spilled from tremulous senile hands. Families pushed baby strollers with polka-dotted, pinstriped, or checkered sunshades. Tourists with cameras around their necks sauntered about in visors and golf shirts. Where were the rides? The amusements? Where was the excitement? I felt it again, the yearning to be back home, to be in a real park with merry-go-rounds, indoor arcades, swinging dragon boats, badminton courts, bumper cars, miniature trains, and Buddhist temples with incense urns several meters tall, decorated with heads of lions and emblazoned with calligraphy.

We arrived at a large shallow pond in the center of the park filled with mallards; in the middle stood a pavilion beside which a semblance of three large cotton balls floated: a trio of swans. There were swan boats on the olive-tinted water operated by men sitting in the back pedaling as if on a bicycle. I thought of the shirtless man I once saw who leapt over the barricade and swam across Pearl River like the ferries that chugged back and forth. Whenever we boarded a ferry, I would stand on the seat, hands on the guardrails, and stare at the waves. When we got to the other side, I would watch with anticipation the collision of old tires tied around the boat and those strung along the dock; the squelching of wet rubber was music to my ears. I always wondered if a stray tire were to come loose and sink down into the murky depths whether some sea creature might eat it for dinner.

My cousins had raced up to the edge of the pond to disturb the snoozing ducks. Don't get too close, you're going to fall in, said Ah San.

31

No I won't! Jia Ming snapped.

What an assertion of independence, I thought. Ma's grip tightened; without realizing, I had put up more resistance to try and slip away.

Look at that one! It has blue feathers on its wing, said Mei Lan.

It takes so little to make them happy, said Shorty.

This one's got purple feathers! shouted Jia Ming.

I wonder what they eat.

Maybe they eat each other.

No they don't. That's not true.

Ba had run off to somewhere. I had not noticed until he came back, crouching beside me. Look what I've got, he whispered, and in his hands, its beady eyes darting, was a pigeon.

Get that away from him! Ma shouted.

Relax, just let him have a little fun. To my surprise, Ma conceded. He handed it to me. Careful...here...put your hands here. Don't let the wings spread or it'll fly away. Don't squeeze too hard, it has to breathe.

I held the precious bird in my hands. I felt its breast puffing and I felt its tiny heartbeat in my fingertips.

Smile! Shorty snapped a picture; the camera whirred, no flash. Come over here, she called. Come and see what your cousin has.

From the corner of my eye, I saw them running towards me; without hesitation, I tossed the bird into the air. Once they realized what I had released, their faces were awestruck, dumbfounded, seething with jealousy. They asked where and how I had gotten it and why I let it go, and they clamored for another one to be caught. I turned away, my lips unable to resist a smile. Too bad for them, they could chase squirrels and admire ducks all they want, but I held a live pigeon in my hands. It was then that I noticed I was free, no longer in Ma's grip. I ran as fast as I could. She heard my footsteps and yelled my name, but I kept running, carried by the momentum of the miracle through a throng of feeding birds that all lifted off the ground at once. For a moment, I saw only shards of the cityscape in the cracks of the fluttering collage, the smell of pigeons overwhelmed my nostrils, and a loud susurrus of wing-beaten zephyrs tickled my face. My mother was calling for me to go back but I did not hear her: the only sound in my ears was the hundred-winged flapping of freedom.

* * *

Ah San sauntered into the house with a bounce in her step, as if dancing, accompanied by the rustle of shopping bags swinging from flimsy plastic handles. She set them down in her room and let out a sigh of fatigued content.

What did you buy?

She shook her head and taunted, That's none of your business.

Tell me, what'd you buy?

Little boys shouldn't be so nosy, she said, almost singing, her words afloat with the lightness of satisfaction.

Let me see.

Shorty and Ma were in the kitchen preparing dinner when Ah San came out in a white button-down shirt, black jacket, and matching pants, and stood before the mirror in the bathroom ogling herself and adjusting her new earrings. She went back inside her room and came out five minutes later in another outfit, a light blue dress with a lacy hem, and stood before the mirror gyrating about the hips, turning her shoulders, and craning her neck.

What's gotten into her?

Who knows?

When Lone Eye came home that night, we heard loud and clear the outburst behind closed doors.

Where did all this come from? Lone Eye asked.

What? said his wife, playing dumb.

You know what I'm talking about, this!

I bought it.

When?

Today.

How much was all this? Why'd you go and—

Because I can afford to. I got a job today.

Are you joking?

I start next Monday as a cashier at the bakery on the corner of S— and K—.

That's good. I mean, that's...that's great, he stuttered, taken aback by the news. I'm happy you found work. How much did all this cost?

I thought you'd be happy for me! I just wanted to treat myself. She burst into tears.

I'm just saying you should've waited—

You think I don't deserve this? You think you're the only one who's allowed to buy anything? We've been here not even three months, and you've changed. You can't even be happy for me anymore.

You're not listening to me, I was trying to—

I know what you're trying to say, I know what you're thinking. You think I went and spent your hard-earned money. I've got news for you. The money I spent today was *my* money, money that *I'm* going to earn. You're not the only one capable of working. This is America. Men and women can both work. Why can't you be happy for me?

With her twisted exaggerations, she had him cornered, and she knew it. Lone Eye knew what he wanted to say but he could not say it. He wanted to tell her that he was happy, happily surprised, and though he was upset at first, the anger had already subsided. He realized that the stress of these living conditions had gotten to her. He was glad that she was starting to see the need for more income, but he was unsure how long this would last. It felt almost too good to be true. His suspicions proved accurate, for within two weeks, it all came to an abrupt end.

They don't like me because I'm new.

Who?

The manager and the other workers, they don't like me. The cash register is always breaking and the customers are insensitive. I'm still learning, I'm doing my best and they just yell and demand things. Those ignorant farmers and their country accents, they can't even speak properly.

Work is hard sometimes.

I don't want it to be that way.

You'll get used to it. Just give it some time.

And you know who else I can't tolerate? The foreigners, the stupid Americans.

He sighed.

All they do is give me a hard time. I can't understand anything they say...and I know they're making fun of me.

How do you know that?

I just do.

You can't work with that kind of mentality.

Of course I can't work.

You need to—

I need to stop, that's what I need. I'm going crazy there. You know what else? The manager makes me wash dishes. That wasn't part of the agreement.

Are you doing it?

What kind of question is that?

If the manager tells you to, I hope you're doing it.

Are you taking his side?

I'm not taking sides.

I also have to wipe down tables and take out the trash and clean the bathrooms. Look at the calluses on my hands! Do you want a wife with rough hands? Can you endure seeing me like this? I can't work...I can't do it...it's all up to you, you're the one who's able to work...I don't know what I'd do if you weren't here...I'm sorry, I'm sorry...I've taken for granted how fortunate I am...I want the boy to grow up and know that if it weren't for his father, so strong and determined and disciplined...I can't do it...I know I sound foolish but I'm so happy we're here together...I feel so fortunate and I realize it more each day...I feel bad for Jia Ming and Mei Lan, they're stuck with me at the bakery in the afternoons. I can't do this.

She quit her job, having won over her husband with nightly grievances and lachrymal torrents. She knew it was the only way. She knew what to say and when to say it. She ended each argument with stream-of-consciousness self-pity and ample praise over his monarchic role as man of the house. There was no choice for him but to feel sorry. She played the distressed damsel too scared to confront the real world of nine-to-five. The only safe place for her was home; the only safe thing to do was nothing. And in the end, what a lift of his ego to know that the foundation of his family rested solely on his ritualistic mornings speeding down four-lane freeways, winding through single-housed, trimmed-lawn, prayer-before-dinner, bath-by-candlelight suburbs, to serve pork fried rice, chicken wings, and teriyaki beef on a stick.

◆

Uncle Hu arrived at our building one Sunday in a sharp-shouldered brown suit. He smoothed the hair on the back of his head with his palm and brushed some dust off his lapel before entering our apartment. He came to take us to his house for dinner. Our mothers declined politely and said that it was too much of a hassle for him to host three families. Knowing that this was an act, he played along and said that he was not going to take no for an answer. Shorty and Ma thanked him for the invitation and declined again, saying that it was too inconvenient for him to shuttle us back and forth. Jia Ming clamored that he wanted to see where Uncle Hu lived. His father pulled him into the bedroom to quiet him down. Mei Lan mimicked her mother and told Uncle Hu that this was too much work for him.

My wife has already started preparing dinner, Uncle Hu continued in a rather stern manner. I closed the restaurant to give your husbands the day off so that we could all eat a nice meal at my house. Get dressed and meet me downstairs.

You shouldn't have come all the way out here yourself. We could've found our way to your place, Shorty said.

That would've been impossible, Uncle Hu said. How would you have gotten there without a car? I don't want to waste any more time. Come on downstairs when you're ready.

We put on our best clothes which had been laid out the night before in anticipation of this excursion. Ma and Shorty seemed slightly taken aback by Hu's directness. He knew that the exchange was a mere charade, yet he responded in a tone that was somewhat harsh, almost condemning, as if he took their mock refusal not as a sign of respect, but its exact opposite. Jia Ming was so excited that he ran around the living room and jumped onto the couch with his head halfway through the collar and only one arm through the sleeve of his new shirt, ignoring all of Ah San's attempts to calm him down. Lone Eye threatened to leave him behind if he did not finish dressing.

That's how you discipline our son, he said to his wife. Don't negotiate with him. Just issue an ultimatum and he'll listen.

Uncle Hu was waiting by his car which stood beside the curb with its hazard lights blinking. Ba went to retrieve one of the restaurant vans that had been parked at a meter a few streets over the night before.

When Ba returned, Uncle Hu asked, How are we going to divide you all up?

Why don't we—

It proved to be a rhetorical question. Before Wei Jian could offer his suggestion, Uncle Hu presented his solution. I felt such a sudden rush of exhilaration when I heard what was proposed that my face convulsed with a wide-arcing smile, which I tried to hide by turning away, not wanting to meet the anxious eyes of my mother. Uncle Hu said that the children ought to ride with him in his personal car; he said it would be a fun experience for us. I would be separated from Ma for the duration of the ride. No matter how much she disagreed, she could not go against Uncle Hu's proposition. The three of us crowded around Uncle Hu's car, an ashen gray automobile with tinted windows and a hood ornament of a trisected circle that sparkled in the midday sun. Mei Lan and I remained composed, but internally, we were beyond delighted. Jia Ming cheered and roared before opening the door and jumping into the back seat. Uncle Hu told my father to tail him with the van, and then he said, One of you can ride with me.

Ma's eyelids widened. The subtle tensions on her face revealed all too clearly what she wanted to do, but she could not act on it. She wanted to be in the car so she could keep an eye on me; that was clear. For a brief moment, I felt dejected, I could not bear to think that the joy I was promised would be so suddenly withdrawn. What I did not know then, but realized many years later one lazy afternoon when I was reflecting back upon that day, was that Ma could not have taken up the offer, that none of the women could have done so; the invitation was meant for either Lone Eye or Wei Jian.

I'll ride with you, said Wei Jian. I can keep an eye on the kids.

Before I got into the back of Uncle Hu's car, Ma gave me her icy glare, a precautionary glance to ensure proper behavior, a prophylaxis against mischief. With our seatbelts on, we were off. The car drove very quietly, the hum of its motor, soft like the purr of a wild cat, soon became white noise. The shaded areas of the leather seat were cool to the touch despite the searing temperature outside. Uncle Hu turned on the air conditioner, and a refreshing glacial breeze rushed out of the vents. A silver pendant engraved with the Chinese character 'fa' dangled from the rearview mirror. Wei Jian said how he never imagined that he would be sitting in a luxury car cruising on the motorways of America. He expressed awe over how successful Hu had become since leaving China and how he managed to build such a successful business in so short a time. Uncle Hu drove on, watching the collage of rocks and trees and signs flit by his peripheral vision like all the ephemeral obstacles that stood before a soul of ambition; he felt like he was the master of his own destiny, rolling through life with sheer determination. Wei Jian envisioned how he would one day assume the driver seat of his own life, taking full control and speeding toward where Hu had already landed; he was immensely grateful to have left his homeland for this country where affluence seemed so within his grasp.

A near-hysterical Jia Ming asked Uncle Hu many questions about his house: How big is it? How many rooms does it have? Where is it? What color is it? Before Uncle Hu could answer him, he changed subjects and said how much he liked the car because only rich people could drive it and how the seats were so comfortable that he wanted to lie down and take a nap. Uncle Hu's self-satisfied smirk flashed in the rearview mirror. He saw all the fragments of his fortune come together: his car, his house, his restaurants, and the look of intense envy in his younger brother's eyes. His success was so obvious that even his six-year-old nephew could see it.

It was all a show, he wanted us to drool over everything he had, it was not some sense of family that brought us to his house that day but a bursting pride, he had been waiting years for that chance to boast and flaunt without restraint, and there was no better audience than his brothers and their wives because they would feel most deeply the sting of contrast between his position and theirs—that was how Ma saw it, that was what she said repeatedly during her arguments with Ba for many years after.

Throughout the ride, Mei Lan craned her neck back to check that the van was still following us. I held on to the excitement that I had felt at the start of the trip, though it was quickly dissipating. I knew that, when we got to the house, Ma would be doubly strict, so I needed to make the most of the time I was free, but it seemed like there was not much to make of it. Several times, Uncle Hu tried to engage us and asked how we were doing and what we thought of our time here in the States so far. We said that we liked it just fine; there really was no other answer. We were all silent for the last part of the commute as we traced the winding road through a small town where houses dotted manicured lawns amidst groves of trees and wild woodlands. There was such abundant foliage that the sunlight appeared green. Wei Jian was most impressed with the amount of unused space between each residence and asked Hu why it was so, to which Uncle Hu responded that it would bring the value of the real estate down if it got too crowded.

You probably don't understand now but you will later on, Uncle Hu said. You've lived in a city all your life, but a nice place in the suburb gives you more personal space, and you'll come to realize how much better that is.

We pulled into his driveway and the garage door started to rise. Uncle, how does the door know to open for you? asked Jia Ming.

How could it *not* know? It's my house, of course it knows.

The garage was illuminated by three hanging lamps. Its walls were lined with shelves of boxes full of old clothing, shoes, toys, and assorted household appliances retired but not defective. There was a lawn mower in a corner that Jia Ming went to examine; he climbed onto the seat, put his hands on the steering wheel, and pretended like he was driving.

Get down from there before your father comes in, said Wei Jian.

It's fine. He won't know how to turn it on so might as well let the boy have some fun, said Uncle Hu.

After Ba parked the van in the driveway, Ma immediately came up and grabbed hold of my hand. They all expressed disbelief over how big and glamorous the house looked. They remarked on the serenity of the neighborhood and how much quieter it was than the city. As we approached the front door, Uncle Hu's wife opened it before the doorbell was pressed. Uncle Hu's daughter shyly peeked at us from behind her mother's legs.

Don't be so shy, her mother said. You've met your cousins before, you played with them when they first arrived, don't you remember? Now be polite and greet everyone.

She took a step forth, closed her eyes, and made a short bow to the amusement of all the adults before running back inside and darting upstairs. As we were shown into the living room, Lone Eye asked about the dimensions and the layout of the house. Uncle Hu began to spout off numbers that he had committed to memory. There was a large television on a stand across from a set of leather couches flanked by matching recliners, one of which Jia Ming was already sprawled on upside down, his head on the elevated footrest and his feet pointing toward the ceiling. Above the television hung a large framed wedding photograph of Uncle Hu and his wife. The ground was covered in beige carpeting that tickled our toes. Jia Ming rolled off the recliner and lay on the ground, pretending to sleep in a fetal position. Lone Eye remarked that the floor here felt more comfortable than the beds we had in the apartment. Uncle Hu's wife came out with a tray of drinks: water, soda, and juice, as well as wine and beer, which our fathers promptly accepted and our mothers refused.

Let me show you all around, said Uncle Hu, still in his suit, looking more like a real estate broker than a family member.

He led us through his house, which upon later reflection was like any other house, but in our naïve childhood eyes and perhaps even those of our parents, it was an infinite labyrinth of decadence. It felt like we had shrunk and entered a dollhouse where everything existed in staged perfection. His daughter came down to join us. Uncle Hu pointed out a painting that he had purchased from an antique gallery as well as a print of calligraphy that a close friend had given to him. He pointed out all the various pieces of furniture in the living room and drew our attention to some decorative statuettes which were gifts from friends who had traveled abroad. Ma said that she liked the placement of the windows and how much natural light they let in. There was a piano in the corner under a red velvet draping. He mentioned that his daughter recently started lessons, but when he asked her if she wanted to play something, she shook her head and ran back upstairs.

On another wall of the house was a fireplace behind a glass door. Uncle Hu said that in the winter, he sometimes lit it for ambiance. We huddled around this architectural curiosity, which perhaps due to an epidemically popular television drama back in China, came to represent the quintessential American home—the single house, as our parents called it. We relocated to the kitchen which opened out to the living room and was separated by a counter with bar stools. Uncle Hu pointed out the refrigerator that was twice the size of ours, the oven and microwave, and the dishwasher which, he joked, saved his wife much time every night. He showed us some fancy cooking equipment: a multi-speed blender and food processor, an electric mixer with a shiny voluminous bowl, and a set of hand-hammered, high-carbon steel knives.

We then went up a flight of stairs to the second floor where Uncle Hu led us through a serpentine hallway that connected the bedrooms, two guest rooms, and an office. It seemed as if there were hidden doors and closets and bathrooms around every corner. In the master bedroom was a king-sized bed laden with pillows on a lacquered wooden frame. I looked at Mei Lan and Jia Ming; all three of us bore the same expression—we wanted to bounce on that mattress and touch the roof of the house, build fortresses out of its sheets and blankets, and have the most incredible pillow fight in the world. There was a private bathroom with a whirlpool bathtub and two individual sinks side by side. The toilet was separated from the rest of the facilities by a sliding door. Everything in that washroom was polished to a pristine gleam, and the smell of a cinnamon-scented air freshener made it seem like we were in some kind of dream candy factory instead.

Uncle Hu conducted the tour with a rehearsed fluency. He constantly alluded to, but never directly stated, how expensive everything was. He emphasized how lucky he was and soliloquized on how quickly and unexpectedly this prosperity befell him. On the way down to the basement which was used for storage—there was an electric wine cooler, an old couch, two mattresses, a bench press, some dumbbells, and an exercise frame with adjustable bars—the question on everyone's mind was finally voiced by Lone Eye: Brother, how much did the house cost?

Hu looked at him and said, You're actually trying to ask two questions. The first is how much I paid for the house. The second: What's its current value? I make sure that all of my investments yield positive returns. Real estate in this country generally trends up so my house is now worth more than what I initially paid. Let me tell you that here in America, it's not polite to ask people how much their possessions cost, not even something trite, let alone a house...but if you must know, I paid well into the six figures for it.

Did you pay it all at once or is there an option to break it up? Wei Jian asked.

Hu briefly lectured his brothers on money lending, credit reports, mortgages, and interest rates. It's all very complex, he said. There are many wonderful nuances in our financial system.

Ah San suggested, seemingly in jest, that Hu ought to let us live in this mansion instead of that cramped, mice-infested apartment in Chinatown. When he ignored her, she persisted, as if trying to guilt him into sharing his excess of riches. She said that he had enough rooms to accommodate all three families, and that sleeping in his basement would be more comfortable than our current arrangement. She pointed out that his daughter's bedroom was already bigger than the total space allotted to her family. Lone Eye's face writhed with displeasure, but she purposely looked away.

Ah San, you sure know how to joke, Uncle Hu said. The reason I brought you all over from China is so that you can make better lives for yourselves.

Then my husband better work hard and buy me a house like this soon, she said.

Uncle Hu led us through the back door out to the porch that opened onto a fenced yard. There was a playground set in the middle of the lawn that consisted of a corkscrew slide on one end and a lookout tower on another; across the top of these two structures straddled a beam with two swings, one of which, like some kind of hanging seesaw, seated two people. Ma put up no resistance and let me roam free on the fresh-cut grass amidst the flowerbeds and the bushes and the three apple trees devoid of fruit. Ma and Shorty sat on the porch and sipped their bottled water. As the sun traced its predictable arc across the sky, stretching and shrinking our shadows, Jia Ming and I sat on the seesaw swing and rocked ourselves into blissful oblivion, back and forth, back and forth—my crippling fear of oscillations vanished for that afternoon—while Mei Lan and Uncle Hu's daughter alternated between the lookout tower and the slide, played some hand-clapping games, and amused themselves with a jump rope, an inflatable rubber ball, and some dolls. Then the four of us played tag, chasing each other until we were downright exhausted. Awash in sweat and with a numbing burn in my legs, I hobbled over to Ma, who had remained on the porch silently staring into the horizon. When I hopped onto her lap, she closed her eyes; I was not sure what for—whether she was trying to sleep, had actually fallen asleep, or whether she had closed her eyes to find something deep within herself. I too closed my eyes. The verdant yard was replaced by a different kind of foliage, a frondescence of sparkling lights against the bleached darkness of dropped eyelids, a darkness that seemed to get darker without changing its hue. All of my other senses heightened for those moments, and I felt as if I were in a different world altogether. I could hear the melodic rustle of trees in the afternoon breeze, the intermittent chirping of birds, and the faint buzz of honeybees; the noises that had become so familiar to me—the honking of cars, the wail of police sirens, the clatter of pedestrian steps, the hollers of passersby, the general commotion of Chinatown—were wholly gone, replaced by the soundtrack of nature.

Ah San came out and told us it was time to eat. Ma vigorously wiped the sweat from my face; I knew she was annoyed that I had made myself look so unpresentable right before dinner. We gathered around the table with napkins on our laps and silverware beside our plates. A large wooden bowl of salad was passed around. I thought how strange that Uncle Hu and his family ate raw leaves like rabbits. There was a stew with barley and potato and chunks of spicy meatball which was unlike anything Ma had ever cooked. Instead of rice, there was bread and butter. The main dish, which smelled better than it tasted, was a pot roast with various root vegetables. The highlight of the meal was a sparkling apple juice that Uncle Hu's wife poured out into plastic wine glasses for the four of us. Dessert was a chocolate pie. By then, I had drunken so much juice that the thought of something else sweet was nauseating.

After the dishes were cleared, their conversation continued for some time. Expressions of gratitude and well-wishes along with handshakes and hugs signaled our departure. Uncle Hu led the way back and Ba tailed behind in the van. Back in our apartment, I fell asleep to dreams of having my own bedroom in a house so spacious that each turn of a corner would lead to unexplored territory, and a personal playground in a backyard filled with apple trees that would bear fruit each fall to make that sparkling apple cider. I wondered if those apples tasted anything like the ones that Grandfather brought to each game of mahjong.

Ma asked Ba if that was typical American food because she said with a chuckle that she left their house hungrier than when she arrived. I don't think I could ever get used to eating food like that, she said. The meat was dry, the vegetables were either raw or overcooked, and that stew was way too salty.

Ba made occasional grunts, either in agreement or mere acknowledgment.

It's a nice house. The suburb is quiet and peaceful, but it's too far from everything. You can't walk anywhere so you need a car...I could never live in a place like that, Ma continued under her breath. It's too remote for me...it's the kind of place where if you die, no one would find your body for days...but I guess it's the American way of life. She continued mumbling softly; I could not tell if she was talking to me or to herself.

Ba was already snoring.

◆

The three of us sat on our mothers' laps in the small, windowless office with rusty filing cabinets, leaning pillars of paper, a desk scattered with paper clips, pens, notepads, and an ash-filled ashtray which reminded me of Grandfather. So crammed were we that our elbows rubbed, our knees touched, and our feet came into playful contact. The woman behind the desk, whose hair was tied into a bun, was busy thumbing through a directory.

Stop it, we're in public, said Ah San, as Jia Ming dug his finger inside his nose and showed the bounty of his excavation to a squealing Mei Lan.

It's hard to get places nearby, unfortunately they're all filled, the woman said.

Are there any openings at all?

There are, but the schools are further away.

How far?

Not within walking distance, some of these are about thirty minutes away depending on traffic.

But we don't have a car.

Don't worry about that, buses will come and pick them up.

What about the school here in Chinatown?

That one fills up very early since most of the teachers are Chinese. In fact, most of their spots for the next year have already been filled. I can sign them up, but they'll have to wait until the next cycle.

Then they won't have anything to do for a whole year. What else is there?

There's H— K— Elementary, that's the closest one still accepting students.

Can they all go together?

How old are they?

These two are six, she was born in April, he in July, and he'll turn six in October.

These two can go...but the youngest one won't be six when the school year starts, so he may or may not have to wait another year.

What? Ma exclaimed. Why is that?

It's just policy. Some schools will let...hold on a minute, let me check. She picked up the phone and dialed a number.

Can you sign up the other two for now? asked Ah San.

The woman lifted her finger, a request for silence, and began speaking in English into the telephone.

Shorty turned to Ah San and said, Should we enroll them so quickly? We don't know if—

If what? If he'll get a spot? Why would that affect us? Mei Lan and Jia Ming both qualify and there are seats open. Why wait? We're going to tell her to reserve those seats.

Good news, the woman said. He can start the first grade this year if he passes an examination. If he doesn't, then he'll go to kindergarten. He can take the test next Monday. I'll give you directions on where to go. Let me go ahead and fill in the applications for the other two.

I was nervous that week, Ma told me later. I kept your aunt on the phone and we just talked and talked. Your aunt kept trying to reassure me, but I was so worked up. That look on Ah San's face, she literally jumped out of her chair at the opportunity to get Jia Ming in school one year before you. It would've been something for her to boast about. I couldn't think about anything else that entire week. The Old Man kept reassuring me that everything would be fine, that you'd pass for sure. I didn't know what to think. I tried to talk to your father, I asked him to take Monday off and go to the test with you and he yelled at me for trying to jeopardize his job.

Monday morning, eight o' clock, fifth floor of a building marked by an X on the photocopied map shown to the taxi driver. Ma sat in the shallow soup ladle of a

49

chair, bright orange, and I in her lap.

Don't be nervous, she said. Stay calm. If you don't know an answer, just take a deep breath and think about it. You'll do fine, I know you will, she repeated over and over, more for her sake than mine.

A tall, myopic woman signaled me to follow her through a hallway into a large room of testing stations. We stopped at one of the cubicles where questions printed on boards were displayed underneath a panel of plastic on a wooden surface. A lady with black hair that had grayed and gray hair that was whitening confirmed my name, and the test began. For twenty minutes, slides were slipped in and out of the plastic casing, and I was asked to point to specific shapes, match objects with their silhouettes, and identify colors, numbers, and letters of the alphabet.

How did you do? Did you understand what they were asking?

I nodded.

The lady came out with me and told Ma that I had passed.

Thank you, thank you! Ma said, shaking the lady's hand with both of her hands.

How did it go? Shorty asked when we got home.

He's starting the first grade.

That's great!

It's such a relief. I was worrying so much. I was so nervous when they came out to take him in.

I knew he'd be fine, he's always got his head buried in a book. Let's not think about it anymore...I was thinking we should go get some groceries at the farmers market before I go to work.

That sounds good, I've only been there once.

Let me ask Ah San if she wants to come.

The six of us headed to the market which was four

subway stops away. Bustling crowds snaked around tables under tarpaulin tents. Loud bargains were negotiated over squeaking scales. Coins clinked into cupped palms. Bruised vegetables were tossed aside and stray fruits on the asphalt were trampled to pulp. Ma and Shorty stopped at various stands and purchased an assortment of produce. Ah San stood bracing herself against the erratic currents of strangers, holding tightly onto Jia Ming who was struggling to run off. We wandered into a shop where circular pies with a splotchy red and yellow surface were displayed behind a curved glass counter. I told Ma, not knowing what it was, that I wanted it for lunch. Jia Ming and I each got a slice in a triangular cardboard box to go while Mei Lan got two cupcakes from a pastry shop nearby. The first bite was repulsive; it smelled of rotting meat and felt like slime on my tongue. I gagged thrice before forcing myself to swallow and then resorted to nibbling only from the crust and the underside.

Why are you eating it like that? Ma asked. She took a bite and spat it out immediately. No wonder, she said, and chucked it into a garbage can.

As we made our way back home, Jia Ming, twenty paces ahead with a bounce in his step, his figure rendered a silhouette by a shifting of clouds, held onto his mother with his left hand and his lunch with his right. This was my last memory of our first summer together: the unwavering image of his sunlight-darkened figure sauntering into the city, a trail of his footsteps transiently imprinted on the sidewalk after he stepped through a trickling rivulet leaking from a fire hydrant, devouring proudly his first slice of pizza as two pigeons flew over him and a white taxi screeched to a halt before the zebra-striped crosswalk under the bright afternoon sun that bleached the orb of sky above into a pale evanescent yellow.

2

MA PACKED MY ELECTRIC BLUE SCHOOLBAG the night before with three spiral-wired notebooks, the pages of which crackled when opened for the first time, a tin box rattling with five sharpened pencils—hexagonal, honey-colored, and with the manufacturer's logo in green foil below the cylindrical silver crown—two large erasers like rubber tofu, and three folders: a red one filled with blank paper white as untrammeled snow, a green one stuffed with lined three-hole-punched paper, and a yellow one that was empty but for an index card scribbled with my name, Ma's name, my address, age, birthday, and telephone number. There was also a bottle of tea wrapped in a handkerchief and a denim vest neatly folded in case the air was too cool for my liking.

I was woken that morning before the others, goaded into the yellow glow of bathroom light to scrub my teeth with bristles coated in mint toothpaste, then ushered into the kitchen where steam billowed from a bowl of egg noodles. After I finished eating, Mei Lan came out of her room, gently picking off the crust around her left eye with her pinky finger. Her mother pulled up the shade to let in the frontier of sun that slowly crept toward Ba's feet protruding off the couch. Jia Ming kept peeping from his room to see if the bathroom was free. Mei Lan was served a plate of steamed buns, and her mother asked if Jia Ming wanted some; he shook his head but Ah San made him eat. With a loud smack, Ma smote a fat cockroach scurrying across the kitchen counter. She picked it up by a contracted leg and tossed it in the trash.

We stood at the designated stop and waited for the yellow bus to pull up to the curb. We boarded the vehicle with our parents on this momentous first day of school. The driver was a fat man with aviator sunglasses and stubble on his chin. As the streets of Chinatown receded and then disappeared altogether, I felt again the epiphany that I had left China for good, and the things that were once familiar truly would be no more: erect cables of bumper cars that grazed the ceiling and hissed blue sparks, hoarse men in limp undershirts riding the ferry across Pearl River, Grandfather's right leg bent and wedged under his left hamstring at the mahjong table, the red motorcycle standing slanted on its kickstand beneath our balcony, aromas of rice congee and fried dough from vendors that made one salivate in the morning—all the strands that wove the fabric of those memories together belonged to a time never again to become the present.

* * *

The classroom consisted of rows of desks and chairs facing a large chalkboard. The instructor's desk stood in the far right corner beside the window within reach of sunlight. We stood by the entrance waiting for Mrs. Lin, the sole Cantonese-speaking teacher of the first grade, a short-haired woman who was so thin that the bump of her ulna shone like a lone knuckle. She approached us in wide strides; her purple dress patterned with pink blossoms swished at her knees. She shook hands with our mothers, gave us a brief introduction and tour of the classroom, and asked if we had any questions.

Opportunity not missed, Ma asked, Can my son sit in

the front? He's so short that I worry others might block his view.

No problem. When everyone's here, I'll sit them by name and I'll put him up front.

Also, he's never been in school before so he might find it hard to adjust at first.

I'll keep an eye on him, don't worry, he'll make more friends than he can count in no time, she reassured.

A girl with a white shirt, cherry red suspenders, and gray sneakers, her hair parted in the middle and braided into pigtails, entered and took a seat.

What subjects will they be learning? asked Shorty.

Reading, grammar, math, and group activities that encourage teamwork...since most of my students are immigrants, I put special emphasis on English and vocabulary.

What about textbooks? How much do they cost?

Don't worry about that. We lend out textbooks every year.

Another girl with straight hair down to her nape wearing an orange sweater came in and sat beside the other; they started pointing, whispering, giggling.

Will they have homework every night?

I usually give out worksheets—

What about lunch? interrupted Ah San.

Everyone will eat in the cafeteria at noon. They'll be given cards with identification numbers to show at the counter so they won't have to pay for anything. In the afternoon, they get time for recess. If the weather is good, I take them outside. Now, if you don't have any more questions, I'd like to take you to see the rest of the school and meet the principal. She's been with us for over twenty years.

As more students arrived, a few with their parents, the room was filled with talk escalating in volume and laughter interspersed with sporadic coughing. I suddenly became very nervous, having noticed two boys staring at us, and fixated my eyes on the ribbon poster of the alphabet above the chalkboard—Aa Bb Cc Dd Ee Ff Gg Hh Ii Jj Kk Ll Mm Nn Oo Pp Qq Rr Ss Tt Uu Vv Ww Xx Yy Zz—the letters all rested on a staff of three lines. Jia Ming and Mei Lan were talking with wild gestures; they seemed so comfortable despite these strange faces around us quietly watching, sharing secrets, and passing judgment. I closed my eyes...

...there were three green mailboxes nailed slanted at the entrance, the staircase was made of wooden planks, and the family beneath was visible in the space between...were the timber to snap, I would have fallen, we would have fallen five meters down into their living room like the dirt, soil, and dust from the bottoms of our shoes each time we marched up...they were a family of three—an old man, an old woman, and a young child—and their visible possessions included two seam-bursting couches, two round stools, one small chair, one clunky refrigerator, a two-tiered shelf of pots and pans, a cast iron wok, a crate of old books, and one table around which they sat each morning to eat oatmeal...we left them, that family downstairs, we left the family upstairs who we never met, we left Aunt and Grandfather and all of Ma's friends, and we fled by plane over land and water spearing through formless clouds laden with typhoons to overflow rivers beneath...I remembered, perhaps through the narrative of my mother, the great storm that swelled Pearl River out of its bed to dissolve cigarette butts in the crevices of the walkway, to cover the roads with greenish-brown algae thick like the sputum of a pneumonic lung, to chain ferries to the pier and render their smokestacks smoke-less, to confine all public transportation to their terminals...the olive green waves ascended and infiltrated the city with lapping fronts, submerging hedges and shrubs until only their tops protruded like leafy scalps, forcing rain-flecked cyclists, their plastic ponchos crackling in the downpour, to shield themselves from the wind with one hand while the other struggled for control of the handlebars as they pedaled their contraptions of rusted spokes and squelching tires under the umbrage of fist-clenched fog through dirty undulations afloat with banana peels, melon rinds, entwined twigs, newspaper pulp, and plastic bags resembling dead jellyfish...the storm finally stopped by which time the legs of ground-floor sofas were tattooed with slime, refrigerators were dead, telephones dead, lights dead, and centipedes, roaches, and mice had found safe haven or drowned, and that poor family beneath us, we knew not what happened to them...perhaps waterfalls had cascaded through the stairs into their living room, disrupted their breakfast of oatmeal, and filled their living space with a soup of dead fish, crushed aluminum cans, kelp smooth as snakeskin, glass cola bottles pregnant with tadpoles...the waters receded, the river summoned back its superfluous extensions, revealing muck on sidewalks for workers to clean, revealing patches of rotting stems limp and wilted black, dead were the flowers in the parks, the kind patterned on dresses, their delicate petals massacred....

Did you hear her? Write your name for Teacher Lin, Ma said. You know the characters. Don't be shy.

They were back from the principal's office. The classroom was nearly filled. I wrote the two characters of my name on a slip of paper and handed it to Mrs. Lin who thumbed through a reference book and jotted down some pinyin on index cards.

How exciting, said Shorty. Now you have English names.

Let me see yours...I have more letters than you, said Jia Ming.

So what? Mei Lan said.

That means my name's better.

No it doesn't.

It'll be a great year for them, I can already tell. I'm going to start class soon. If you think of other questions later, please call me anytime. Let me show you the way out. It's a short walk to the subway station, or we can call a cab for you.

Ma leaned down and said, We're leaving now, you'll be here with your cousins, remember, pay attention to the teacher, came here for this, remember? She stood up to leave but knelt back down and gave me a hug. What are you crying for? How can I go if you're crying? Hush up, your cousins are watching, the students are watching, everyone's watching. Come on, dry your tears. She got up to leave, taking an eternity to traverse that dreadful hall, and turned to wave goodbye one last time before rounding the corner; it was the first time she had ever left me.

* * *

Who can tell me the first letter of the alphabet?

A throng of hands shot up.

I can, someone said.

So many of you! Just yell it out then.

A!

Who can give me a word that begins with A?

Apple.

Ant.

Who can tell me what the next letter is?

B! Then it's C.

Can you sound it out?

Buh.

Kuh, like a cough.

Why did I have to leave? The mechanical woman who came to life at the push of a button could have taught me this. I could have sat at the wobbly table, its surface pictured with flowers, stamens erupting like peeled bananas and pistils protruding from marigold petals encapsulated by lime green leaves, with my vocabulary book and cassette player out on the balcony that creaked on windy nights. On the eve of one Lunar New Year, Ba taught me to fold helicopter seeds from strips of old newspaper. I constructed hundreds, thousands, maybe tens of thousands of paper propellers which I dropped, twirling like ballerinas, down two stories into a mountainous heap for the lady in a wide-brimmed straw hat to sweep up the next morning with an enormous dried palm leaf, the tip of which slanted upwards like an upside-down comma. In celebration of the new year, we ate dinner at Grandfather's house and stopped on the way for colas in slim glass bottles. I remembered the hiss of tiny bubbles that rushed up to form a layer of foam. I wanted to board a plane back to our creaking balcony and our yellowed wallpaper and our hardwood bed covered with blankets. I could just as well learn English at home, and watch Grandfather play mahjong, anticipating the sound of his approaching steps. In the summer, he came in a plaid shirt, sandals, and shorts, his thick brown calves were mottled and covered with wispy hairs, the nails over his pinky toes were ingrown, the soles of his feet were lined with wrinkles resembling an aerial view of sand dunes, and he always brought two large bags of red apples. Grandfather's here! he would shout, and I would run downstairs, push open the gate, and offer to carry them upstairs. They're too heavy, he would say, his breath reeking of tobacco. If you drop them, they'll roll through the city into the ocean and float all the way to America, and then we'd have to swim all the way there to get them....

Let's give someone else a try, anyone else? Mrs. Lin looked at me and did not turn away. Could she tell that I knew?

Jia Ming pointed at Mei Lan. Call on her, she's a know-it-all!

Mei Lan looked away, embarrassed. A smile on Mrs. Lin's face appeared, her lips a crescent moon as my hand went up slowly.

Eh-lo. Luh.

After some brief moments needed for comprehension, laughter erupted all around.

Good try, remarked Mrs. Lin. It's pronounced *ell* not *eh-lo*. There's no *lo* at the end, but good try. Who can give me a word that begins with the letter L?

Someone screamed, Where's the *lo*? Is he going to cook us something?

The taunts evoked the blackened chimney-like column back home crowned with fire to heat a wok of vegetables, a pot of soup, a pan of marinated meats, the remains of which were fed to the cat who stealthily trotted into the house at the clink of chopstick on ceramic. I had entertained them with my immigrant English; I never would have guessed that a homophone for *stove* could garner so many laughs.

The parade of pronunciations grew softer as I

followed the hands of the clock above Mrs. Lin's desk and traced the plump bumblebee cutout buzzing motionless in a dotted line to the third brass hook on the wall from which hung a black jacket with three white stripes down the arms and white elastic band fringes at the pockets. A parallelogram of sun shone on the girl with thick, pink-framed glasses who sat several feet closer to the chalkboard than the rest; her hair, static-buzzed, was tied into a ponytail that swung every time she turned her head.

There was a bathroom break after the lesson. We filed to the facilities in two separate lines. Though I needed to go, I felt queasy about relieving myself in the midst of strangers. Jia Ming was prancing around, talking loudly, and inspecting all the different stalls after he finished. Having decided that I would rather hold it in, I walked out of the lavatory. When we got back to class, I watched the minute hand of the clock run laps around the hour hand.

That was a preview for those who don't know the alphabet yet. Some of you know it very well, but we'll learn it together until everyone knows it by heart.

The clap of a metal drawer yanked open then slammed shut, someone burped, a ruffle of yellow-colored blue-lined papers, a whir of metal teeth sharpening pencils, the screech of chalk on slate dusty with the pale remains of previous markings, a voice like the tinkle of pendants on a necklace, someone hiccupped, the soft buzz of the white lights hanging from the ceiling....

We had a period of designated playtime during which Mrs. Lin introduced all the board games available and all the books we could read. I watched the rigidity of the classroom melt away as students left their seats and gathered in small groups around various activities. I remained in my seat looking at the pink flowers on Mrs.

Lin's purple dress...

...not unlike those fading on the wallpaper on the second floor of that slumping tenement I used to call home...was it now peeling off or had it already been stripped away to reveal the indented tracks of termites?...I watched the girl with pink glasses scribble something on a piece of paper and recalled the shadow on the wall years ago (the silhouette of a stiff-stemmed upside-down flower) of my hand learning to hold a pencil at night by lamplight: it was Ma's number one claim to fame...she boasted to her friends how she spent one whole month teaching me to write the number one at the age of one, to grasp the pencil with stability and make that straight line...she told me several times during my adolescent years how I chose the brush on my first birthday and how she knew then that I would walk the path of a scholar, how on that day of celebration before the feast of noodles and pastries baked into the shape of peaches, I was placed before an assortment of objects laid out on the bed before all of my relatives—a handful of coins, a toy car, a calligraphy brush, some candy, a ruler, a Buddhist tome, an abacus, a blank ledger, a sheathed knife—and how I made the choice that milked tears from her eyes and made her heart beat so fast that she almost fainted...I remembered pages upon pages of ones, slanted, curved, undefined, all with some kind of flaw, until they were crafted with certainty using the same up-down stroke. Why did I have to be here? I still could not figure that out.

The morning had departed without farewell; the hands of the clock, now fleeing, now pursuing, finally rested upon each other for a moment, northward. At the sounding of a bell, we filed down to the cafeteria and waited in line for lunch. Mei Lan and I stood together

61

moving a few steps forward at a time. I asked what she thought of school, and she said she liked it. I asked if she missed her mom, and she said sort of but not really. I asked why not, and she said she would see her soon enough. She said she was excited to be here. She said many other things but I had stopped listening. Then she asked me if I missed my mom. I said that I did; I said I wanted to be home, and she asked why, and I said I did not want to be here.

The clamoring in the cafeteria got louder as more students came in. A single large window, interrupted by shadows of the gridded frame, illuminated the whole cafeteria which also doubled as an auditorium for ceremonies and speeches. The window overlooked an empty road with a big rift in the asphalt that made cars go CLUNGK CLOONGK, flanked on the left by weeds, dandelions, and some saplings, on the right by a rusty chain-link fence, one border of the playground where recess would take place later that afternoon. I asked Mei Lan if she liked Mrs. Lin, and she said yes; she asked if I liked her, and I also said yes. With trays in hand, we approached the food in metal tubs that fogged the curved glass and we each exited the other end with a square of pizza, a small carton of milk, a half-ladle of corn, and an orange.

I took the last seat at the end of a table across from a girl in my class. She had almond-shaped eyes and skin like mother of pearl. At the adjacent table, a loud Jia Ming had already made new friends. I stared at the pizza, its fumes insufferable, and remembered that day at the market after the test. I thought, What if this is all they serve? What if I have to eat this tomorrow and the day after and the day after? I looked around at all the students happily munching on their vile slices. I picked it up with my fingertips, held my breath, and began to nibble at the crust.

Are you new? she asked suddenly. It took me some time to realize she was talking to me.

I shrugged. What do you mean?

You weren't here before, right?

Before I sat down?

No. She laughed. I mean last school year.

I shook my head.

That's why I don't recognize you.

Do you recognize everyone else?

No, but a lot of us were here for kindergarten.

What's that?

The grade before first grade.

Zero grade?

There's no such thing. What's your name again?

I'm—

I remember now. You were the one crying this morning!

I nodded.

Why were you crying?

I wanted to go home. I still want to go home.

You don't like it here?

No.

Do you know who that is? She pointed to Jia Ming.

That's my cousin.

She signaled me to lean across the table and then whispered into my ear, He had this booger sticking out of his nose earlier, and when he sneezed, it landed on his shirt. He didn't even know...why do you eat pizza like that?

It was my turn to motion her to lean over. I whispered into her ear, I don't like it, I really don't want to eat it.

You don't *have* to eat it, she replied in a tone saturated

with the obvious.

I don't?

Just throw it away when the lunch ladies come by.

Really?

She nodded.

I won't get in trouble?

She shook her head.

What's your name again?

I'm Mandy.

That doesn't sound like a Chinese name.

That's because it's my English name.

Did Mrs. Lin come up with that for you?

What? No, why would she? My parents did. Don't you know anything?

She kept asking me questions, and I kept answering until a lunch lady in eye-magnifying glasses and a thin hairnet wheeled past an industrial-sized trash barrel—the kind that Ba used at the restaurant to make duck sauce from plums and apricots—into which we dumped the remains of our lunches.

I'll be back, Mandy said after getting permission to use the restroom.

I too needed to go but I did not know how to ask, so I remained in my seat, thinking that when Mandy came back, I would ask her to ask for me.

Hysteria emanated from the crowd around an animated Jia Ming whose tentacle-arms and flapping tongue had snared the attention of all those in his vicinity. One boy was gumdrop red from laughing so hard—one of many in a mural of cackling faces. Out of that chaos flew an action figure, a turtle with a torso of steroid-puffed muscles and a sword across its olive shell; this plastic monstrosity was the object of a monkey-in-the-middle game. Watching them, I too wanted to laugh; my cheeks widened and my lips stretched, its corners turned up, as the turtle was tossed back and forth in parabolic arches between grease- and tomato-sauce-stained fingers.

Give it to me! someone screamed with hands outstretched, knocking over a milk carton and spilling a small puddle soon wiped up by someone else's sleeve.

Give it here.

Keep it away! Keep it away from him!

The toy slid off the table and landed with splayed limbs, spinning on its shell right before my feet. I bent down and snatched it up.

Give it to me. Don't give it to him!

I laughed and threw it back into the jungle of reaching hands.

Give it back, lunch is over, you'll break it, said the boy in the purple shirt.

The turtle slid off the table again, this time, out into the aisle. Without thinking, I dove for it—and collided with another boy. I looked up, a grin still on my face, but before I could see who it was, we collided again. I hit something, or something hit me, and the turtle was now some distance away. I soon realized that I was shoved, pushed away by the boy I had hit; he was much taller and had gold streaks in his hair.

Sorry, I said, looking for something to say.

He responded in cinematic-gangster Chinese, You stupid fucker…I'm going to beat you 'til your mother can't recognize you! Nobody crosses Leung Chau Wah! He pushed me again and walked away, running his fingers through his hair.

The boy in the purple shirt picked up the turtle and put it in his pocket. There sounded the electronic ringing of a bell, the clatter of chairs pushed under tables, a scraping of metal on tile, and a stampede of sneakers as the cafeteria emptied.

If someone steps on you, say sorry, Ma had always told me.

I did nothing wrong. Why such a grave threat? Did nothing, meant nothing, willed nothing. All I could think about were those boys and their turtle and my stupid cousin; it was his fault for getting them so rowdy, for getting me involved. I saw for a brief moment a deluge of fists.

Chau Wah's the biggest bully in the whole school. He's in the fifth grade, someone said on the way up. I heard he shoved some kid's head into a toilet once.

If someone steps on you, say sorry—that was what Ma had taught me.

I curled my shivering fingers into a fist, soft as a bruised apple…

…they're too heavy, if you drop them, they'll roll through the city into the ocean and float all the way to America, and then we'd have to swim all the way there to get them…

I wanted to raise my hand and confess the whole story from start to finish. There was no way I could fend for myself in a fight against someone so much older. I hunched over my desk in deep regret of my failure to resist the laughing crowd.

My bladder, swollen, made itself felt, then subsided.

Why did I have to be here? To think a bell would ring, the bus would come take me home, I would sleep on the floor beside Ma, and wake up the next day to repeat all of this…until when? I would rather learn my lessons with audiotapes on a typhoon-whipped balcony and sleep on a hardwood bed surrounded by centipede-infested walls any day. I was in bed one night some years ago, my arm comfortably wedged in the cool underside of the pillow, as was and still is my inclination, to feel the soft caress of a thousand valleys and hills of stitching, until a piercing sensation woke me crying. Startled, Ma turned on the light. There was a red mark on my left index finger. She lifted the pillow, slapped thrice, crushing the culprit into a pulp of writhing legs, and fetched me a glass of water. Slow down, you're going to choke! she said, while inspecting the swollen digit. It's just a little bite, you'll be okay...here, go pee, then go back to sleep. I said no, but she said go, and I said no, but she picked up the metal spittoon stenciled with crimson flowers, the vessel that resembled an upside-down bell with no pendulum, and she claimed that the bug was inside. Let's see if you can hit it, she said. I pulled down my pajamas and tinkled in the music of xylophones. Behind my veil of tears, I saw no bug, so I directed my stream at the flared circumference of the spittoon, spraying a mist. Stop that! Aim into the bowl, she said, and slapped my buttock, the sudden motion left a streak of urine on the bedroom floor. I laughed, she scolded, and I laughed harder, until the last jets were squeezed out and I crawled back into bed next to Ba, who had woken but pretended to be asleep....

Mrs. Lin's dress ruffled as she walked toward the blackboard and started writing numbers.

What if he kills me? I said aloud, unintended.

What was that?

Nothing.

Are you sure?

I nodded.

I thought I heard you.

I shook my head. In the time between silences and the silences themselves, I saw his prominent cheekbones and his expansive forehead traversed by a thin blue vein crossing diagonally over the left temple. What would he use? A knife? A bat? A gun? Or plain bare knuckles? I pictured his chapped lips, buttonhole eyes, stubby nose, and his hair, gold-splashed, the hair of gangsters and rebels. Just confess to Mrs. Lin, tell her the whole story, let her know, she could stop it, she's the teacher, she would know how.

How are things going? You look like you have something on your mind.

I looked up.

Mrs. Lin was huddled over my desk during the second break while all the students were out of their seats mingling over board games. How do you feel?

I want to go home.

You'll be home soon. It's okay so far, right? Not so bad? She stooped on one knee, her chin near desk level, her dress draped across her thigh and fanned out onto the ground. It was her smile, it had to be, for it seemed in that moment that everything would be all right.

Reluctantly I nodded.

Good, let's have you meet some classmates. She led me by the hand over to some students. Why don't you guys teach him to play?

Mandy, sitting cross-legged, told the group my name and said that I was her friend.

I'm going to see how your cousins are doing, said Mrs. Lin.

Moments passed, and the moments that followed became carefree. The rules were simple: the object was to be the first to reach the end. They asked which piece I wanted. I pointed to the green one. The round commenced; two dice, released from enclosed fists, somersaulted across the board, and the corresponding game piece was moved along the path. Over the course of the game, some skipped ahead on ladders and others backtracked over snakes.

One, two, three...

...at the market on the other side of Pearl River, snakes were held in chain-link cages shaped like doughnuts...Grandfather handed the merchant some *renminbi*, a wriggling reptile was yanked out by rubber-gloved hands and shoved into a plastic bag tightly knotted to be brought home, bled to death, skinned, and boiled with dried tree bark and bitter seeds and herbs...

...four, five, six, seven.

When it was my turn, I tossed the dice, picked up my piece, and lightly grazed it over each square—up, down, up, down, in a smooth bobbing motion like a stone skipping over water.

There was commotion behind us so I turned around. Staring at me like well-timed mockery with its dual specks of eyes on its pea-sized head and its fat little deformed grin was the sword-wielding turtle, this time given life via impersonations. We turtles don't know the meaning of defeat, the boy in the purple shirt said as he stood it on unreliable legs.

I saw his face again, the furrowed brow, the gold highlights in his hair, that smirk of arrogance. What I would have given to have time rewound, to have said, Pleased to meet you, I'm innocent, let's be friends, I'm so-and-so, you must be so-and-so, before this encounter, I never knew you, you never knew me, and let's just keep it that way. How warped could one's face become? How many drops of blood make a puddle on a sunny afternoon? Would he wait for me after class? Would he greet me with a cannonball fist? Would he get on the same bus? Follow me home? What if his whole gang joined in?

Another figure emerged, a semi-masked man garbed in yellow and blue, a tri-pronged claw on each hand. A fight ensued; the figurines, held firmly by their owners, rammed into each other. Sound effects emanated from the other boys. The masked man was bashed against the turtle until the boy in the purple shirt dropped it and withdrew his reddened hand.

You boys there keep it down. No mock fighting, said Mrs. Lin.

The boy picked up the turtle, inspected it for scratches, then rubbed his index knuckle and said, I'm not playing anymore.

What a coward, said Jia Ming.

The swelling in my bladder made itself felt again and, upon acknowledgment, persisted this time.

Go tell her, tell her to call Ma to pick you up and leave and never come back, tell her how it happened, all of it, everything, she's the teacher, she'll listen, there's still time. You stupid fucker...you stupid fucker, I'm going to beat you, beat you 'til your mother can't recognize you...beat you 'til your mother can't recognize you...nobody crosses...nobody...beat you 'til your mother can't recognize you anymore. Just speak and it will tell itself. Why did I stumble that instant and not one earlier or later? Be tough, just fight him, harden your fist and fight him. It's Ma's fault, it's her fault for raising you to be so timid. Say sorry if someone steps on you...say sorry.

The coalescing of beads in temporary suspension blurred my vision before they coolly splattered onto my wrist. A tingle of the nostrils. A rough dryness of the tongue. Mrs. Lin came over and ushered me out of the class and asked what was wrong. I replied with some coughs stifled by the heavy weight in my throat that I wanted to go home.

She stooped on one knee, invited me to sit on the other, and spun a soliloquy on the importance of finding comfort in strange places, the inevitability of leaving home, and the necessity of departure for discovery. She had taught many immigrant students and all of them, she assured me, felt scared and nervous at the beginning, but it would get better with time. You'll even look forward to school soon, she said.

I wanted to tell her I had no desire to leave home and see the world, that I missed Ma and wanted nothing more than to be with her, and that I did not understand why I had to be here or what was so special about this place. I wanted to tell her there was a balcony at our old house where I listened to audiotapes and filled the grids of exercise books with math problems. I wanted to tell her that I was curious once and licked the tip of a pencil; it had a sea-brine flavor, the taste of tears, and with the point in my mouth, suddenly taken by an urge to show off my new discovery, I turned to Ma, sucking on the pencil. Don't you want to try this too? my eyes silently asked, and Ma snatched it away and yelled, Rinse your mouth! That's going to make you sick!

But Mrs. Lin...I wanted to say, I should have said but did not say...the gold-haired bully made it clear I'm not welcomed here.

You'll see your mom soon enough.

I nodded.

Just think, she'll be so proud of you for getting

through the first day, you'll get used to it, trust me, you'll even make friends, this place won't seem so strange tomorrow.

What was Grandfather doing now? What about Aunt? And the lady who bought our cat? They were all on the other side of the world, sleeping, snoring, dreaming on termite-gnawed beds with centipedes hiding under their pillows.

The sensation in my lower abdomen grew to that of a bloated pain and felt on the verge of bursting...the clock hands lapped nauseating circles as they had done all day, taking their eternal time...maybe it would pool on the seat, overflow onto the floor, and darken the fabric over my crotch...like the residue of those blossoms in my lap, I did not know their names; having fallen overripe with thick velvety petals, they occupied in my memory a throne of permanence...I remembered the wooden seat Ba constructed after hours of sawing and hammering and drilling in the space beneath our balcony where, on a certain New Year's Day, a million paper ballerinas once heaped; the seat was attached to his bicycle between his triangular seat and the handlebars, and when he rode toward Pearl River, I held on over his steering hands and directed him over manholes so I could listen to the echo of their metallic clatter as he pedaled past the shadows of strangers, invisible chirping crickets, empty benches, overflowing garbage cans, and the glow of white spherical bulbs hanging like full moons from poles to drench the pavement in mesmerizing silver puddles...he would remind me of those evening excursions sixteen years later...when I outgrew the seat the following year, he dissembled it and made a new one, which he fastened to the rear of the bicycle during my third summer when the trees were in bloom, when Ma learned a new recipe for a medicinal broth of assorted herbs, mango pits, and those nameless reddish purple flowers...I remembered sitting in the living room on a short stool, the mangoes slick and slippery after Ma peeled off the yellow skin spotted with moles, and greedily burying my teeth into the sweet golden flesh, the fibrous threads getting caught between my teeth, the honey-thick syrup trailing down the sides of my mouth, fingers, arms, luscious drops that hung for a moment from my chin and elbows before staining the newspapers spread on the floor; the large oblong seeds were collected and pierced and tied with string to coat hangers hung on the balcony to dry (dangling like the angled wings of spangled paper cranes, her origami birds that got tangled and mangled by three wrangling boys and left her teary-eyed and jangled)...Ba and I gathered the reddish purple flowers at the park, those fallen we picked up, the un-fallen he knocked down with a stone tied to the end of a rope which he twirled above his head, aimed, and released...he put me on his shoulders and I swirled my wrist like he taught; it made whooshing sounds but fell fruitless each time to the ground...Next time, he said...When you're older, you'll get it, he said...after accumulating a bounty deemed sufficient, he pedaled back to the house while I sat in the back, my arms around his waist, a heap of dying flowers covered in soot and embalmed in their own juices uncomfortably stacked on my lap, staining my crotch with the color of bruised blood that evaporated to turn bluish black for Ma to scrub off in a tub with brush and soap...how embarrassing it would be if I were to wet myself in this room of strangers and two not so strange....

We stopped by the bathrooms—it brought such momentous relief that even the fear of Chau Wah was abated, though for too short a time to be relevant—on the way down to the fenced expanse of asphalt, a plain black field of tar upon which was drawn with chalk some hopscotch squares by a previous class. The gym instructor, a dark-skinned, bowlegged man with sinewy arms dressed in a plaid short-sleeved shirt, jogging pants, and a baseball cap, brought out a netted bag of red dodge balls. As the games commenced, I remained a distance from the crowds on constant surveillance for Chau Wah in case he sneaked out of his class—or simply walked out—for an opportune confrontation.

Don't you want to play? We're jumping rope, said Mandy.

I shook my head.

If you change your mind, we're over there, she said.

Some duration of time had passed before Mrs. Lin approached. Recess will be over soon, why don't you go join the others?

I shook my head.

Did you know that I came to America fifteen years ago?

Fifteen years, I thought. I could not imagine it, I'd be twenty, what would I be doing then?

I became a bilingual first-grade teacher because I wanted to help all the new Chinese students, and I'm still doing that...I'll probably keep doing it for as long as I work.

It was true what she said. I went back to visit her the summer before college. We walked in during a math lesson. She was in the same classroom and her desk was in the same place. She had not aged much, her face was more tanned, and she was much shorter than I had remembered. It was all hugs and handshakes and congratulations, and then we stood for a picture, Mei Lan and I, with Mrs. Lin between us in a forest green dress with egg yolk yellow flowers and a big disbelieving smile on her face.

Do you still have family in China?

I nodded. My grandfather and my aunt, I said.

You must miss them. You can always go back and visit when you're older. The school day's almost over. We'll head back inside soon. Now be honest, the day wasn't so bad, right?

I did not answer her.

A swarm of feet gathered around the gym teacher. The dodge balls were returned to the netted bag that resembled an oversized bunch of grapes when stuffed full. One of the boys jumped in the air, arched his back, let out a dramatic scream, and dunked his ball into the sack; his fingers caught the netting and pulled the sack right out of the man's hand. A couple of balls tumbled out and started to roll away. The class was in hysterics. Had they been apples, they would have bruised, they would have leaked juices for ants to feast.

Back inside, at the sound of the last bell, Mrs. Lin congratulated the three of us for making it through the first day, bade us farewell with a smile and a wave, and said she would see us tomorrow. We followed the rowdy tide down the stairs and out to the buses parked beside the curb. I kept turning back to check if I was being tailed, and I swallowed my saliva far past the point of anything to be swallowed. Then the worst of all possibilities dawned on me: What if Chau Wah rode on the same bus?

With unsteady legs, I climbed the three steep steps and took the first seat behind the driver whose arm dangled out of his window with a cigarette in hand. The bus gradually filled with students, the volume of noise escalated with the volume of bodies, but I remained deaf and numb. My eyes were fixated on the door. What if he shows up? What if he sits next to me? It was a full ten minutes of suspense, a rude halting of time, an eternity of tiny eternities until the driver dropped the burning stub, revved up the motor, and closed the doors. The plastic windowpanes clapped over each crack and pothole all the way to Chinatown. As if waking from a dream, everything around me—the un-swept floor freckled with hardened gum, a girl's thin strands of static-electrified hair, the stop sign flashing red by the side mirror, impatient motorists slamming on their horns—all appeared with refined resolution, edges distinct, corners sharp, colors bright...but nothing, nothing was clearer than the smile of my mother. When I got off the bus, she took hold of my hand and we walked home together.

* * *

—Teacher Lin called me earlier today...I can tell by the way she talks that she really cares...what?...she said it was hard for him today, he was crying...she said it was expected since it was his first day...the others?...she said they fit in just fine...I hope he wasn't too much trouble...she really kept an eye on him, I could tell, I thanked her over and over for her reassurance, it's fortunate to have a teacher who's so caring...he's always been like this...he's already shy and quiet...this is the first time he's been by himself in a new place...I couldn't focus at work this morning, I kept thinking: What if he's not warm enough? What if he didn't eat enough for breakfast? Will he raise his hand to ask questions?...I was so happy to hear from Teacher Lin, but then to be told that he was crying...I don't know...what?...I have to give it some time...there are still conflicts, nothing's settled, I just try to avoid her, she finds fault in every little thing and exaggerates...let's not talk about it, it's not convenient...don't even bring him up, he's as obnoxious as ever, they don't know how to control him...anytime she yells at him, he insults her back...I haven't been feeling too well lately, I doubt it's anything serious but these last few days, I've just been sick, I threw up twice last night, just an upset stomach probably...he's yawning every five minutes so I'm going to put him to bed right after dinner...tell the Old Man he did fine, he'll be happy to hear...

* * *

After a dinner of rice, squash soup, and canned dace, followed by a bath, Ma spread the blankets out on the living room floor and turned out the lights. The sun had not fully set when I crawled under the covers feverish with the desire to confess, to tell her all that had transpired despite the numerous chances during dinner: Did you like school today? Was the teacher nice? Did you understand what was taught? Were you full after lunch? Were your classmates friendly? I answered all her questions with simple positive affirmations and avoided the truth like a sinful temptation, the furious truth longing to be heard and desperate to be told. Perhaps a confession would have implied betrayal. What if she were to think: Off to school on your first day and you've already gotten yourself in trouble; how can I trust you, ever? I wanted Ma to call Mrs. Lin and tell her I would no longer be attending her class.

I nurtured the agony in my blanket, for there was no place to leave it, and stayed awake most of the night but for some scattered dozing sharply interrupted by flashes of pummeling fists, slashing knives, and swinging baseball bats. I could not banish images of death from my mind. The more I tried, the more vivid they became—not of my death, no, but of capital punishment in old Chinese movies...of the betrayer, murderer, trickster, or wronged innocent laying supine, eyes to the turquoise sky futilely seeking divine mercy while the townspeople gathered to watch the great unifying spectacle of a gruesome death, the criminal (always a man) with his limbs and neck tied by rope to five horses that galloped across dusty plains at the flick of the whip after the judge stroked his beard with emphatic finality, the dramatic music, the last pleading echo, and then an armless legless headless torso, a five-pronged fountain spewing crimson...of the adulterous woman with bound hands and feet, screaming if not gagged, screaming innocence or regret or apology, squirming inside a woven cage hanging from a bamboo pole across the shoulders of four court officials, two in the front, two in the back, garbed in blue and black, with twirled mustaches and black sedge hats tipped with stiff red plumes who marched with synchronous strides into the river, her deafening pleas suddenly vanishing into a delicate ascension of bubbles....

In the darkness of the living room, I stared at the gravel-textured ceiling that at times appeared inches from my face and, other times, miles away, starless and flat. Someone sometime came out to urinate, left the bathroom door ajar, and did not flush. Cockroaches scurried out from under the dispensers of sugar, salt, and monosodium glutamate over the tinfoil-covered stovetops, sounding soft crackles. The refrigerator hummed, footsteps thumped, and Ba snored in a crescendo-decrescendo pattern, his arm dangled over the couch, its outline visible in the waxing-waning moonlight filtered through the shade. There were intermittent screeches of braking rubber tires over asphalt, a car alarm on repeat, and twice in the night, or early morning, there was a staccato honk (both times) followed by a man whistling (the first time) and a shouted greeting (the second time), then a clicking of heels (both times), and the open-close of a car door, the VRREAUOVVVV of a depressed gas pedal, and a screeching swerve around a corner. Also heard: the faint ticking of our clock, several ambulances (or police cars or fire engines), the distant cry of someone's baby, the ding of the elevator with no accompanying footsteps....

The next morning, I brushed my teeth and washed my face before a steady column of cold water that gushed out of the rusting faucet.

Good morning.

Good morning to you, Mei Lan, Ma said.

I'm so excited to go back to school.

That's good to hear. You're the oldest of the three, so make sure you keep an eye on your cousins and keep them out of trouble.

I certainly will.

After a breakfast of stale sponge cupcakes, Ma and Shorty walked the three of us to the bus stop and waited until the bus pulled up, the last chance for my confession gone with the squeak of the closing doors. How I prayed that Ma would come to school with me! I could not tune his voice out of my mind: You stupid fucker, I'm going to beat you 'til your mother can't recognize you...nobody crosses Leung Chau Wah...beat you 'til your mother...beat you 'til your mother...your mother...

Mandy took the seat beside me one stop later. We drove out of Chinatown and burrowed into the tunnel of tiled walls the color of desert sand, lit by tubes of orange and yellow lights. Blackened pipes spanned arched ceiling to crusty floor. We emerged onto the elevated highway, our skin warmed by the caress of the morning sun through the clattering plastic windows. Unprompted, Mandy extended her left hand. Take a look.

I looked.

Can you see it?

I shook my head. I could not see it because I did not know what it was, but she assumed I would notice it, and having noticed it, could tell it from the rest.

Here, she said, showing only her ring finger. A spark of sun reflected off the nail, freshly cut and filed, gleaming with a crescent moon cuticle. I still was not sure what she wanted me to see.

I smashed it when I was three.

Smashed what?

My finger. She began to tell me (her first memory, she claimed) of the day she went out for dim sum when a new family was moving into her building. A woman trying to hold the door open and funnel suitcases through at the same time accidentally let the door slip.

I didn't cry. The pain was like an itch at first, like a feather tickling the inside of my finger, and then it turned into a deep throbbing. There was a bloody imprint on the doorframe. My parents took me to the emergency room.

Didn't it hurt?

Of course it did, but I didn't cry.

I don't believe you.

She shrugged her shoulders and said, The bone wasn't broken but the nail was crushed. It cracked in half and fell off. The doctor said it wouldn't grow back, but it did, and now it's shinier and smoother than the rest. She fanned out her other fingers for comparison and it was true.

I told her how I hit my head once against the corner of our mailbox on the way back from dim sum, and I cried and cried...I remembered the clink of chopsticks on porcelain bowls, bamboo baskets stacked in towers wheeled along in steaming metal carts, each kind of food written in red calligraphy on white rectangles and shouted out by waitresses: shrimp dumplings, spicy tripe, phoenix talons (chicken feet), preserved duck egg and pork congee, and honeyed tofu. Ma and Ba were arguing, and I complained that I was too tired to walk. There were no seats on the ferry so I had to stand. There were no poles within reach so I had to hold on to Ma's dress. I was careful not to step on the foot of the gaunt hunchbacked man whose chapped big toe, earthen brown, and crowned with a blistered yellow nail protruded from his tattered shoe like a hatching alien; I could not stop looking at it, at its sparse crinkled hairs like the legs of a dead spider. Don't depend on others and learn to do things yourself, Ma shouted. You can walk, let's go...but before she could finish, Ba snatched me up in his arms defiantly and carried me the rest of the way home. We approached the foot of the stairs, up the first step, up the second, then a deafening scream, my eyes squeezed shut and the darkness was spinning around me. Not doing something helpful? Then don't do anything at all! Ma screamed as Ba lowered me to the floor to check my head. She grabbed my arm and pulled me up the stairs. She boiled an egg, peeled it, removed the yolk and put in its place a silver ring. Then she wrapped the egg in a handkerchief and rolled it over the bruise on the back of my head, tender and bubble-soft as if ready to pop. She fed the egg to the cat afterwards and showed me the ring. Its once shining surface was no longer silver but a swirl of deep blue and purple. The ring sucked out all the bruised blood, she said. Another memorable bruise was the one I got after I somersaulted off the couch out of sheer boredom and landed on the ground smack on the left side of my forehead—that was not until years later at a new apartment, and that time I did not cry. The bruise swelled and subsided, leaving behind a hardened lump noticeable in select angles of lighting that later distorted the fit of baseball hats. And then there was the bruise in the middle of May's forehead: she was standing on the bed against the window watching the blizzard as if in deep meditation with hands pressed against the cold glass that afforded a silvery myopic view of the city—the rooftops of its skyscrapers shrouded in clouds, its roads unplowed and devoid of cars, its sidewalks unmarred by footprints, its trees coated with snow like sweet frosting—and I, lying between her feet and the window, rolled over. She toppled and gave a laugh, her knees dug into my side, and her forehead slammed into the window frame. The bruise came and went but the scar came and stayed, a canyon-like sliver visible every time she smiled...Ba took the blame for it by telling Ma that he had dropped the telephone on her when she was sleeping in his arms; as ridiculous and comical as that sounded, it was the truth she knew until I told her the real truth many years later when I would no longer get in trouble for it.

At the start of class, Mrs. Lin handed us a printout. Follow as closely as you can, I know most of you can't read it, but just follow along. When you do this enough, you'll have it memorized.

All the students were lined up by height, shortest to tallest, facing out from each classroom, hands placed over our hearts. The loudspeaker in the ceiling sounded and the principal's voice was heard. We followed her recitation: I pledge allegiance to the Flag...

...dangling motionless from a hollow dowel jutting out from a stone column...

...and to the Republic...

...my worries had temporarily settled for I had realized that, even in extreme pain, one could be free from fear...would I be able to recall my beating with that same shrug of a shoulder?...

...one Nation under God...

...I pretended to mouth the syllables of the verses spoken too fast...

...and justice for all.

I half-followed the morning lessons and half-watched from some impossible vantage point our things being sold off or given away: one olive-colored couch, four black-streaked stools, one mahjong table, one video cassette recorder, one television with dust-matted antenna, one small folding dinner table with three warped plastic chairs, one hardwood bed, two lamps, one dented dresser with five drawers, one shiny red motorcycle, and the refrigerator we left behind—imagine if it were to slip from grip and cartwheel down the stairs rending apart walls, it would rock the earth on impact...once in the middle of the night, I remembered, or possibly dreamed, that for a few seconds a tremor in the ground woke me and sent me running to the living room to see our balcony rise and fall like a ferry on stormy waters against the backdrop of thousand-punctured skies bleeding silver...another time—a dream for sure—there was a quake of such magnitude that our furniture was uprooted, the walls collapsed, the doorframe cracked, the stairs shattered, yet there were no screams, for everyone had fled, and the centipedes, termites, ants, geckos, and mice were pouring out of the crevices and fissures to hurl themselves over the balcony in one big vermin waterfall...I rode on their slimy backs all the way to Grandfather's house for refuge...

...we were at Grandfather's saying goodbye, and

though it was a warm day, Ma made me wear the one-piece turquoise jumpsuit, its fabric suctioned tight onto my skin. We exchanged tearful hugs and blessings and farewells. We were all there together, and then we were not there anymore...we were outside the train station where Shorty took out a camera and said, One last picture before we go. I stood with my cousins at the corner of the sidewalk next to a traffic light. The three of us held hands, Mei Lan in a plaid dress and matching vest, Jia Ming in a sporty brown jacket, and I, a turquoise figure of wax with sweat-matted hair, an abomination from the sea glistening in the smog-diffused sunlight. Smile! she said, but I did not smile. There was a click and a flash and a whir, and then we made our way to the bustling platforms. No degree of complaining on my behalf would have led Ma to believe that I was about to get heatstroke. My outpouring of sweat that soaked the collar of the jumpsuit all the way through finally convinced her the outfit was not appropriate for the weather. I changed in one of the public bathrooms. For the rest of the way, Ma held onto me with one hand; the other was placed firmly over her purse where in a hidden pocket was the exact sum of one thousand American dollars, the totality of our monetary assets, half of which came from Grandfather. We stood beside the slumbering train surrounded by officers in uniform conversing in various Chinese dialects, the smell of fuel, the whir of helicopter fans hanging from steel rafters overhead, a perpetual collage of rolling suitcases, and a suspended billboard of the schedule denoted with numbered plastic cards that droned on like dragonflies' wings. With a searing hiss and the sound of a mechanical yawn, the train arose, the conductor sounded its horn, the doors opened, and we departed for a neighboring city where we were to stay overnight at a hotel...

...slowly steadily silently inevitably insistently irrevocably my fears returned, seeping in between the minutes to distract from the lessons and the recollections, a hovering presence amongst the rattle of pencils removed from tin boxes, the sonic flipping of new textbook pages, the distribution of acid-smelling yellow sheets to be filled with abecedarian inscriptions...I kept turning to see if Chau Wah was waiting for me outside the classroom...

...if I had real fists, they would clench; real veins, they would bulge; real muscles, they would flex...

...the train cruised on, silent as the landing of a cat tossed from a two-story balcony...

...I should've told Ma, I thought. At least I should've warned her. I'd be back dead or faceless, pounded into anonymity by adamant knuckles...

...speeding forth on a raised pair of parallel rails over a bed of fist-sized rocks and wooden planks flanked by fences to keep out roaming chickens and tail-flinging livestock, speeding past weather-slashed mountains and children shouldering bamboo poles strung with buckets of water and slouched laborers on emerald rice paddies roaming with water snakes...

...sly, manipulative and wicked, Ah San was born in the year of the snake...Chau Wah must have been too...

...on the creaking balcony with my alphabet book in hand, its cover snot green and flayed, I pressed the dust-caked play button for the voice of the woman to echo syllables against the susurrus of a hundred thousand dead ballerinas being swept...

...consecutive triplets, three of a kind, and a pair of eyes—once he won twelve times in a row, and one of the players said sarcastically, Make sure you don't tell us what your grandfather has next round...

...how are you feeling? asked Mrs. Lin—again a chance to confess, again a chance forgone. You don't want to play board games with your classmates?...

...no, I said. But Ma insisted, Drink some water, you'll get dehydrated. She twisted off the cap, tearing its tiny plastic teeth. The water tasted stale, warmed by...

...the sun traversed its usual parabola, a parallelogram of light on the brown carpet tracing the same path as yesterday...

...even if he had a pair of *hongzhong*, I wouldn't tell you, I boasted...so what choice did Grandfather have but to sigh, exhale smoke, and throw the dragons away?...

...the train pulled into the station with a high-pitched squeak. We got off and hailed two taxis to a nearby hotel where doors were numbered and elevators dinged at the press of each button, an inconsequential chime...

...sounding consequentially from the loudspeaker was the tone that signified lunch; I shuddered, refusing—or, rather, unable—to stand up. As the other students filed out, I remained in my seat, a frigid statue, unmoving. Mrs. Lin looked up. You're still here?

The long-awaited outburst in fragmented words between fragmented sobs: He's waiting downstairs...gold hair...he threatened...they tossed...they were laughing...he pushed me...the toy turtle...my cousin...but everyone was leaving...I don't want to go...I don't want to go...I don't...

She knelt on one knee and embarked on a monologue about growing up and dealing with new people and new settings. I heard not a word; my own membranous sniffing was much louder. I tried to listen, but I was too focused on the impending disaster. I bawled and begged her to let me stay, but she insisted that I had to eat. I told her I was not

86

hungry. She assured me that nothing would happen.

How do you know?

Don't worry, you'll be okay.

Can I have lunch up here with you?

I'm just eating crackers.

I like crackers.

You're a growing boy, that won't be enough nutrition.

Can I bring my lunch back up?

I don't think that's allowed. Come, I'll take you downstairs. She took hold of my hand and brought me down to the cafeteria, voicing more words of reassurance along the way before the final abandonment.

I stood in a line stuttering toward the humidity of rectangular steam baths for a circle of processed meat between buns, a limp stalk of broccoli, a small carton of chocolate milk, and a few wedges of canned pear. I looked for Mandy but could not find her. I took the same seat as I had yesterday, this time across from a short short-haired girl greedily eating her hamburger, the ketchup smeared like devil horns on her cheeks, a clown's fake smile.

Are you one of the new students?

I nodded.

Did you come with the other two?

I nodded again.

After each gluttonous bite, she asked a question which I answered without any words while looking around in all directions.

What are you looking for? Why do you keep turning your head?

Should I tell her? The whole story? The offer was tempting. Have you heard of Chau Wah? I asked. He's in the fifth grade.

She shook her head. I don't know anyone in the fifth

grade. Who's Chau Wah? Why are you looking for him?

I'm not looking for him...he's looking for me.

What does he look like? I can help you find him.

No, I don't want him to find me.

You're weird, she said, taking another big bite out of her hamburger.

We ate in silence until some compulsion made me say, He's got gold hair.

I don't know anyone with gold hair.

She started to ask more questions, her voice becoming one of the indistinct hundreds. I stopped listening. I did not understand why I had to be there, in that cafeteria. What purpose did it serve? It was for my schooling, that I understood, but I could have easily learned everything at home. I could sit alone with my books and cassette player, and there would be no unfriendly kids and no unpleasant food. I thought back to the dog-eared vocabulary book, the letters of the English alphabet in large block print, four to a page, each letter accompanied by an object that started with it. I thought back to the flimsy exercise books and the pages of little squares, which I filled with ones and twos and threes and so forth. I had already memorized Chinese poems from an old anthology of short verses, classics written during the dynasties. Over the years, I had forgotten not only the poems but the very fact that I had even learned poetry. The memory of memorizing poetry remained inaccessible and undisturbed in some recess of my mind for more than twelve years and was resurrected during my freshman year in college one autumn day when my Chinese teacher distributed a poem, *Jing Ye Si*, to be read aloud. After the first line, I heard myself declaim the last three without looking at the handout and realized in a state of absolute bafflement that I had learned it before. It was the only one from the anthology that I could recall because I used to recite it so often, loving the very sound of its words—*chuang qian ming yue guang / yi shi di shang shuang / ju tou wang ming yue / di tou xi gu xiang* (before my bed the moon is bright / seems like there is frost on the ground / head raised I look at the bright moon / head bowed my thoughts are homeward bound)—composed by the immortal Tang poet who drowned, legend accords, trying to embrace the reflection of the moon. I can see him now: flushed with the warmth of drink, rowing through a valley of misty mountains past daring overlooks, lone pavilions, and abandoned pagodas, he sings to the melody of undulating waves and the rhythm of his chirping oars. The cool night air is fresh and clear as the heart unburdened. Thin clouds part to reveal the moon rippling in the water, a full white orb glowing with promise and temptation. Suddenly he feels a surge of love—love for the solitary, love for the serene, love for the timeless—a love so pure as to beckon his leap...he falls like a plucked feather, sounding a whispered splash, and after the ripples subside, the boat remains afloat on a pristine reflection of star-speckled sky.

The lunch ladies circulated for the last time to make sure that the tables were cleared. I looked, I kept looking, but I could not spot him. The loudspeakers in the ceiling sounded the dismissal bell, and the crowd rose, heads bobbing, necks craned, mouths agape with laughter and chitchat; they were like the crowds on ferries that sailed over musty green waves, they were like the children at amusement parks licking ice cream that ran down cones, theirs was the camaraderie of sweat-beaded couples on badminton courts and ping-pong tables shaded under giant ferns, their shouts were the vocal emanations of joy from

89

swinging dragon boats, the clatter of chairs pushed under the tables sounded like the eight-handed scrambling of mahjong tiles....

My cousin sauntered by with his arm over another boy's shoulder—buddies they had already become. For a moment, I saw them as two old men with false teeth and white hair and ragged goatees, meeting each other in the street decades from now, slapping one another on the back, and throwing high-fives.

I joined the jolly tide that flowed out without worry. I looked, and I kept looking. Each step I took, I took with caution. He was nowhere to be found.

And then I saw him. He was there.

I wished I had told Ma to let go of her dreams of my accomplishments, her dreams of raising a good son. I wished I had told Mrs. Lin to part with her optimism. I was blameworthy for bumping into him. What had given me the audacity to touch him? He was untouchable—I knew that now, but I had not known before. He was going to rend my limbs apart; my stumps would spew blood like the criminal condemned. You little fucker...I'll beat you, I'll beat you 'til your mother can't recognize you...not father or brother or sister or aunt or uncle or cousin, but mother, devout, passionate, selfless, milk-bearing, life-giving mother.

I saw his hair, a keratinized candle flame. He turned toward me. I stared him in the face. I saw the reflection of myself in his eyes. His fist inflated, expanded, came closer, closer...I winced, my cheeks scrunched up...but there was no fist; it was a mere trick of timid eyes. I waved my hand without knowing why, tracing a half arc, and shyly, softly, muttered, Hello.

He turned to his friend, a tall slouching figure with an

oversized nose and undersized eyes, and said, Who's this idiot?

I don't know, just some punk, the friend replied. They cackled, imitating each other, and walked on. They cackled and walked on. His gold-streaked hair blended into the sea of heads. The threatening light extinguished.

That was it, the whole of it. He had forgotten, that dumb amnesiac. I merged into the formless parade of feet and exited the cafeteria back to class, an irrepressible smile on my face. What did he say? He said, Who's this idiot? The idiot you forgot. Who would have thought? Not I, and I thought all day and night. He would never remember me and I would always remember him. I was ready to smack a big kiss on Mrs. Lin's cheek, I was ready to listen now to her monologues of perseverance and affirmation, I was ready. I raced up the stairs, laughing, skipping every other step. There was recess outside, there were games to be played: cops-and-robbers, hopscotch, freeze-tag, and dodge ball. Ma would pick me up later, maybe with stray threads in her hair...and he would never remember...

...our hotel room had a queen bed flanked by two lamps on two nightstands, a table and two chairs, and a big curtained window. I sat on the edge of the bed. It slumped; I jumped. Jia Ming dashed into our room exclaiming, The bed is soft! I asked Ma if I could go to his room. After a slight hesitation, she agreed. She told me to come right back for bed as our flight to America was early next morning. We met Mei Lan in the hallway and went to her room instead. We climbed onto her bed, the three of us, and defied gravity; the force of our calves and the force in the compressed springs sent us soaring toward the ceiling that none of us quite reached even with tautly-stretched arms at the point of nil acceleration. Who knew there was such thrill in jumping on a soft mattress? We were used to blanket-covered hardwood beds. We jumped and jumped until all knowledge of time and place was forgotten, until we were transformed into creatures that knew only how to laugh, laughs that twisted our stomachs inside out and squeezed ripened tears from our eyes—up, down, up, down, up, down—until we were flat out of breath and lying on the wrinkled sheet with arms raised in surrender, giggling in spasms, our bellies desperately rising and falling, our sweaty faces gleaming in the warm lamplight.

Mrs. Lin was right; everything would be all right. Confronted with such an unexpected outcome, I no longer disagreed with her. For the rest of the school day, I was elated, jubilant, filled with an effervescent happiness. I no longer cowered before each present moment as if the weight of merely being there were too much to bear. There was a newfound buoyancy in my steps. I was overwhelmed with a sudden sense of lightness, like the moment an airplane leaves the ground. I was reminded of my first bicycle, dark blue and bright yellow with shiny spokes and untouched rubbery handlebars. It was a surprise that Ba brought home one night after I passed the test to start the first grade. We went for an evening stroll through the park. Along the way, Ma kept yelling for me to watch out for other people and held onto my handlebars at each crosswalk. I knew she was giving me the glare, but it was too dark to see. At the park, I raced ahead. The wind blew through my hair as I pedaled faster and faster. I could feel the burn in my thighs, I could feel my heart trying to pound its way out of my chest, and I loved every moment of it—it was a joyride as unforgettable as that first jump on a spring mattress.

3

CRÈME YELLOW AND BABY BLUE SHEETS bought on clearance to cover a queen mattress and box-spring on a yo-yo-wheeled frame, for three....

* * *

We moved to a studio apartment next door. Ma thought it was important to live, if not comfortably, then not uncomfortably, and that meant distance from the conflicts foreseeable since that ace. The rent cost the entirety of her salary plus a fraction of Ba's; add electricity, telephone, food, and other expenses, and we were lucky to break even every month. Under extreme scrutiny, stray dollars could be saved, but maternal instinct preferred hook-hung butchered meats to canned shelf-lined meats, the antithesis of Ba's philosophy that every cent was categorical, money was life, and the avoidance of cost was like cheating death....

* * *

Leaves turned crispy brown, acorns rained for squirrels to horde, birds departed in V's overhead....

* * *

In the woodlands of modest suburbia streaked with motorways flanked by rain-worn telephone poles connected via dipping cables, something hopped over the railing—Ba recalled its antlers, majestic scepters of bone that shone with a primitive energy—into the right lane and stood still (gloss-eyed, a wondrous calm gaze) as the vehicle decelerated with a screech and exhaled burning rubber. It lay quivering on the asphalt, brilliantly red. The shock and surprise of the situation quickly gave way to a calculated practicality. They rolled up their sleeves and lined the back of the van with newspapers and plastic bags. On the count of three, ready? One, two, three.

Did you serve it at the restaurant? I asked.

Of course not, Ba said. We ate it ourselves.

* * *

Walls were repainted white by white men in jeans stained with white curlicues, commas, comets....

* * *

—It's better though not by much, at least there's no more of Ah San's bickering...no, just next door...we were lucky, we applied for subsidized housing and got approved...it means that the American government pays for part of the rent, in our case, it's actually most of it, if it weren't for that, we wouldn't be able to afford it at all...what?...no, I took only the stuff we brought along...I bought a new bed, new cookware, and a table...the previous family left the couch and it's very clean, but they don't need to know that...I don't need to give that bitch things to talk about...I can almost hear it: She took this with her, she took that...

* * *

The window overlooked the adjacent building, the roof of which was studded with pebbles and cluttered with rectangular chutes, vents, smokestack-like projections, circular sewer grates, and fans under rusting domes, a singular blade of which my eyes would follow on slow afternoons until it appeared still and it was the world spinning around it....

94

* * *

A resumption of tensions long held in restraint; the intermission was over. My parents welcomed back the nights of discordant opera, for now there was privacy and space to fill with arguments. Every night was the same routine, an encore of the night before, a rehearsal of the one to follow.

* * *

—He can do his homework now without being disturbed by Jia Ming, that demon child...the farther, the better...if we never crossed paths again with Ah San and Lone Eye, that would be ideal...I still run into them...no, that wouldn't be wise, I keep it to myself...I'm learning that masks are necessary...what?...what about the bastard?...don't get me started, nothing has changed, his habits haven't changed a bit, he treats his brothers' wives better than he treats me, he pays more attention to their children than his own son...

* * *

I want you to remember what you said to me. I want you to remember your words. What did you say? You made a big speech about starting a new life, you wanted me to dream, to imagine, to envision—those were the fancy words you used. You told me to think about the life for our son, a world-class education for him. You said we'd start anew, build something from nothing, climb up from the bottom, remember that? To stay would be meaningless— that was what you said, and I believed you. I left family to come here. I left my whole family to follow you. Who do I have here? No one! You have all your brothers, and you have a secure job. Look at Wei Jian—everything he does he does for his wife and daughter, but you? You come home every night thinking the whole world has turned on you, blaming everyone but yourself. You treat your brothers' wives better than you treat me. What is here that we can't get back home? A better education? Sure, but he still would've gone to school. He'd grow up in a loving family with his aunt and grandfather. Before I left, the Old Man asked me if I really wanted to come, if it was a good decision. I can help you raise him here, he said. Of course he didn't want me to leave, why would he want that? He kept asking, Are you sure? All the way there? It's not another town or city, it's a different country, in fact, a whole different continent. You've no idea their customs, you have no friends or family there, you can't speak the language, you've never gone anywhere so far in your life, and he has a big advantage over you: He's got family and you've got no one. Are you sure you want to do this? You don't have to go with him. You don't have to say yes. We can figure something out. Every word he said was true but I shut him out. I was that foolish...I ignored a voice of reason, and for what? For what? For you? To be treated like this?

* * *

—I haven't been feeling well...everything makes me nauseous...don't tell the Old Man, I don't want him to worry, I'm sure it's nothing serious...

* * *

Glass-encased mercury dropped below the red tick marks. Before we left China, Aunt had stooped down, brushed the hair from my forehead, and asked if I was excited about seeing snow. Snow? Ma had interjected. What's so great about snow? We're not going all the way there for the snow.

* * *

Ba worked the same job on the same days, departed in the same van with the same workers, stood at the same spot before the same twenty-four-inch wok which he cleaned between orders with a thick-bristled brush under running water, then drizzled oil and tossed in the next set of ingredients to crackle for the next customer at the counter, before returning the same time each night for another verbal tango of angry crescendos. He wanted her to shut up, but she wanted him to talk. She complained about his distance and lies, and he her expenses and complaints. She wanted facts, but he thought deceit simpler. One remained silent while the other yelled until accusations became too exaggerated and required immediate objection; then the one-sided dialogues would become dual monologues. Neither listened, and neither responded except to disagree—that was the trademark of their verbal clashes. Their fights settled nothing. He always ended with the proud threat of divorce, assured it could not be fulfilled, for he knew she had no money and no nearby kin. He knew she held dearly onto the integrity of family and the shame of separation.

* * *

A long coat past the knees with a pastel green exterior and an interior lining of pink hearts inscribed in blue hearts, a wrong-gendered bargain from the downtown wholesale retailer that replaced the turquoise one-piece when its feathery insulation sank to the legs after wash number three. This one's perfect, she had said. It's long, it'll keep your legs warm, it's got a zipper and buttons and a hood with drawstrings, your neck will be covered—come, feel it—and the price! After a few rounds in the laundry, the coat flared out at the bottom like a dress. Waddling onto the bus each day, warm and self-conscious, I pulled back the fabric from the inside with pocketed hands in an attempt to reduce the conical protrusion....

* * *

—I'm very thankful for Teacher Lin, she's a godsend, she calls me once a week to let me know how he's doing, he's adjusting...remember those first few days? He was crying, I just worried and worried, I couldn't stop worrying, but it's better now, she says he's still very shy but fitting in well and making a lot of progress with his English...I was so scared, I kept thinking, What if he's too shy to learn?...if you don't speak English in this country, all you're good for is physical labor...he's learning it fast, very fast, she said he's doing better than some of the students who were born here...all those lessons on the cassettes must have helped...

* * *

In the still hours between arguments when her mind spiraled into regret and doubt, Ma found refuge in her other pastime: Cantonese pop music. She distracted herself with catchy melodies from the audiotapes and sang along, pitch perfect. Does this bother you? I can turn it down. I shook my head each time, and she would say with a sigh, That was why you picked the brush on your first birthday. Your grandfather was right. You were meant for studies. I couldn't open a book if you showed me how, let alone read it.

* * *

I should've listened but I ignored him. I shut my ears to his reasoning. He was wise. I was stupid. He saw right through you, but I didn't. What can I blame it on other than being too optimistic? It was silly of me to think things would change. I look back at everything and laugh—how can I not? I must be the dumbest woman on earth. Before

98

the marriage, you were already so proud over nothing. I paid for the entire wedding, the dinner, the rent for the apartment, all our new furniture...I even made your suit...and what I did get? Nothing! There was no ring, not even a cheap fourteen-karat band...

* * *

In an office hung with framed diplomas, a potted tree stood in the corner, its leaves with pearly white undersides and its trunk covered with snaky entanglements. Come on in, he said. The sunlight through the window scattered by the foliage created a bristling fractal-like shadow on the floor. Come on in, he said again. The doctor sat cross-legged with his coffee, milk-swirled and sugar-melted, the knot in his tie lopsided, his white coat draped over the back of his chair. I have some news for you, he said, shifting through some papers in a folder. He sneezed into the crook of his elbow and repeated, I have some news for you.

* * *

No memory of first snow; instead, a conjured image to fill its place: shadows of falling snowflakes projected onto our window hazy with condensation...I thought of dandruff, the dead skin of itching scalps; I thought of a giant haggard homeless man with legs in the ocean and torn jeans salt-soaked up to the knees, bent at the waist, hunched over the coastline furiously scratching his head with yellowed fingernails....

* * *

When your brother told you he was going to sponsor us over, you preached such great things, you made the future look so lofty. I listened, I listened and believed, I really thought things would change for the better. The Old

Man asked if I was sure I wanted to go with you. He warned me, You've no one there, no one, he'll have all the say, he'll be in control, his brothers will all be there, and you'll have no one. It was the truth but I ignored him. I'm just wasting my breath on you, I don't need to say any of this, you already know....

* * *

Blinking snowplows paraded to clear the newly fallen snow as she watched from the irrevocable distance of the present the one-in-infinite set of circumstances of the past, obsessing over each moment that could have turned out differently but did not....

* * *

Ma remembered how she crossed Pearl River by ferry one overcast morning and made her way through congested streets under clouds clumped gray like bruised knuckles. Her destination was a round table covered with a tea-stained, cigarette-burnt tablecloth on the third floor of a dim sum restaurant where a sole strand of smoke was twirling steadily upwards from a cigarette wedged in the nick of a glass ashtray. On the way over, she repeated the words that had been repeated to her the day before: You ought to meet him, a gentleman, a real gentleman. You'd like him. Give him a chance. Don't pass up the opportunity. Marriage isn't too far in your future.

* * *

Storms made telephone wires sag with icicles, obscured curbs, and accumulated pools to soak inattentive boots. Rolling tires spewed jets of ashen sludge to stain the bases of snow-mounds punched deep with footprints of shortcut-seeking pedestrians....

* * *

—I could've married someone else, anyone, but I ended up with him...It's getting to that time, they were all saying...You ought to be looking, he's not bad, he'd make a great father...everyone had something to say...I know there's no point in regret, but I can't help it...

* * *

I remembered all the men dressed in suits. I was wearing a blue and gray sweater, black pants, and polished black shoes, sitting on the edge of a chair frowning without intent into a camera that blinked its silver eye and sounded a whir to capture a light-inverted print of me sitting before a collage of gold proverbs printed on red rectangles—'*yi fan feng shun*' ('one sail smooth wind'), '*long ma jing shen*' ('healthy as dragon and horse')—while everyone else was giddily scrambling about...no, a mistaken memory, an anachronism; not having existed before my parents' marriage, I could not have possibly witnessed their marriage....

* * *

Ma left the textile company and found a new job at a nearby grocer. The hours were better suited and the pay was higher but the work was more laborious: stocking shelves, cleaning floors, organizing storage rooms, unloading crates from delivery trucks, stacking boxes of oranges, apples, and pears onto inclines outside the store with the price scrawled in noxious-fumed marker on rectangles of cardboard, transporting shipments of frozen wontons, dumplings, meats, and bags of ice into the freezer, displaying colorful boxes of dessert wafers, sugar-glazed crackers, exotic fruit-flavored candies, shredded dried squid, shrimp chips, and pretzel sticks with chocolate and strawberry dipping along the cashier line to spur spontaneous purchases...no more swollen feet and sore ankles, no more pedal accelerations and strips of thousand-punctured cloth, no more thread stuck to the bottom of her shoes....

* * *

—I'm eating things I never liked, tart and sour things, pickled mangoes especially, pickled cucumbers, dried prunes, dried figs...I've started putting dried orange peel into some of my soups, I never used to do that...I just started soaking a new batch of pigs' feet and eggs in sweet vinegar and ginger...with him, it was cool and sweet fruits I craved: honeydew, cantaloupe, and watermelon—I remember those watermelons, you kept saying it wasn't a good idea to eat so much watermelon, but I didn't care...

* * *

Torrential torments, nocturnal internal monologues: Dare I bring this child into these circumstances? Into this family? she kept asking herself. Could she be back? Did she come back? Could I do it again?

* * *

Her skin was stretched taut, a large flesh-hemisphere bulged from her abdomen, unnoticeable at first, but it became apparent in the months to follow. The nurse lifted Ma's shirt and draped a sheet over her legs. The shades in the air-conditioned room were down. An ultrasound device was wheeled in. The technician squeezed some jelly onto Ma's skin below the belly button. Upon contact with the sensor, an image appeared on screen, a scrambled sea of wavy lines and flickering dots, a blizzard of electrical snow....

* * *

—She would've been two and a half? No, three, she

would've been almost three...I'd felt so much guilt...I can't do it again, I can't...I was required then by the government, but here in the States, there's no such policy, I have a choice here, and I can't...I don't know...what?...why would I talk to him about it?...he has no say, he's not the one going through it...it'd be pointless, he'd just find a way to turn it into an argument...I don't think I can do it again...I felt so much guilt then, it was like some form of torture, I couldn't sleep for weeks after, and every time I closed my eyes, I heard accusations from the gods in heaven and from the spirit of the girl, I had so many nightmares that I'd wake up in the middle of the night crying, I'd go kneel before the altar and beg Guanyin Pusa for mercy, I told her I had no choice...these are not the best circumstances, the timing could not be worse, I don't want to bring her into the world to suffer, but I can't possibly...maybe she's back this time around, maybe this is my chance to atone...

* * *

Her belly swelled as jars of pickled mangoes emptied....

* * *

—We're doing well, how about you?...your grandson wants you to stop smoking, his teacher's been telling him how bad it is...what do you mean what business does she have?...you need to quit, we've been saying it for years now...I wanted to tell you...the doctor gave me a grainy picture of my womb today, he pointed out her head and arms and legs, I'm looking at it right now...

* * *

Have you been taking the vitamins I prescribed?
Yes.
Good...and you don't smoke or drink?

No, never.

Good. My secretary will set you up with the next appointment. Any questions?

I'm sorry doctor, she said. What if...what if I don't...?

* * *

Ma had a recurrent dream, she told me many years later, of a faceless fetus, or something faceless, speaking without a mouth—or perhaps its back was turned, she could not remember. It was speaking gibberish, and then it started to shout and snapped her out of sleep. Its words quickly receded from the grasp of memory, and the next day she thought and thought about what it had said but could not recall anything at all. I asked her what she thought the dream meant. She told me she did not know but that it made her feel the guilt all over again, yet she also felt like she was being given a chance at redemption. She said to me, The gods understood there was nothing I could've done but I knew I was being forgiven because she had come back for a second chance at life.

◆

Wei Jian was trained in carpentry and interior remodeling. With no culinary background, employment at Hu's restaurant meant reading off orders into the phone: Bean sprouts ten boxes, broccoli twenty boxes, bok choy twenty boxes, soy sauce five boxes, drumsticks fifteen boxes, sirloin steak fifteen boxes, pork belly ten boxes, jasmine rice twenty-five bags...he also signed for deliveries, transferred shipments with dollies from the truck to the walk-in fridge, peeled buckets of peapods until his fingernails were green, rinsed vegetables in enormous sieves, marinated tubs of chicken thighs, cleared tables, emptied ashtrays, washed windows, and refilled salt shakers, soy sauce dispensers, toothpick holders, and napkin tins.

Wei Jian knew he had to get out of there. He confided this to no one but his wife. It was neither the foreignness of the restaurant business nor the monotony of the work—he was able to overcome all sorts of drudgery with his unwavering work ethic; he found solace in knowing that all of his sacrifices were made for the sake of family—but the fact that his skills were not being utilized at all that became the root of his distress. The repetition of thankless tasks that he thought any primate could be trained to do gnawed away at him. He craved affirmation in the work itself; he wanted some sort of inherent reward—in short, his ambitions were too lofty for this kind of mindless labor. There were other aspects of the job that bothered him, namely the lack of an upward climb. He was started on the same salary as his other two brothers but he knew that any increase in his wages would not be from merit but out of charity. He was as replaceable as the next immigrant in line in need of a quick dollar. Around the six-month mark, Uncle Hu supposedly named Ba head chef of the restaurant and gave him a substantial raise with the incentive of encouraging his other brothers to work even harder. It was this, as revealed by Shorty in a candid conversation with Ma, which ultimately spurred Wei Jian's exit. Contrary to Uncle Hu's expectations, Ba's promotion, instead of being something positive, not only hastened Wei Jian's transition out, but further widened the chasm between my parents and resulted in the hurling of an empty cup that smashed to pieces after ricocheting from cranium to wall.

Of the four brothers, Ba was the only chef by training. He had earned a culinary degree at the age of eighteen and worked at various restaurants in China. His three cookbooks of traditional and gourmet recipes printed in top-to-bottom right-to-left calligraphy on laminated pages which he brought to the States rested atop our refrigerator at home to collect dust. The volumes turned out to be dead weight. There was no time here for authentic or refined cuisine; this was not a place for double-boiled silkie chicken and abalone soup which was rumored to relieve the pains of arthritis, not a place for air to be pumped through the necks of ducks to separate skin from flesh before being glazed in syrup and roasted in an oven heated by burning sorghum straw, not a place for gelled aspic to melt inside pork and minced crab dumplings steamed in bamboo baskets, no, here it was all about speed and efficiency; no books were needed to learn how to stir-fry an assortment of vegetables and meat in a wok with noodles or rice in under two minutes. Lone Eye was assigned to man the fryer and oven and made appetizers to order: chicken wings, teriyaki beef, crab rangoon, chicken fingers. He suffered frequent burns from the unforgiving splatter of oil which left little pockmarks all over his hands and arms. He learned to carry a tube of antibiotic cream and aloe vera in his back pocket.

All three brothers were subjected to the same misery at the restaurant, but Wei Jian, like all ambitious men, thought that the pain was exclusively his and that he somehow had more at stake than the others. Behind a calm demeanor, he frantically plotted a way out, never once revealing even a hint of his intentions, never once speaking about his perpetual frustrations. So perfectly did he hide his resentment that his sudden departure left everyone bewildered for the weeks that followed. It was a thorough shock for many reasons, the most significant one being that he took such a major step toward independence within less than a year of arriving in the States. It was not until some time had passed that my father and Lone Eye both came to appreciate just how daring a move it was for their brother to change jobs and how much mental preparation it must have required. Unlike watching a fledgling leave the proverbial nest for the first time, Uncle Hu's reciprocal emotion was not pride, but a hushed indignation. He had committed years of time and energy to sponsor them over, found them affordable housing, and provided them with secure jobs. Wei Jian's audacious departure could have been interpreted as an insult, a slap in the face, the rebellion of an ungrateful child, had he not carried it out with such tact and premeditation. Uncle Hu did not anticipate this sudden loss and must have felt some anxiety; how much sleep did he lose that night wondering whether his other two brothers would follow in Wei Jian's steps?

What had started as fodder for daydream—a different trade, a new manager—during those hour-long rides along tar-paved motorways, during those long hours restocking inventory and cleaning the dining area, began to take on the temptation of a possibility when some of Wei Jian's acquaintances mentioned to him that a few places in Chinatown were looking to hire. The more he tried to ignore them, the more fixated he became. The notion of transitioning out quickly shed its guise as a hypothetical and emerged as a very real obsession. He spent many a waking minute engaged in mental calisthenics, cartwheeling back and forth between whether or not to make his exit, and agonizing over how he would go about it. He paid closer attention to job openings and even signed up for a couple of interviews, which he would go to on his days off, telling no one but his wife who was sworn to absolute secrecy. With sweaty palms and a slight stutter, he met with various supervisors, paying no attention to the questions asked but wondering the whole time whether or not this was a good idea. Early on, he left these meetings without giving a moment's thought to the impression he left; instead, he walked away with an undertow of guilt and also a kind of thrill, as if he had stolen something precious or gotten away with a crime. One informal meeting with a home improvement contractor in Chinatown coupled with some words of recommendation from his friends, who happened to be on close terms with the manager, landed him a two-week probationary trial to see if he would be a good fit.

He found himself in quite the dilemma. He discussed the possibilities with his wife that night but Shorty could only offer emotional support, reassuring him that she would agree with whatever decision he made. In terms of practical suggestions, she was a dead end. I don't have enough experience in things like this, she said. Why not just be up front with Hu? Why don't you ask him for two weeks off so you can try out this new place? Wei Jian shook his head. One of Wei Jian's personal mantras was an old Cantonese saying—'*ke ngau wan maa*' ('ride an ox to look for a horse'). One ought to secure a better substitute before prematurely letting something else go at the risk of losing both. How could he break the news to Hu? What would he say? He played out various scenarios in his mind but they all ended with him being immediately replaced by another worker. Honesty was not an option, despite his natural tendency; he was sure there would be unintended consequences. Determined to keep everything confidential, he realized that he could not ask Hu for a temporary leave without fabricating a lie. For the next few days, he appeared distractible and withdrawn, unable to focus, and he even became neglectful of various duties at work. His brothers and coworkers all noticed and asked about his overall health to which he responded with assurances that nothing was wrong. Amidst all of their concern regarding his wellbeing, an obvious solution had presented itself. The easiest way to get time off, he realized, would be to feign illness.

Convinced that this was his best option, he assumed the role of a sick man without hesitation. He confessed to his brothers that he was having chills, muscle aches, nausea, and loss of appetite—in short, an overall malaise. Uncle Hu told him to take a couple of days off to recover. On the ride home that night, his mind was the clearest it had been since the interview. The timing worked out perfectly; he could go to his new job, leaving the apartment after everyone was gone and returning before anyone came back. The only slight obstacle was Ah San since she was home during the day, having entirely given up on finding work, but she was the least of his worries; he knew she would be out shopping most of the time and was too self-absorbed to know or care about what was going on around the house. After he told his wife what he had done, she was thoroughly conflicted but did her best to keep her composure. She wondered whether or not this would all end in disaster. Mei Lan, who really believed that her father was sick, brought him cups of hot tea to drink and wet towels to place over his head in the evenings. Since school ended before he got home, he told her that he was at the doctor's office getting more medicine whenever she asked where he came back from. Shorty was pained to see Mei Lan so stressed over her father's fake illness, yet all she could do was reassure her daughter that everything would be fine.

At the new job, Wei Jian exerted himself beyond capacity, doing everything he could to impress his supervisors. Right from the start, he demonstrated a tenacious work ethic, an eagerness to learn, and a humble approachability. Though the atmosphere was foreign and half of his colleagues did not speak Chinese, he felt more comfortable here with blueprints and buzzsaws than in Uncle Hu's kitchen with wonton wrappers and chicken wings. By the end of the first day, he already had a firm grasp of some of his expectations. The telephone rang every night, calls from Uncle Hu and his coworkers all wondering how he was doing. He told them he was coming along but still not back to full health. Uncle Hu told him to take as much time off as he needed for recovery. Wei Jian wondered if it would have been better to just tell Hu the truth. Would Hu really not have given him a temporary leave? It seemed to be a preposterous presumption, especially in hindsight, but he was so far into this lie that there was no turning back. He even had the next step planned out. He was going to call up the manager and tell him a version of the truth: that he was granted only a week's time off from the restaurant and needed to know soon if he would be offered an official position. This was not the ideal scheme, but it was the most conservative. He could not in any way risk losing his job at Hu's. The immediacy of the situation called for action; he did not have the luxury of time to debate alternative options. He also wanted to end the farce as soon as possible, especially since his daughter took his feigned illness quite to heart and Ah San was beginning to get suspicious. Wei Jian lay sleepless in bed rehearsing the best answers for all possible questions, plotting out the imaginary conversation with the precision and exactitude of the diagrams he worked from, preparing himself for disappointment though he could not help but feel a faint, lingering hope; he was unsure whether this optimism was grounded or whether he was merely projecting his desires upon an otherwise desolate situation. Armed with a mental flowsheet of potential dialogue, he made the call on a Friday night. Before Wei Jian had a chance to say anything, the manager offered him the job right then and there. He told Wei Jian that he would make a great addition to the team and that he had already drawn up all the papers for him to sign. In between repeated expressions of gratitude, Wei Jian negotiated a later start date so that he could properly quit his job at Hu's. Shorty burst into profuse tears when he hung up the phone and told her the news.

Having secured the reins of this new horse, he was ready to ditch the blundering ox. He spent all weekend mulling over how to make the cleanest possible break. He let a few days pass after his return to the restaurant, and then informed Hu in a matter-of-fact tone with a businesslike attitude entirely devoid of sentimentality (he neither thanked Hu for the privilege of working for him nor expressed any sadness about leaving) that he had taken another job more suited to his skills. Hu, keeping his reflexive emotions in check, responded in like manner: he did not ask the reasons for leaving nor did he voice his suspicions about the sick leave, but simply smiled, firmly shook Wei Jian's hand, and wished him the best of luck at his new employment.

The truth was that all three brothers, whether they acknowledged it or not, felt perpetually indebted to Hu for the new life he had given them; working for him to the best of their abilities day in and day out was an obligation and a constant source of stress. To the envy of my father and Lone Eye, Wei Jian had severed his chains of servitude in one quick swipe without threatening the bond of fraternity, at least not outwardly. Wei Jian did not give any more thought to the possible consequences of his decision; what was done now was done. Galloping off with reins in hand, he was not going to look back.

* * *

Shorty came by and chatted with Ma over tea. He's much happier now, she said. Better hours and better pay. He's home in time for dinner every night, and he's doing something he enjoys and knows. It's made a world of difference.

I'm so happy for you, Ma said. What does he do?

Similar to what he did back in China from what I can understand, remodeling apartments and houses, renovating office space, interior decoration, things like that.

Are they Americans?

Who?

His coworkers.

Some of them are...but the boss is Chinese.

How does he talk to those who only speak English?

I'm not sure. I think all the information he needs is in the diagrams and blueprints. He gets along with everyone, and he's picking up English words here and there. I can't believe he's working fewer hours than before but making more money. Expertise in something really opens up a lot of doors, even for us unlearned folks.

If I could speak English, I'd have a more comfortable job as a secretary or something. I could sit in an office and answer phones instead of moving boxes all day.

There are beginner English classes starting at the—

That's not for me. I wouldn't be able to concentrate in

a classroom, in one ear and out the other. I guarantee it.

Maybe it'll be a good distraction.

I doubt it.

Anyway, the real reason I came by...I wanted to tell you...

What?

I'm expecting as well.

You, too? Ma exclaimed. Stand up! Let me take a look...I can barely notice...do you know if it's a boy or girl?

Not yet.

What perfect timing...and with his new job!

I know, Shorty sniffed, wiping a tear from her eye with the apex of a pale knuckle.

Ma thought for a moment and then said, You're very fortunate. Not without reservations at the revelation of personal troubles, she did let this one slip: I'm so happy for you...you know, we're still struggling here...we'll barely make the rent in a few months when I have to stop working.

Stop being so modest, that's not true. We all know your husband makes about nine hundred dollars a month after his promotion to head chef. That's four hundred more than the others so I'm sure you're not struggling *that* badly. Don't tell anyone I told you, but I think Wei Jian really considered leaving after your husband got promoted because he realized he wasn't going to advance anywhere. He wasn't meant to labor in the restaurant business and...

Ma stopped listening. All she had heard was: A promotion...four hundred more...four hundred more...four hundred...and not a word after that.

...with his salary alone, you should be fine, and the great thing about America is...

Ma stared at Shorty's moving lips and thought back to

113

the days of pulling weeds, laying bricks, and wheeling manure, of bleak sunrises over communal shacks and straw-stuffed mattresses infested with bugs and hunchbacked laborers tilling fields, of maggots festering in the blisters between the webbing of her toes from standing knee-deep in feculent mud.

...they've got programs to help families in need, you just apply and...

Four hundred dollars more after a promotion—was it really true? How did Shorty know? This is the first time I've heard of it, Ma thought. Almost nine hundred dollars...that's nearly twice as much as what he...it can't be...something doesn't add up. All Ma could think about was the five-hundred-dollar check that Ba brought home every month. There seemed to be a clear discrepancy between what she thought he was earning and what he was actually earning.

...they'll give you weekly coupons for baby formula, eggs, juice, and milk.

Four hundred more, Ma thought. How did Shorty know?

The teapot went dry; the moist leaves settled at the bottom.

It's getting late, Shorty said. I should go...don't worry so much...things will work out, they always do.

Ma smiled in acknowledgment and accompanied her to the door.

In bed that night beside the white noise of Ba's dream-filled snoring, Ma remained awake, wondering how Shorty knew about his promotion while she herself was left in the dark. How did someone outside of immediate family know about his raise while she, his own wife, did not? When she looked at it that way, it was obvious that he was lying to her about money again, a resurrection—or rather, resumption—of an old habit. She suspected that he was bringing home just a fraction of his wages, and that the rest was paid to him in cash.

* * *

That first meeting, I could've said no, she told me many years later. The second meeting? Same. And the third? I didn't know what to think anymore. He started to seem pleasant, and it went on and on, and then he proposed. I was undecided, but everyone insisted. I was undecided, but I said yes. And then he confided to me that he had no money. Our new life was to start on my savings alone. His brothers had paid for their own weddings, so he could do no different. He was on the verge of tears that night when he told me—of course, now looking back, it was all an act, but he played it convincingly. I told only the people I could trust because I didn't want any rumors to spread. The Old Man paid for the wedding from his own savings and we got some help from your aunt as well. What did we get in return? Not a thank you, not a single nod of acknowledgment, nothing. You know, I even made a suit for him to wear. He never bought me a ring, not even a cheap fourteen-karat gold band...I'm not talking about diamonds, that was far beyond our means. He paid for the bed, that was it. I reminded myself that material wealth was not important, his commitment was all that mattered, but he couldn't even give me that. In no time, the lies started. Everything he said was a lie. It was like a disease he suffered from. He was incapable of telling the truth. He lied about even the most minor things. He was never home when you were a baby. I was up every night pacing the room with you in my arms. You cried all the time, you woke up every night and cried for no reason...and you were always sick, if not at the beginning of the month then at the end...do you remember what happened when you were six months old? You had such a high fever that we had to rush you to the hospital. I packed a few bottles and diapers and ran to Pearl River with your aunt. They were about to unhook the ferry from the dock, and we screamed for them to wait, waving our tickets in the air, and luckily they let us on. When we got to the hospital, I handed you over to your aunt—my arms were numb from carrying you—and right at that moment, you clenched both your fists, your eyes started rolling back, and your arms and legs stiffened. Some nurses were nearby and brought you into a room. They urged us out to the waiting area. We'll take it from here, we'll take care of this, the doctor's been paged, please, we'll come get you when things are calmer, they said. So we waited, and I kept pacing back and forth until finally the doctor told us you were okay, that your fever was coming down. When I saw the intravenous needle in your forehead, I almost fainted. That night, I went to the bathroom every ten minutes. It's a funny thing—when I get nervous, I have to go like there's no tomorrow, every ten minutes. I mean, where does it all come from? And where was your father during all this? Probably cuddled beside some whore. That bastard lied to me about *everything*, nothing truthful ever came out of his mouth. Do you know the kind of stress that puts a person through? Do you know what a nightmare it is to live with that kind of man? He's the one you're to spend the rest of your life with, he's the one you're to depend on in difficult times, and everything he says can't be trusted—do you know what that feels like? We were struggling financially, right from the start. He contributed nothing to the wedding, but

116

he took all the credit...and I let him because I knew it was important for him to look good in front of his brothers. You have to keep face, you don't flaunt your disgraces...a poor man should eat leftovers behind walls, not in public. Your father told me he made three times less than he did and kept the extra money with Lone Eye. He told me so himself after I bought the motorcycle. He's a good man, he'll provide for you, he's caring, and he's handsome too, they had all said. But he's not a good match, I told them. They kept urging, It's getting late, it's getting late, if you don't find someone now, you might not find anyone. So I gave him a chance. He had me fooled with his sweet talk. Your dad's quite an actor. I wonder why he didn't go to drama school with those talents. He can be quite the charmer if he wants to, doling out compliments like candy on New Year. Everyone thought so well of him. I always thought there was something fake, but no one else noticed, and eventually they all had me convinced he was a great guy. He was rotten inside, crawling with maggots. If I'd known your father would turn out so, I would've backed out, no matter the consequences. He changed, he really did, almost overnight. He lost his temper over little things, he lied about everything...he treated me like a burden to be shed. At first I thought it was a phase, but I couldn't have been more wrong. He had secured himself a wife and now there was no need to keep a mask on anymore. It's remarkable how I've managed to endure it all. I can recall no happy memories with your father, not a single one. The joy of family is most apparent on birthdays and holidays when everyone gets together to celebrate...you had turned two, it was New Year's Eve, everyone was out, everyone was happy, people were lighting firecrackers in the streets to scare away evil spirits...I phoned the Old Man that night

117

and told him your father wasn't coming home. Working late again was his excuse. How stupid did he think I was? Restaurants don't open on New Year's Eve. Everyone's home with family. How stupid did he think I was? Your grandfather said, Just bring your son over and eat with us, there's plenty of food. All along the way, the streets were filled with the laughter of families, whole families, mothers and fathers holding their children, laughing, shouting, lighting firecrackers, the kids were all running around in new clothes and carrying lanterns, the sun had just set, and the night sky was burning red...I couldn't help but imagine your dad snug in some other woman's bed...I mean, where else could he be? We got to the Old Man's house, and he opened the door before I even knocked. He asked me what was wrong, why my eyes were red, and I said, Nothing, nothing, some dust got into them. He looked at me for some time and didn't say a word, and then he said, Come on in and eat.

* * *

Shorty came by again for a chat over tea, something she started doing almost every week after we moved out. Did I tell you? she said. I quit my stupid job. I had issues with the management all summer, and after what my husband did, I decided to take that step myself. I mean, what's the worst that could happen? I was getting charged for missing items each month. I said, Boss, my pay's been going down, this is getting out of hand...

...in the summers, an assortment of trinkets was laid out on tables in the street...each morning, Shorty tried to sell off the organized clutter of bronze statuettes, miniature vases, good luck charms, gold-on-red prints of proverbs, pinwheels, toy cars, keychain ornaments, action figures, dolls, incense urns, belly-protruding Buddhas with

118

earlobes shaped like chicken drumsticks, Japanese comic books, Chinese martial arts and romance novels, plastic bonsai trees in blue and white porcelain dishes filled with opal-textured pebbles, faux gem necklaces, finger-traps...but few things were sold, and at the approach of winter, everything went back into storage. There were cuts in her paycheck for missing items; she was responsible for any discrepancy in the inventory...

...he accused me of stealing, he accused me of taking that stuff for myself! I said to him, I'm sorry, sir, but what the hell would I do with mobiles and old books and toys? Those things can't feed my family. And he just shrugged. I've never seen such a pitiful attempt to make a few extra dollars. He might as well just take it right out of my purse. Then last week, some money went missing from the cash register and he confronted me about it. He said he would withhold my next three paychecks if I didn't return the money so I quit on the spot.

That sounds awful.

I was so upset. If he didn't want me working there, he could've just fired me. It would've been much easier. Anyway, I went and got hired at the hotel on K— Street as a janitor.

Another new job? You and your husband both seem to be running laps around Chinatown's job market, Ma joked. How did you land one so fast?

I had a friend fill out an application for me, and I showed up for a supposed interview, but they didn't ask anything and told me to start the next day. They didn't care that I didn't speak English. There are some Chinese workers there, so they've been helping me out.

How fortunate.

I'm still upset over my ex-boss. How low do you have

119

to sink to extort money from those you hire?

At least you've got work. I told my manager that I wouldn't be able to work in a few months and asked if he could hold my spot. He said, If I take you back, then I would need to fire whoever I hire to replace you. Ma paused for a moment before continuing, Truly we're in a world run by the dollar. You know what else he said? He said, What if every woman here decided to get pregnant, then what? I'd lose my business if I held all their spots.

That's harsh.

He said he'd give me a week off at most.

At least your husband can take care of everything in the meantime, Shorty said before taking her leave.

That statement lingered in Ma's ear. It was timed so perfectly that Ma was beginning to wonder if it was intended, if there was a seed of malice behind Shorty's visits. Twice now she had come over for a friendly talk only to leave Ma in such a state of agitation—four hundred more...a promotion...you're not struggling *that* badly...your husband can take care of everything in the meantime— that she resolved to clear the issue once and for all.

Ba came home from work at his usual time. He showered and went straight to bed before his hair had fully dried.

You're going to get a headache like that, Ma said.

I crawled in between them, Ba to my left, his face to the wall, and Ma to my right facing the window left slightly open to counter the malfunctioning radiator.

He told me he won't hire me back, Ma said.

Ba did not respond.

Did you hear what I said? He told me he won't hire me back. He didn't say it outright, but he implied it. Once I leave, I'm as good as gone.

Ba, still facing the wall, finally said, There are other jobs out there.

I know that, but things will get more difficult. As it is, we're barely—

Just find another job.

I'm not...that's not why I'm—

He turned around with a suddenness that made me jump. What do you want me to do?

I'm telling you what the situation is.

And I'm telling you the solution. Get another job, it's simple.

She got out of bed and flipped on the light. I know I can just get another job, but it's not that easy. Why are you being so hostile? I won't be able to work soon, and when the baby's due, it'll be even harder to make ends meet and—

He tossed aside the quilt and stood up. I work like a slave ten hours a day in the heat of those damn woks! I come home with a paycheck. That's the duty I fulfill every month. What else do you want?

Don't raise your voice like that. Listen to me, I'm—

I don't know what else you're expecting. I stand for ten hours without a break in that infernal kitchen—

Do you think I have it easy? Do you think work is a vacation for me? When I come home I do all the housework, all of it, dusting, mopping, scrubbing, cooking...I work just as hard as you—

I earn my share and give you the check every month. It pays for whatever it pays for, and that's that. I'm capable of nothing more!

You think you're the only one suffering—

You complain every night—

I didn't want to bring this up. I wanted to let it go like

I've let so much go before—

Why don't you get to the point?

She paused for a moment and then asked, How much money do you actually make?

He was stunned, not at the question, but at its unflinching directness. There was a moment of contemplative silence before he quoted the number printed on his last paycheck, and the one before, and the one before, the repetition intended to mock, and hide.

I know the number on your checks. I'm asking how much you actually earn.

I just told you.

I'm going to ask you one more time. Are you hiding money from me?

I'm not hiding money from you if that's what you're thinking.

I think you are.

If you're not going to believe me, then I've got nothing to say.

But why not? Why don't I believe you?

Who the hell knows?

I don't believe you because you're lying.

That's a circular argument. That means nothing.

You know full well you're lying to me. I know all about your promotion.

I'm tired. I'm not going to talk about this anymore.

When are you not tired? When is there ever a good time to talk? If you don't want to keep arguing, then just answer me: How much money do you make?

I've already answered your question.

You haven't.

He paused, the black holes of his eyes widened. You really think I'm lying to you?

Your silences reveal more than your words. You can fabricate your words but not your silences. How can we raise a family if there's no trust? What am I supposed to do about the bills when my job ends? How can we take care of a new baby? I don't understand how you can be so selfish—

He stormed toward the door, twisted the knob, and flung it open. It slammed against the wall with a mighty thud, yielding a view of the paint-chipped wall of the hallway bathed in white phosphorescent light. The only sound heard, the only thing felt, was the reverberation of the pivoted-door-to-wall collision until he screamed with a force as great as he could summon, I don't want the fucking baby! Get rid of it!

I sat on the edge of the bed, my butt numb from inertia. What followed I recall only in pieces, a shattering of sequential moments. I started to cry, an unintended mirroring of Ma's response to his words.

Jia Ming stuck his head into our doorway. Then Shorty appeared and pulled Jia Ming back. What's going on here? This is grown-up business...you go back inside.

It was a show for his brothers' families and the other neighbors, she told me years later, a show with no cost of admission.

He spoke again with a voluminous lead actor kind of fervor. Get an abortion! I don't want the baby. Who knows if it's even mine?

What did you say? You bastard! You fucking bastard!

Ah San, Lone Eye, Shorty, and Wei Jian were all standing at the door watching. Ba took three sudden steps—a motion so quick my eyes did not catch—and Ma was on the floor before I could hear the slap. I want you to take that son of yours and go the fuck back to China.

Crawl back to your father's! Get the hell away from me!

She struggled to get up, her belly protuberant, her arms flailing like the legs of an upturned beetle.

I began to bawl, my cheeks drenched with lachrymal waterfalls.

You fucking bastard, you think you're a real man now?! She grabbed the closest object, an empty cup on the table, and hurled it across the room. It ricocheted off the corner of his right eye, leaving a heated pulsating bruise, and smashed to pieces against the wall. A complete suspension of time coupled with an impenetrable silence followed the last echo. The lamp was dim; their faces were drenched in equal parts light and shadow. I sat stiff-jointed on the edge of the bed, knees bent at right angles, soles parallel to the floor, my heels lightly resting on the edge of the box-spring, watching them: she on one side of the room, he the other, and the space between an irreconcilable distance. Somewhere buried in that exhibition of familial discord was the root of their growing separation: not the suggestion of infidelity or abortion, not his theatrically violent assertion of masculinity, not even the seed of doubt planted by Shorty, the logical conclusion of which Ma arrived at and realized clearer than the light of day that he was hiding money from her—no, it was never the money that Ma cared about; it was the lack of trust.

Shorty rushed into the living room and snatched me off the bed. I screamed and thrashed as she carried me out. I screamed and thrashed, convinced I was being kidnapped, convinced that if I left that door, I would never see my parents again. Then I was in their living room sitting on the couch Ba used to sleep on, a mug of hot water in my hand. What happened? What happened? What happened? they kept asking.

The cup left its mark, but so did his slap. When May was born, there was a dark smudge on her left wrist. Ma said it was from the impact, that she was trying to break her fall inside the womb.

I want you to take that son of yours and go the fuck back to China. Crawl back to your father's. Get the hell away from me, Ma recited to me one lonely night; those words resonated in her memory for the next sixteen years. That's what he said to me, and I knew, I knew that moment that I would leave him.

That day, the end of his wait—or rather, her wait, for he did not know he was waiting—came right after my college graduation. Twenty-four hours after walking across the stage to receive my diploma, I sat in a courtroom to hear a judge confirm their names, dates, and places of birth, and date and place of union, and ask whether there was an irretrievable breakdown of marriage to which both parties answered yes. The judge signed some papers and said the divorce would be official in ninety days, a pronouncement sixteen years from the flight of that empty cup.

◆

It was a cloudless day, the kind where the sun's reflection off dewy grass made one squint. While I tried to explain in fragmented English that we had missed our stop, Ba traced the outline of a rounded belly, hunched over to pull an invisible object from between his legs, then made a rocking motion with his cradled arms. The driver, unable to resist a laugh, understood and told us to sit in the front on the reverse route so he could let us off at the hospital.

We waited at the terminal, the early rays warming our faces, the crisp morning air smelling faintly of exhaust. When his coffee break was over, a twist of the key woke the vehicle with a sputtering shudder and bore us on our way.

Through a series of white-walled halls separated by doors stenciled with semicircle windows, we found Ma's room. She was in bed, attached with wires and stickers to a looming monitor where peaks and troughs paraded steadily on. Her water had broken overnight. She had been brought here by ambulance. I asked how she was doing because it felt like the right thing to do. She smiled and said that she was fine, that things were coming along. She was wincing on occasion and pacing her deep breaths, in and out, in and out. Contractions, I later learned, of the uterine wall to expel its mystery nine months in the making.

We waited for hours; the clock hands circled (the antithesis of vultures), welcoming life with the beat of their temporal wings, soundless and delicate, an incremental march toward miracle. The windowless room was dim; the filamentous embers seemed to burn with difficulty. We were surrounded by a dull glow and a metronomic beep, our family of three, four to be. I took a seat in the rocking chair and began swaying back and forth, rocking nervously upon two arrow-less bows, back and forth, back and forth like the pendulous throes of her labor.

I knew when Ma felt pain because her hands would clasp the railing until her knuckles turned white. When the contractions became more frequent, the doctors were paged. Someone wheeled in a cart with shallow drawers stocked full of little glass vials and plastic-wrapped syringes. Ma was instructed to sit up and hunch over, her legs hung off the edge of the bed. Her skin was cleaned

126

with swirls of iodine and a sterile sheet was draped over her back.

I got off the rocking chair and stood beside Ba. It took a few seconds for the feeling of seasickness to go away.

Just a pinch, tell her she'll feel a tiny pinch, tell your mother to hold still.

There I was, not yet done with the first grade and already put on the spot to translate for my mother. Both Chinese interpreters in the hospital were away; one was out sick, the other on vacation. The words were heavy; I had to hurl each character out of my mouth with herculean effort. You'll feel a small needle, but don't move, I said.

She won't feel anything afterwards, said one of the nurses.

The resident ran his finger along Ma's spine again before inserting a longer and thicker needle. She let out a suppressed scream. Her hair was disheveled, her breath reeked of stagnancy, and her gown, loosely knotted, had fallen off her shoulders.

Hold her, hold her tight, she's squirming.

I can't. She's the one holding me. I can't even move, she's grabbing onto me, said the nurse.

Readjust and try again, said the attending anesthetist.

I'm hitting bone...I can't—

Pull it out.

The beveled tip was withdrawn, a pinprick of blood emerged from the tiny hole. He drew up more lidocaine. For the second time, the glint of needle met the glint of sweating skin. She let out another scream and jerked her whole body forward.

Is she in pain? asked the doctor.

Are you in pain?

Yes!

She feels pain, I said.

I'm cold. Tell the doctor I'm very cold.

She feels cold.

The room was sweltering. I stood next to Ba, my fingers grappled onto a pocket of his jeans, his hand gently resting on my shoulder.

Pull the needle back, then move it a little to the left. Tell her we're almost done. After this, she won't feel anything.

What are they trying to do? I asked Ba.

Let me feel. Okay, right here, you're off the midline. Try again. Are you getting resistance? Pull it back, shift it to the right.

Ma howled in surrender.

Why is she in so much pain? Nurse, keep her still please!

She's holding on very tightly.

Two other nurses stepped in to help. The trainee's hands were now visibly shaking. Another nurse, heavier set, came to take the place of the one Ma was bear-hugging. The whole ordeal was beginning to feel fictitious and dramatized, like a staged play, the lights dimmed for effect.

What if they don't get it right? What if they mess up? What if they can't...? I stopped mid-sentence, not knowing what they were trying to do. I did not want to watch, but my eyes were fixated. My arms were wrapped tightly around Ba's waist; the side of my cheek dug against the side of his hip. He looked down at me but said nothing. I became desperate. What's taking so long?

If only you knew how advanced Western medicine is, you'd have no reason to worry, Ba said in a calm omniscient voice. She'll be fine.

It's in! It's in! exclaimed the resident whose forehead glistened with beads of sweat.

I guess sixth time's the charm, said a nurse sarcastically.

He withdrew the needle after threading a catheter through and pulled off his gloves with a resonant snap. A nurse retied Ma's gown.

Giving birth to your sister, that was nothing. Do you know how difficult *you* were? she asked me years later. I was on oxygen, and there were six nurses, three doctors, three students, and your aunt all in the room, encouraging me, counting my breaths. When you finally came out, I really thought I had died and reincarnated. When your aunt held you in her arms, you reciprocated with a lovely golden stream. Serving me a cup of tea already? she had jested.

When the chaos had settled and everyone was gone, I went back to the rocking chair and, despite my aversion to oscillations, rocked myself into a precarious sleep.

* * *

Her legs were splayed; her thighs vast and white like two snowy tundras. The obstetrician told Ma to start pushing after she examined her cervix and deemed it sufficiently dilated.

Push! Push! Come on, one, two, three! chanted the nurses.

Ma strained, her fists gripped onto the retractable banisters. I stood beside the bed and clutched the railing while Ba stood in the corner of the room.

Does it hurt? Are you okay? I asked.

It's just pressure. There's no pain, she said. Tell the doctor I only feel pressure.

I don't know how to say pressure in English.

That's okay, she said, grimacing and grunting, an orchestral arrangement of the jungle, her breathing unpredictably erratic, at times long and drawn out, at other times short and sporadic. Her legs were spread like the wingspan of a carnivorous bird, majestic, ready to soar. Saliva thick as egg white pooled at the back of her throat. She defecated. A nurse discarded it into a small pail hanging at the foot of the bed. I can't believe I'm going at a time like this, she said, laughing out of embarrassment.

Push, come on, push!

Here it comes! I can see the head.

Deep breath...now push!

I stared at the patch of hairy flesh gaping like a big butchered eye struggling to wink, the folds of elastic skin stretched, the swelling crater grew to the size of a half dollar, a golf ball, a fuzzy blushing peach...pink membranes sparkled in the dim light, tearing, torn, and the blood of cracked vessels oozed forth in bright red rivulets, lapping upon the shorelines of her thighs.

Here it comes! Keep pushing!

Her head slowly emerged, a giant wet prune crowned with sparse black hair. With expert hands, the doctor lifted the baby out, lubricated with pink and yellow secretions, an eight-and-a-half pound skin-shriveled creature that sounded a piercing cry neither of despair nor joy but of life, of pulsating biological life.

Ba had left the corner and was now standing at bedside. He snorted and chuckled. Now that's a *big* healthy baby! he said with a glow of such incredible warmth on his face as I had never seen before.

The only thought on my mind was how small she was, how perfectly she fit in the doctor's palms. A plastic clamp was placed on the umbilical cord two centimeters from the stump of her belly button. The doctor handed me a pair of scissors. Do you want to cut it?

I reached for the scissors with a teeth-boasting smile.

No! Give those back to her. I don't want you to mess it up. Just let the doctor do it.

What did she say?

I handed the scissors back.

I guess she doesn't trust you...what about you?

Ba took a step back and shook his head.

The obstetrician snipped the cord without hesitation and carried the baby to a cart padded with blankets and warmed by an overhanging lamp. Her tiny fists batted, her tiny feet kicked, and her cries filled the room as she was inspected from head to toe. After the placenta had passed, the doctor handed the baby to Ma. She gazed upon the new child, now quiet, and it was Ma who started crying.

Ba approached her with flattened lips, suppressing a smile, and Ma passed the baby to him. He rocked her gently in his arms and looked at me. Sit down, he said, and placed her on my lap.

What are you doing? Ma's voice was hoarse, fatigued, its fire expended. Watch him, please. Make sure he doesn't drop her...I'm so tired...just be careful...I'm so tired...

I felt the weight of my new sister on my lap. Her skin was damp and her nose was studded with little yellow dots. Her mouth was toothless, her gums red and smooth, her lips moist and slightly ajar. Human features indeed, but an alien still, the most alien thing I had ever held. When she started to cry again, Ba picked her back up. I looked over and noticed that Ma was getting stitches.

Doesn't that hurt? I asked.

The anesthetic hasn't worn off.

You can't feel the needle?

No.

Then what do you feel?

Nothing.

Nothing. She felt nothing. It was then that I understood why they held Western medicine in such high regard. I watched with fascination as the needle curved its way in and out, pulling along a strand of black thread...and my mother feeling none of it.

What's the baby's name?

Ma turned to me. What is she saying?

The name, she's asking for her name.

The proclamation of a name, a philosophical ideal sculpted with a tightening of vocal cords and taps of the tongue, transformed into ocean-wading electrical signals to traverse along wires across thousands of miles of lapping salt water and emerge back on land through walls to the plastic receiver in Ma's hand one night, her name had been nominated by Grandfather, a name with meaning and significance, an imprint of a certain hope. But she had no English name, so my mother, on sheets soaked through with sweat, still breathing deeply, gave no answer.

What's her name? the nurse asked again.

Ma shook her head.

The nurse left the room and returned with a list of girl names in alphabetical order. We need a name so we can identify her in the nursery. Ask your mom which name she wants.

I translated what I thought she had said.

Ready? She began to read from the list.

Within seconds, Ma lifted her hand. That's it, tell her that one.

Is this the one? the nurse asked, repeating the name.

She's asking if that's the one you want.

Ma nodded.

Because it was simple, I later learned, just two easy syllables for Ma's Chinese tongue to pronounce. That was how her English name came about, three letters almost alphabetically equidistant from each other, a name that I later morphed into another by swapping the order of its letters, a move of such cleverness then that I smiled for days, for its rearrangement spawned another word: a homophone of *little sister* in Chinese, and also, the month of her birth.

4

WHEN MAY WAS TWO-AND-A-HALF MONTHS OLD, Ma went back to work at a new teahouse and seafood restaurant adjacent to the Chinatown gate. Its front doors were flanked by four display windows, two on each side, boasting crystalline tanks of lobsters with rubber-banded claws, crabs stacked in pyramids perpetually crumbling and reassembling, sandstorms of translucent shrimp, planar-eyed flounders, and cod with a sheen of green. Behind the reception booth where a suited man stood with a walkie-talkie in hand was a glass case displaying, falsely, the world's third largest shark fin, a massive triangle of dried and wrinkled pelt that looked like petrified wood.

Ma left us home alone because it was too expensive to hire a babysitter. One of our neighbors, who worked afternoons, checked on us in the mornings. Throughout the day, Ma would call several times an hour with repetitive questions, her voice loud above the backdrop of commotion, her concern never waning. During her lunch hour, if time permitted, she came home to check that the stoves had not turned themselves on, that there was no smell of gas in the air, that the phone line was still functioning, and that my sister was fed the bottles of formula left three quarters submerged in a pot of hot-turned-lukewarm water. She checked and double-checked and triple-checked that the door was locked before rushing back to her carts of sweet egg tarts, mango jelly, and congee with fish and peanuts. For the first couple of weeks, this became the source of innumerable arguments. One thing was certain: she would not turn to Ba's side of the family for help. Ah San was home all day, but she was not going to ask her to look after us.

What the hell are you thinking? Ba asked. What happened to your common sense? You're leaving a six-year-old at home with a newborn? Are you out of your mind? I know that we can't afford a babysitter, but do you think leaving the children by themselves is the best alternative? We could get arrested. They could be taken from us due to parental neglect. I don't understand what the big deal is. Ah San is home all day, why won't you ask her to help look after them? If you don't ask, I'll ask her myself. What's happened to you? You're always going on about family this and family that, so explain this absurd lapse in judgment. You keep saying, though he's only six, he's a very responsible boy…I know that, you don't need to keep repeating it, I know that he can feed her and burp her and change her and rock her to sleep…I know all of that, and believe me, I know how much of a blessing it is that our son is so well-behaved, but are you aware that you're putting the whole family at risk by not getting help? Any slight mishap, and I mean anything, and we're in trouble. What if he drops her? Have you thought about that? That's not so hard to imagine, is it? Let me say this clearly so that you see the truth for what it is. If he drops her or if he gets hurt himself trying to take care of her or if someone finds out they are home alone, they would be confiscated by child protection services and we could land in prison. A six-year-old can't tend to all the needs of a newborn girl without any accidents. If anyone finds out, the children will be taken from us and given to foster parents. Do you understand? What you're doing is counterproductive and

135

potentially criminal. I don't see what the big deal is. Why won't you ask Ah San for help? Is it all because of this grudge you're holding against her? Why are you being so stubborn about it? If Ah San wants money in return, we can pay her. I'm sure she won't ask for much. She understands that we're all struggling here.

It was the first and only time Ba had ever been so worked up during an argument.

First off, stop telling me all the horrible things that could happen because that accomplishes nothing. I already know all the pitfalls of leaving them home. I worry and think about it all the time—every minute of every day while I'm at work—it's the only thing on my mind. Why do you think I call several times an hour to make sure they're okay? I run back here during my lunch breaks to make sure everything is fine. When did you start showing interest in the children? When did you have this epiphany that you're a father? Maybe instead of sleeping all day or burying your head in a newspaper on your day off, you should play with them. You have no right telling me how to raise *my* children when you yourself do nothing. Don't tell me what to do when you don't contribute anything yourself. I know that leaving them at home is a terrible idea, but you don't seem to understand that I have no choice. We just can't afford a babysitter. And you keep bringing up Ah San...I'd rather send my children to a slaughterhouse than lead them straight into the mouth of that snake. That bitch will corrupt them for life. Are you so dense as to not see the malice she harbors against me, against us? Of course, you don't. You look for the easiest solution, the one that burdens you the least. You don't understand the complexity of the situation we're in. You think to yourself: Ah San is free, she can help us out. It's not that simple. Do you think you're fulfilling some moral duty by telling me how everything could go wrong? I get no support from you, I have no other family here, and all we ever do is argue. I'm doing the best with what little we have. Don't you dare make me out to be the negligent mother. When school starts up again, we'll definitely need a babysitter. We can't pay for one now, but by then, hopefully I'll have saved up enough to hire one. Don't you think I've thought about just staying home and taking care of the children? But if I don't work, we won't have enough money, it's that simple. I asked for a later start date, but the boss wouldn't give it to me. He said there were plenty of people waiting for that spot. So I had to take it. The hours were too good to pass up. I'm home right before school ends, it's perfect. I'm the one trying to juggle all of this. I call up my father and sister every night, and this is all we ever talk about. They're my only support, yet they're all the way on the other side of the world. I don't know why I ever came to this country with you. This is a living hell for me. My life is just one big stress after another. All you do is undermine me. Your son here, this six-year-old boy who's taking care of his sister all by himself, is the *only* person I can trust. He's the only one who will do a good enough job. I have more trust in him than anyone on your side of the family—that's the truth— and if you don't understand why I'd say such a thing, then you need to take a long and hard look at the situation. This isn't ideal, I know. What six-year-old boy spends his summer taking care of a newborn? But this is how we have to manage for now. I taught him how to feed her, to make sure that the formula is neither too hot nor too cold, what position she should be in when she's asleep, how to clean her up when she soils a diaper...I personally taught him all of those things, and I've watched him do them, and I have

137

more trust in him than any babysitter I could ever find. Don't ever mention Ah San again. It's not a grudge I'm holding against her. It's not some little playground resentment. Have you not seen the way she's treated us ever since we arrived? The very fact that we're renting this apartment, this place of privacy where you can be your true self, where you can shed that mask and be the bastard of a man you really are—you can thank her for it. She made it impossible to live communally, so we had to move out and dig ourselves into this financial hole. Even from the beginning, she schemed with her one-eyed husband and cheated us out of the bedroom that was rightfully ours after drawing for it under conditions that *they* set themselves, so no, it's not just a grudge, it's because she's the most malicious woman I've ever met. She is rotten to the core and full of bad intentions, and I'll never let her near my children, let alone take care of them. I've thought about quitting my job and staying home with the kids, but I can't. Do you really think the money you bring back is enough for this family? But don't worry, I have a solution. I can put a stop to these troubles. Do you want me to hire a babysitter? I can do that right now. I know how much they cost. I've asked around for the cheapest ones—in fact, I have phone numbers written down, so if you want, I can go ahead and call one of them up and she can be here five days a week starting tomorrow bright and early. Do you want me to do that?

Why are you even asking me? Go ahead. Call someone up! That's what I've been trying to say. He had stepped right into the trap, even though it was there in plain sight. He knew what she was going to say next.

I can do that, and I know how we can pay for it. Do you want to be a good father? A loving husband? Do you know what you can do to help out? In case you don't know what I'm getting at, let me say this loud and clear: Stop hiding money from the family! I know all about your promotion. I know that Hu is paying you more than the others, and I know that—once again, like you did in China, because old habits never go away, and because you value money more than anything else in this world, even over family—I know without a doubt that you're hiding money from me. So, if you want to be all fatherly and caring and supportive, then be truthful about your earnings. With the extra cash you're hoarding, we can afford the babysitter with some to spare.

Ma had this in her ammunition all along, and she was waiting for the opportune time; because of this trump card, she was always the puppeteer of their arguments. She controlled when the fight ended; she had the power to silence him whenever she had said or heard enough.

He sighed and said nothing.

I thought so. You're a real bastard, you know that? I can see right through your mask. You're a despicable man. You're the biggest mistake I ever made in my life...marrying a man who cares about money more than family, what the hell was I thinking? Why are you so quiet? Where's all your concern now? Where's all that lead actor energy? You disgust me. You're a hypocrite and a miser. Don't you ever walk in here and undermine my decisions. Don't you ever call me a negligent mother. I put my children before everything else, before my happiness, before my health, but you? You can't even be honest about your earnings. I applaud you in one sense, to be so stubborn as to hold onto a lie like this even in the face of irrefutable evidence. Your brother's wife has told me on multiple occasions about your promotion. Do you think Shorty would just make up something like that? You'll never admit to it because that would mean admitting to every single lie you've told about your wages in the past. You'd have to concede that you were wrong to argue with me all these years. I've come to accept your twisted mentality. I know that will never change. So, let me give you some advice: A man who values money over his wife and children is in no position to question any of my decisions. Don't you ever think I'm a bad mother. Don't you ever make judgments like that about me again. Don't come home every night acting as if the whole world has wronged you. Your brother Wei Jian was wise enough to leave that job, and he's doing fine. In fact, he's making more money and working fewer hours. Why don't you follow in his footsteps instead of taking out all of your frustrations on me? Isn't it obvious to you by now why your brother Hu sponsored you for immigration? Do you really think it's because he's a generous man at heart who wants us all to experience the good life? No! You're here to provide labor for his restaurant!

♦

Ma took an immediate liking to Mrs. Song because she knew the meaning of discipline. She was a short, stout woman with an elliptical face, a protuberant stomach, eyebrows sliver-thin amplified by two carefully penned eggplant purple lines, lips shaded blue, bluer on certain days than others, and hair that gleamed auburn under phosphorescent light. If there was ever a face of distilled unpleasantness, hers was it. She was strict, almost tyrannical, always ready to yell until her face flushed red and her voice cracked, until she spiraled into a coughing fit, blamed us for it, and summoned her voice to yell again.

Mrs. Song was a regular customer at the new teahouse. Every weekend Ma would tell me how she ran into my teacher and how they talked about my conduct and effort at school. It was knowledge I could have done without; I felt I was under more scrutiny than all the other students.

If you need to hit him, go ahead—anything to make sure he doesn't act up.

Teachers can't hit children here, but it's good of you to support it.

Thank you for making sure he doesn't fall in with the wrong crowd. I'm sure understand the reasons we're all here.

I dragged the dead weight of my feet every morning to the classroom, though not with total reluctance. Due to the number of chairs in each row and the alphabetic distance of our last names, Mandy's seat ended up being next to mine. We seized every chance at conversation, and when the circumstances were not conducive to speaking, I slipped notes to her in crumpled-up pellets or neatly-folded squares, random notes remarking on random things.

One day, someone caught chewing gum was made to sit in the corner to copy out an entire article from the encyclopedia by hand. The rest of us were sentenced to a period of quiet time. I drew a caricature of Mrs. Song: a large beach ball of a body topped with a small head. I made her eyes bulge and added some stick figures for students. Having thoroughly drifted into my project and paying no attention to the class, I gave a sudden jump when Mrs. Song screamed aloud, Who didn't pass in homework? I'm missing one from...you again! A double stroke of bad luck for the kid in the corner. I'm going to talk to your mother about your behavior. Do you want to grow up to be a beggar?

I penciled in thunderbolts shooting from her eyes and fire coming out of her mouth and handed the piece of paper to Mandy. When she saw the drawing, she cupped her hand over her mouth to stifle a burst of laughter, the tail of which escaped and resembled a fart.

Who's making noises? Who was that?

The amusement drained from Mandy's face as she assumed a stoic mask. I was able to control myself until I saw the blank look on her, and then I almost became hysterical. It was the funniest, blankest look I had ever seen: the skin was taut at the corner of her lips, her eyes stared ahead with a deep vacancy, and her eyelids were flared beyond necessity. I bit my bottom lip as hard as I could to fight off the laughter with pain, but I was still smirking. Pencil in hand, I lowered my head and pretended to write.

Who made that noise? Do I need to send all of you to the principal's office? She walked back to her desk threatening to cancel recess if there were any more disturbances.

Mandy put the cartoon in her pocket and took it out during recess when we were alone in a section of the playground. We had a long laugh over it until it was no longer funny. Do you want it back?

I shook my head.

She put it in her pocket and said, I'm going to throw it away at home so Mrs. Song will never find it.

Everyone was running about on the open field of asphalt. They were playing freeze-tag: immobile immunity with the crossing of arms, a dead body upright. We decided to join the game.

Look who it is, said Jia Ming. Are you two done professing your love to each other?

I felt a warmth rush over me. I looked at Mandy, who looked away. I wanted to push Jia Ming to the ground and sink my teeth into his forehead.

We're here to play. I'll be on one team and he'll be on the other so—

So you two lovers can chase each other? He trotted around us in a circle and cackled. Did you two kiss yet?

Someone called a timeout. Since you're both joining, one of you two will be the new 'it.'

We played rock-paper-scissors, and I won, but Mandy lunged forward and tapped me on the shoulder. You're it! She ran away, then turned around and flashed a smile. Her figure receded and the sound of her steps echoed across the playground.

* * *

Do you know how much the sitter costs? Do you know? Now that he's back in school, we need a sitter for the girl. There's no alternative. I give the woman all of my instructions every morning, and I keep wondering whether she's doing a good enough job. Do you think I get any rest at night? Every day my mind is flustered. I go to work and mull over every possible thing that could go wrong. Maybe I'm sick in the head. I don't know. I can't stop, and then I start thinking about other things. Is the boy learning at school? Is he asking questions? Is he being too shy? Has he really adjusted? What if this? What if that? And then I think to myself, There's nothing here for me. Why did I come? For what? For this? For you? People at work tell me, I saw your husband the other day. He's such a polite and handsome man, he must treat you so well. And I laugh. I laugh to myself, and I think, How wrong they are! They don't know what I come home to. They don't know about your lies. All they see is the mask you wear so convincingly. I know you're hiding money and wasting it on scratch tickets like all those other despicable kitchen men. I ask myself every night, What did I do to deserve this? How did I end up here?

So Ba retrieved for the nth time from the ice-room of his memory the one response self-evident for the audience of himself in the grand cinema of his mind, the silhouette of his lone head watching on screen the repetition of his days: handfuls of bean sprouts, diced onions, peapods, stiff-stalked broccoli, strips of marinated chicken, and noodles pre-kneaded pre-powdered pre-packaged, all tossed to pop, sizzle, and crackle, to be shuffled and scrambled and poked and prodded with a spatula and then portioned onto plates...the wok was tilted and scrubbed with a thick-bristled brush under running water to wash off the residual grains of rice, the last snippets of vegetables, the unwanted bits of charred meat, remains washed away by eddying currents toward the sieve above the gutter to be scooped up and thrown into the dumpster for rats and raccoons to scavenge overnight...repeat, repeat, with no respite, for the spectacle-wearing, cane-bearing old man who parked his pickup truck with headlights still on, for the skinny woman who ordered enough for one three times her size, for loved kids and lovely families and loving couples...a surge of orders during the prime hours of five to nine in the evening: jasmine rice plates served on red trays covered with a printing of the Chinese zodiac or packed into boxes and brown paper bags with fortune cookies and packets of soy sauce...once I overheard him telling Uncle Hu over the phone about some construction workers—fat jackasses, he called them—wearing baseball caps, paint-stained jeans, and sour sweatshirts, who ate half of their food and threw some cigarette ash into the remains to force a full refund…from the ice-room of his memory, his response: I stand for ten hours in that kitchen, I can barely feel my legs at the end of the day, and you think I'm hiding money? Do you think I have a separate bank account? Do you think I have a hidden safe in the freezer at work? Maybe I have to defrost the bills before spending them! I've said it before, I'll say it again, and I'll keep saying it: I'm capable of no more!

* * *

Mandy missed school several times a month because of her tendency to get sick. She was excused with notes signed by her uncle, a physician trained to discern diseases by the pattering of pulses and the texture of tongues. The notes were legitimate since both Mrs. Song and the school principal frequently sought her uncle for remedies. The clinic was located in the back corner of a shop in the heart of Chinatown that specialized in Buddhist ornaments and decorative vessels, attracting residents and tourists alike with its eclectic selection of Buddhas. Its shelves were lined with statues of the Buddha in various reincarnations, all featuring upturned soles, floppy drumstick earlobes, radiant smiles, and swollen bellies, as well as statues of the merciful goddess Guanyin Pusa in a flowing white dress holding a golden vase, and the red-faced, long-bearded general Guan Yu with *guandao* in hand—Ma had adopted him as my guardian and protector back in China, and to this day, his statue stands behind a golden urn between two red lamps on a small altar in my mother's apartment. The walls of the shop were hung with prints of proverbs for health, wealth, and happiness, three-dimensional plaques of dragons and phoenixes grasping pearls in their talons, scrolls of landscape art and calligraphy, and calendars with mythical figures in watercolor. They also sold wood etchings in glass displays, bonsai trees in white and blue porcelain bowls, horoscope books for the present year that featured (interspersed between the text and to my absolute fascination) drawings of human faces and palms dotted with dissecting lines, an anatomy of superstition. The main display window was saturated with rows of cross-legged Buddhas, lighting the street with their smiling deluge, laughing the silent laughter of the immortals. The left wall of the store was lined from floor to ceiling with hundreds of brass-handled wooden drawers stocked with dehydrated longan pulp, twigs of Chinese tamarisk, dried pomelo peel, sweet wormwood, ma huang, strychnos seeds, lingchi mushrooms, cockleburs, croton seeds, dried wolfberries...in the glass counter were plates of dehydrated seahorses, ground scorpion, snake slough, ginseng roots, dried sea anemones, powdered geckos, turtle plastron, and the gonads and phalluses of various animals...behind the counter, Mandy's aunt, with scale in hand, retrieved and measured out the combination that was specified by her husband, who saw his patients in the back corner behind a white curtain and wrote out in longhand the recipe for a slow-boiled medicinal broth to be consumed once, twice, or three times a day. The ingredients were collected and piled onto squares of brown paper, folded up into packets to be brought home and emptied into a clay pot shaped like a girl's head with two protrusions like erect pigtails, one a spout for the steam to escape, the other a thick handle. I remembered my first taste of Chinese medicine: sitting on a stool in that apartment back in China and forced spoon by spoon to drink the bitter brew, it made me throw up more times than I could count. This is good for you! Ma yelled, hitting me with the wooden end of a feathered duster...despite my uncontrolled bawling, I managed to drink an entire bowl and spent the next hour making sure that I kept it down.

* * *

Autumn departed, and winter arrived. The fallen snow, sprinkled with sand, dirt, and cigarette butts, liquefied into slush on warmer days only to harden back to ice. Before the dirty mounds punched with deformed footprints could fully melt, another freight of frigid winds dressed the ground in flawless white and adorned the stairs of fire escapes with icicle fangs.

Our routines were unchanged. At the end of each school day, marked by the ringing of a bell, we welcomed the sting of cold air that made our breaths visible, our legs jittered their way out of the building, and our heads, laden with hats and earmuffs, were the targets of snowballs flung by hands in polyester gloves and knit mittens. We crammed onto the yellow bus that roared over uneven roads—each pothole triggered a rambunctious rattle, a vibration of green vinyl seats, a clapping of plastic window panes— across the suspension bridge that looked out toward the vast unreachable where ships floated on a pointillist sun-tinted blanket of shimmering crests. We filled the bus with unrestrained shouts, and our conversations struggled to be heard. The driver, an old stuttering man with curly white hair, stopped before a red light one day, put the bus in park, and walked down the aisle chastising us for our misbehavior. The angrier he got, the more his words crumbled, and the more his tongue wrestled with itself.

Uh uh uh uh I'm an idiot buh buh because I can't suh suh suh speak right, and you kids won't leh leh leh leh leh listen to me, mocked Jia Ming.

We were one rowdy crowd. Because of the cold, our recess was replaced by forty-five minutes of hushed play inside the classroom. Under Mrs. Song's scrutiny, excitement was held in check and dialogue kept to a minimum; the only moments of vocal freedom were lunch and the commute to and from school.

* * *

—It's cold here, even colder than last year, the heat doesn't always work...three nights ago, we all wore our winter coats to sleep...it wasn't this bad last year...what?...there's always snow on the ground, the people at work tell me it hasn't been this bad in years...it's so cold that I don't want to leave the house...every step I take, I have to be careful not to slip, it's tricky, especially when the snow melts a little and freezes again, then the whole road is covered with black ice, I've seen so many people fall...just the other day an old lady lost her balance and sprained her ankle...what?...it's slow in this kind of weather, nobody comes out to eat, we used to get six dollars in tips a day during the week, and maybe up to nine on the weekends but now we're lucky if we get three...all the old folks stay indoors...on the weekends, if the streets aren't so hard to walk through, we'll get...where would I find another job now?...it wouldn't be much better...I can't speak English, so I'm basically crippled here, I'm limited to whatever's in Chinatown...that's why I tell him all the time to work hard in school so he can be his own boss...the teacher this year is very strict, I see her once in a while and she keeps me up to date with his progress...what?...I don't keep in touch with them...no, Shorty hasn't been by since that time...I don't blame her, if I were her, I wouldn't come by either, why volunteer yourself into another family's dysfunction?...I know he's hiding money again, but what can I do about it?...he's never going to admit it...Shorty already told me that he got a big raise after being promoted to head chef, but he denies such a thing ever happened, he's clearly lying, he gives me his check every month, but I know that part of his salary is being paid in cash, and he wants to keep that part all to himself...it's incredible to think that in such circumstances, he could be so selfish...I just accept it, nothing's changed and nothing's going to change...if you want something, you get it yourself, if you want to go somewhere, you go on your own...that's why I insisted on working over the summer, it was terrible leaving them home, but I had to...you've no idea the kind of stress it puts a woman through, to be in a marriage like this...why do you think I'm forcing myself to work so hard?...I need to save up money and become independent...if I had to depend solely on him for money, imagine the power trip...what?...now he leaves the apartment earlier and comes home later because of the weather, the snow doubles his commute time, but it's better that way, it's quieter, less time around him means less time to argue...I can be in the greatest mood, and the moment I see his face, I turn sour, and all I feel is this rush of hatred...enough about him, the girl's doing well, did you get the most recent photos I sent you? I mailed them two weeks ago...isn't she just beautiful?...she has those big bright eyes just like her brother...coming home to her after a long day at work makes it all worthwhile...she's a natural motormouth, she's been babbling since she was four months old and now all she does is try to talk, it's adorable...she's great with the babysitter, she's not afraid of strangers...on the contrary, she smiles and tries to talk to anyone who holds her, it's remarkable, she'll grow up to be a socialite, I'm sure, I've

149

never seen a baby so comfortable with strangers...did I tell you the other day she tried to mimic me? I was wiping up a spill on the table, she was sitting by herself on the bed and she started wiping the mattress with the doll in her hand and then she toppled over, I laughed so hard, it was the cutest thing...I have to keep things extra clean now, she's been teething and she chews on anything she can find...the pediatrician says she's meeting all of her milestones on time and coming along just fine...yes, I know, she's much heavier than her brother when he was her age, it's a difference of night and day, she's plump and healthy and he was thin and always getting sick, I don't know what they put in the formula here, but it's working, she's packing on weight like you won't believe...I'm supplementing the formula with solid food, I buy fresh vegetables and live tilapia at the market, I cut up the greens into fine bits, steam the fish, and pick the meat off with my fingers and make sure there're no bones, and then I cook it with rice into a thickened porridge and add just a sprinkle of salt, you should hear the way she smacks her lips when she eats it, she goes through several small bowls a week, even the boy loves it, he's always asking me to make him an extra portion...the doctor said to watch for mercury levels or something, I don't know, the Old Man made that for us and I made it for my son and we all turned out fine...what?...she was sitting up with support a few weeks ago, but now she can almost sit up by herself, and she's made a few attempts at crawling...she causes me so much stress, but I wouldn't give any of it up, the way she lights up when I come home from work and greets me with a string of babbles just melts my heart, nothing puts a smile on my face like her smile...I thank heaven every day that she's healthy, she's so much easier to take care of, she sleeps through most nights unlike her brother who used to cry all the time...it's a blessing how easy she is compared to him, I'll never forget having to run to the hospital either at the start or the end of every month when he was a toddler, I'll always remember that time he seized because his fever was so high, that was terrifying...I thank heaven every day for giving me such a healthy baby this time around...she always wants to play, she loves peek-a-boo...she responds to her name, she's done that for a while now...she waved goodbye to me the other morning, it was sad and sweet at the same time...what?...no, I still worry at work, I try to be calm, but I can't, I call the house several times a day to check in with the sitter, I told her that I'm just too high-strung, and she understands, she doesn't take offense to it...I'll tell you what's not ideal: the apartment is too small for four people...no, we're breaking even every month, my boss did give me the raise as anticipated, the restaurant was bringing in consistent business before the weather got so cold, it'll pick up again in the spring...luckily, we have subsidized housing, and heat and hot water are both covered, otherwise we'd be in debt for sure...tell the Old Man we're doing fine, I don't want him to worry, I have many things to be grateful for...things could be much worse, but I guess you could say that about any situation...

* * *

Yellow blobs lodged between teeth turned the enamel yellow, then brown, then black and spawned bacteria with sharp fangs that bit the gums with lightning streaks. The camera zoomed out. The kid was crying. His cheek was swollen and red and throbbing. Then it was off to the dentist who strapped him into a recliner under white lights beside a tray of knives and drills and picks. The door closed to the sound of maniacal laughter. The screen

151

blackened, the credits rolled on the left, the toothbrush and toothpaste sang a tune on the right: so ended the video on oral hygiene one non-particular morning.

You saw what happened, affirmed Mrs. Song. I expect you all to brush your teeth every morning. If I catch any of you with bad breath...

The next morning, I performed with near perfection the up-down strokes and the side-to-side strokes and then scraped my tongue clean, reaching as far back as possible, evoking multiple gags, empty wretches, expectorating globules of saliva and phlegm mixed with toothpaste that stuck to the side of the faucet, refusing the call of gravity until my hand redirected the flow of water to wash it down.

Show me your teeth, I said.

Mandy grinned.

Now stick out your tongue.

The ruby protrusion quivered, too organic to be a gem yet too pristine to be flesh.

Your tongue's red, really red!

I brushed it for a long time this morning. Your turn.

I showed her my teeth, then stuck out my tongue.

Yours is really red, too.

Teeth and tongue comparisons became our morning ritual. Mandy's teeth were always spotless, her tongue smooth and slick like a misshapen strawberry without seeds. One morning, I woke up late and had to forgo oral hygiene and breakfast in order to catch the bus. When she told me that my tongue was red like hers, I knew she was lying. I grew restless over her comment, baffled at why she would lie to me. Was she trying to be polite? Had she been lying all this time? The next morning, after brushing my tongue until it was almost raw, I too decided to be untruthful.

It's mostly clean, but there's a small white patch in the middle, I told her.

She looked at mine and said, Your tongue's a little white, too, also in the middle.

The next day I made up another flaw, and the next day, another, and my suspicions were confirmed. She was merely repeating what I said, matching compliment with compliment and criticism with criticism. The following week, I told her not only was her tongue white but that her teeth were yellow as well. She looked stunned and remained speechless for a few moments and then told me that my teeth were really yellow and that my tongue was covered with germs. I said her teeth were brown and crawling with worms. She said she could see the mounds of plaque accumulating on my gums. I said I could see her teeth decay into little black nuggets right before my eyes. She said my breath smelled so bad it might kill her. The next morning, with a most serious expression, I told her there was a piece of food stuck between her two front teeth. She let out a loud gasp of embarrassment, turned away quickly, and tried to pick out the nonexistent morsel with her fingers.

Who's making noises so early in the morning?

We both looked down at our desks.

If I hear another sound, there will be no breaks today. I hate distractions when I'm trying to organize my lessons. I'm going to go make some photocopies, so when I come back there better be complete silence.

After she left, an eraser flung from Mandy's hand hit me on the cheek and fell to the floor. I picked it up and placed it in my pocket. She extended her hand, and I shook my head. She extended her hand further, and I smirked and

153

shook my head harder. She looked at me with knitted brows and mouthed some words under her breath. I took out the eraser and handed it to her, but when she reached for it, I withdrew my hand and plunged it back into my pocket.

* * *

You can't catch me.

Where are you going?

Anywhere I want.

I just tagged you.

That was my jacket.

Delirious laughter, streaks of blinding lines shimmering off the asphalt, giant plumes of smoke from distant smokestacks, the first day of outdoor recess, the first triumph of spring....

Don't go up there. Come down! That's not part of the playground.

You can't get me up here.

I already tagged you.

No, you didn't.

Mrs. Song might see you. Come down now!

She's too far away.

Just get down, it's dangerous.

And what are you guys doing here? asked Jia Ming, who appeared at the bottom of the steps.

Hello Jia Ming, said Mandy.

Don't hello me, he snapped with false authority. You guys aren't supposed to be here. I'm going to tell Mrs. Song right now.

We were just leaving. Don't tell, pleaded Mandy. The tremor of panic in her voice goaded me down the steps faster.

Five more steps, each one half my height. I lost my

154

balance on the last step and crashed to the ground, scraping a large hole over my right knee. Jia Ming laughed so hard that he hunched over to hold his stomach in. Before running off, he said, Are you going to be a cripple now? You two are such idiots!

I rolled up my jeans to reveal the skinless flesh over my right knee. It remained a light tan color, and for that duration, I was hopeful—hopeful that there would be no blood, no mark, no proof of blunder. Then it sprouted, hundreds of tiny flecks coalescing into garnet drops that slid down my shin and stained the rim of my sock. Mandy handed me a tissue from her pocket, and I wiped away the blood.

Does it hurt?

No.

It doesn't hurt at all? Not even one bit?

No.

I think it might hurt later.

Her prediction came true the moment it was spoken. It was a slight pinch at first, and then it became an intense burn.

Is it hurting yet?

No, I lied.

If the cut's too deep, it might leave a scar.

The gravity of the accident started to settle in. What would I tell Ma? What if Jia Ming told on us? What if—

I felt a tap on my shoulder. You're it!

I chased Mandy, wincing with each step from the pain. All of a sudden, she swerved to the left and let out a scream. Jia Ming was fast approaching from the right. He jogged beside me and said, It seems like the cripple got his legs back. To prove he could run faster than me, he ran faster than me.

I stopped and watched him chase Mandy all over the playground, purposely slowing down to let her get ahead, then catching up to her with powerful strides. Did he tell on us? We were not at the steps anymore so there was no proof. What would I tell Ma? That I fell? Yes, a simple fall, it was true. I would hide it from her for as long as possible; the later she found out, the more the scrape would have healed, the less serious it would appear. It was still unsettling, the prospect of having to endure her disappointment, the anticipation of her reaction, for I was always the one to blame whenever I got hurt: if I slipped on a puddle of water, I was faulted for not watching where I was going; if I stubbed my toe against the foot of the bed, I was faulted for being careless.

You didn't catch me, Mandy said when we filed back to class. You were too slow.

The game shall continue tomorrow and you will be tagged, I said.

She laughed. We'll see about that.

The next morning brought rain and dark clouds and whipping winds that turned the playground into a slick field of puddles. Without the promise of recess, time trudged slowly forward; the hands of the clock became weary and arthritic. By the afternoon, the sun was out, and a mature wind sent clumps of broken clouds racing across the sky like adrenalized stallions. I drank in the light with my eyes until my retinas were bleached, until everything was circumscribed by flaring halos and kaleidoscopic shards vividly shapeless.

On the way home, we freed our pent-up voices. When I got off the bus, I stared at Mandy with winced eyes and furrowed brows, a concentrated look of evil. She understood immediately and without hesitation bolted down the sidewalk. I ran after her. Get back here! You're not getting away this time!

We wove through a maze of shoes, sneakers, tapping canes, baby strollers, honking horns, lampposts, rain-cleaned display windows, soggy cigarette butts, sewer grids submerged in precipitation...the calm and composed chaos of a city street on a stormy-turned-sunny afternoon was smudged formless like a watercolor mural. The only point of distinction was Mandy's hair, undulating like a black flame in the wind, her arms rhythmically swinging with the stride of her legs, her laughter ghostly trailing.

It became the pinnacle of our day: the chase! Every afternoon, we would sit in the same seat, I by the window, and she by the aisle. We would leap off the bus at the same stop, our feet would hit the ground running, and I would run toward the flickering flame of black hair, toward the soothing voice that silenced all my protests, toward the memory of her who at first encounter suggested that everything would be all right in this strange place. When we reached the traffic light at the corner, she would press the finger-polished button for the WALK signal, for the motionless green man in stride to appear, and we would stand together, hunched over, hands on our knees, panting and laughing before parting, she to her uncle's clinic and I home.

* * *

Do you want to know your future? Jia Ming asked me.

You can't tell the future, said Mandy.

Yes, I can. It's easy.

Prove it.

I will. He took hold of my hand, palm up, and began to inspect the lines, his eyes darting back and forth. I see you're going to be rich one day.

That sounds good, said Mandy, moving closer to observe.

You'll have a big house right here, he said, pointing to the middle of my palm. And you'll have a front yard here and a backyard here...and a big swimming pool. Where do you want your swimming pool? In the front or the back?

In the back, I said.

HHRRAUCKK PTOO...wish granted!

* * *

Do you know the Chinese school on P— Street?

P— Street? The one that smells really bad in the summer?

She nodded.

Chinatown's dirtiest street was notable for a hair salon owned by a fat woman, a grungy eatery where greasy noodles and soggy rice were kept warm in metal pans over hot water, a tofu factory that operated out of someone's basement, a company that helped illegal immigrants find jobs, and a fenced-in playground with a swing, a slide, and a saddled dinosaur on a coiled spring. On both sides of the street, with the illusion of great height, stood residential quarters of three or four stories, its residents seldom seen, the window shades always down. The road, lined with parked cars and cachectic trees, was too narrow for garbage trucks to fit, so trash accumulated in fetid piles. Yet what contributed most to the rancid corpse-stench was the trampled pulp of a mysterious fruit that fell from the trees and littered the sidewalk at the start of each summer.

Did you know that the school's haunted?

No.

No one's told you the story?

I shook my head.

They say that ghosts of dead children haunt the bathrooms in the basement. I went down there once. It's the scariest place I've ever been. The lights kept flickering, and when I was on the toilet, they just turned off on their own. I was so scared I just ran out. All the stalls were creaking, and there were scribbles on the walls—

Scribbles of what?

I don't know, ghost writing maybe.

Why's it haunted?

A long time ago when the school was first built, a serial killer hid in the basement. When kids went down there, he caught them and strangled them to death. But that's not the worst part. He had nowhere to hide the bodies, so he hacked them into little pieces with a big butcher knife and flushed them down the toilet. Now the place is possessed by the ghosts of the murdered victims. Innocent children get lured down, and they disappear forever.

Why don't they just close the place down?

Because the teachers don't believe it's true.

If someone's missing, how can they not believe it?

Who knows? Do you know about the brick building across from that school? Do you know why the door is barred by a green fence?

No.

Mandy told another captivating tale of decapitation: It used to be a mahjong club...

...the owner was a madam whose curled hair was dyed a squid ink black. Her club provided cheap beer and cigarettes, lent money at lofty interest rates, and attracted a reckless kind of crowd. It became the eventual site of a shooting by three masked men that left nine dead. At the sound of the first gunshot, she dropped to her knees and

159

crawled on all fours. Weighed down by her dress of purple flowers soaked with the contents of a surrendered bladder, she embarked on the longest journey of her life, the twenty-second crawl to a back room. She blockaded the door and waited until all was quiet before emerging to see shattered glass, upturned tables, scattered tiles of dragons and winds and flowers, and nine gelatinous pools of blood spilling from desecrated heads to stain the grout between her tiles. She ran across the street and vomited before the bronze statue of Confucius who looked on with his scholarly beard in hand. She hired a geomancer to get rid of the spirits, and he told her to guard the door behind a metal fence painted green.

* * *

An electric blue sky with a single fiber of cloud, a spring day of summertime in disguise, a day so fine as to escape the erosion by time—perhaps it was this clarity that blurred so well the events of that afternoon which began with a temporary defiance of gravity from bus to sidewalk, the prelude to pattering steps that brought us past the freckled old man walking feebly by with a bamboo cane, who yelled, Watch it, young lady! His tobacco-hoarse voice reached my ears, and perhaps he heard it, too—or he heard it first, and then I heard it, too.

Mandy jumped off the steps, then I did; that I was sure of.

Jia Ming, having witnessed our daily afternoon chase over the weeks, abandoned his usual seat and took one near the front of the bus.

She jumped off, and then I did; that I was sure of.

She ran, and I ran.

He turned to me and said, Watch me catch the girl of your dreams.

160

So we ran, all three of us, sneakers pounding on the sun-warmed asphalt.

I heard Jia Ming's taunts...from behind? Or was he ahead? I did not recall, cannot recall.

We passed an old woman pushing a cart of groceries, a father who held a daughter in each hand heading to pick up the third, a tourist couple holding hands, and the woman said to the man, Look how cute they all are.

Under the caress of pristine sun, there was the smell of burning rubber...

...memory fades a little before resuming lucidity...

...we crossed the street, Jia Ming and I, with the calm of ordinary people crossing streets. The crosswalk swelled with strangers spilling forth from all directions. The light was red. They swarmed around the silver car stopped on the zebra stripes.

She's dead! She's probably dead, that stupid girl! Jia Ming cackled and waved his arms in the air.

We walked down the alley that led to our apartment building. Jia Ming was in a rapturous state. He spoke so fast that I could not understand a word he was saying. I...I think...I think I left something behind...you go on ahead, I stuttered.

Was he behind her, or was I?

I took reluctant steps back to the crosswalk, both hands in my pockets, my index finger hooked around the thread-tangled key ring, my middle finger rubbing the jagged teeth of the keys. My legs felt like stilts made of spaghetti. Jia Ming's laugh was still audible, echoing through the alley of blackened fire escapes that dangled precariously overhead, a ten-foot drop between the last step and the ground.

Who was behind her? He or I?

Approaching the street, I heard the cyclic wail of sirens. Red and blue lights encased in rectangular prisms atop black and white police cars swirled amidst the dense crowd. The silver sedan remained in the middle of the street. The driver standing by the side of the road was being questioned. Policemen waved cars through with hand signals, and onlookers were urged to disperse. Another siren was borne, this time from the white ambulance that merged into the stream of stuttering traffic; its horn blared with urgency as it receded out of sight. I turned around and ran back home, my eyes focused solely on the ground beneath my feet.

At dinner that night, Ma said, You don't look well. What's the matter?

I shook my head and continued eating.

She waited a few minutes, then asked again, this time with such motherly concern that I had no choice but to tell her. A girl in our class got hit by a car. She had to go to the hospital.

When?

Today.

How is she?

I don't know.

How did it happen?

She was crossing the street.

Poor girl, Ma said, shaking her head. How unfortunate, I hope she's okay. Take this as a lesson yourself. You need to be careful when crossing the street, do you understand? Cars have no eyes, and drivers are reckless. Make sure you pay attention. It's worrisome to hear such things...why are you shaking? Are you cold?

No, I answered, unaware I was shaking, became aware, and stilled myself.

Remember to watch where you're going. Don't take your eyes off the cars. Look left and right before you cross. Cars have no eyes.

I nodded and finished my rice in silence. Ma went to the kitchen to heat up some soup.

She ran out into the street, I said.

The girl?

I nodded. She ran out into the street, I repeated.

Why did she run? Was it green for her?

I could see her pendulous black hair and the churn of her piston knees...a smile inverted, a cessation of the comic at the sight of the oncoming vehicle...she must have let out a shriek, like the shriek of brakes that halted the car not soon enough...she must have been thrown to the ground from the collision in obeisance of physical law. What was the sequence? What was the order? Was he behind her, or was I? The harder I tried to recall, the more elusive everything became, until what little fragments of certainty I had receded too into the distance of non-distinction. My memory of the afternoon was but one swirling myopic distortion of sight and sound. Perhaps it went like this: a bumper decelerating, tire marks branded onto the road, gasping mouths, bugged eyes, stunned hearts, Mandy flung to the ground, rolling, rolling...but this I remembered for sure: we got off the bus, Mandy first...then who? He or I? I was behind; was I behind? I was ahead...Jia Ming caught up, and turned back to me yelling, Watch me catch the girl of your dreams. He ran ahead—I remembered his legs and the legs of everyone else...I remembered the screech that preceded her scream, and then I heard his taunt and his laugh. I replayed the sequence in my mind: I am screaming, I am at the curb and he is behind me...now he is at the curb, and I am behind him...I see the car, I see the car try to stop...he sees the car hit her...only his words remain clear: She's dead! she's probably dead, that stupid girl!

There was no walk signal, I answered.

That means she crossed at the wrong time. These stories make me worry. You should always look both ways when—

He said she was dead and then he laughed.

What are you talking about? Who said that?

Jia Ming was chasing her.

What?! Why didn't you tell me this before? Did you have anything to do with it? Her tone suddenly became hostile.

They both ran past me, and she ran out into the street and got hit. Jia Ming kept laughing and said she might've died.

Ma shook her head. I'm going to ask one more time: Did you have anything to do with it?

No.

I did not want to ask, but the words slipped out before I could hold them back. What if the police find out that Jia Ming chased her? What would happen?

Who knows? Maybe they'll arrest him and put him in jail. He deserves it.

Was I involved? Had I lied? Was he ahead? Was I ahead? We were both running after her, so did it matter? Thundering through my consciousness was a tempest of guilt—I saw myself run; I was not ahead; I was running, but I was not chasing; I was chasing, but she was not fleeing; I was running, and she was fleeing, and he was chasing; she was fleeing from him, not from me; yes, she was fleeing from him, not from me. She's dead! She's probably dead, that stupid girl! How did I know there was no walk signal when she crossed? I must have been at the corner. Did the light change? Was I watching from afar? Was I running toward it? Where was he? He was ahead; yes, he had to be; he saw the accident, and he uttered those words. Those were his words—that I was sure of, sure of each word in its order, in its place.

I stayed awake all night into the early hours. The stagnant air was tickled by snores. The dry-leaf rustle of May's diaper periodically sounded. The ceiling at times appeared inches from my face, at other times miles in the distance. I heard twice the lone tenor of a passing car and once the sound of breaking glass. I kept thinking that Mandy would board the bus in the morning, take the seat beside me, and we would talk like we always talked. When Ma woke up, I pretended to be asleep so I could pretend to wake up when she woke me.

The next morning, Jia Ming, contrary to his inclination, stood away from the crowd at the bus stop. Someone approached him, followed by a few others, and then a few more, until I was the only one standing by the curb. They all seemed to be engaged in intimate conversation. I waited for Mandy who, proof of the frailty of hope, did not come. I prayed for some alignment of the stars, some glitch in the fabric of time, some act of divine mercy, to render yesterday undone. The bus approached and squeaked to a stop. I hesitated to board, intently watching Jia Ming, a grin on his face, his arm slung over a friend's shoulder. Once I took my seat, I stared out the window. I imagined the sound of her feet jogging on the pavement to merge with the shrinking line. I imagined we would stick out our tongues to see whose was cleaner. The doors slammed shut, a strain of acceleration, and my heart sank to fathomless depths: What if she was dead? Not moving, not breathing, dead.

Her seat remained empty when attendance was taken. Does anyone know where Mandy is? Is she out sick again?

No answers.

I swear her parents keep her home for the tiniest ailment.

Between our pledge to the flag and the start of the first lesson, a voice on the loudspeaker requested Mrs. Song to go to the principal's office.

The class was unusually quiet, but perhaps it was a trick of the ears. I knew why the teacher had been summoned by the principal. But maybe I was wrong. I told myself, rather convincingly, that it was for another, more trivial, reason. And though my heart was pounding and my hands were tremulous, something assured me that all would be well; perhaps it was a trick of the mind. When Mrs. Song returned, the snippets of conversation immediately hushed. She looked different, the contours of her face traced disgust and shock, or perhaps it was a trick of the eyes. Maybe it was all a collective trick of the senses because I was privy to knowledge that others were not. She sat at her desk shuffling through some papers and then, startling the calm that had settled, spoke with an unwavering harshness, Jia Ming, come out here with me!

The whites of his eyes glowed whiter to match the pallor on his face as he followed her out to the common area. We all watched with craned necks, but none could hear what they were saying. When they came back, she called for someone else, the boy whose shoulder Jia Ming slung his arm across that morning. The boys looked directly at each other as they crossed paths. There had never been such silence in the classroom. I felt like a sneeze interrupted. My palms were sticky with sweat, my toes were stuck to my socks, and I could feel my heartbeat in my fingertips, the dreaded pulse of time, a bomb ready to ignite in a grand lamenting explosion.

Come over here, Mrs. Song said to me after Jia Ming's friend went back to his seat.

I stood up, my legs wobbly like cobras rising to the sway of flutes.

Do you know why I called you out?

My tongue remained immobile. She eyed me with pointed daggers aimed to maim. I don't know, I said.

Sure you do.

I could not bring myself to say anything more, so I said nothing.

You really don't know?

I shook my head.

Why do you seem so nervous?

Again I said nothing.

Let me ask you this—I want you to answer truthfully—did you chase Mandy out into the street?

I ran after her, I thought, but I did not chase her out into the street, so yes was not the correct answer. I thought for a moment back to Ma's spankings with the wooden handle of a feathered duster, beatings meant to instill in me a sense of respect and fear. Exile from school would prove the vanity of her efforts...a gavel-pounding sentence, a clang of metal bars, frayed stripes, inked numbers, and mush clinging to an upside-down ladle...how was Mandy doing now? Was she awake and talking or trapped in a coma she could not wake from? No, I finally said.

You chased her, she asserted.

I could no longer say yes, for I had already said no. If I changed my answer, then she would know for sure that I had lied. I said nothing.

If you didn't chase her, then who did?

I don't know.

You don't know, or you don't want to tell me?

Her face up close, distorted by her scowl, was ugly—the ugliest thing I had ever seen. My eyes began to dampen.

Mandy was hit by a car yesterday. She's in the hospital.

I wanted to die. I wished for a quick sudden death, a heart attack or a clot to the brain, anything to end this interrogation. I imagined her body crushed and mangled on a blood-stained stretcher. I began to bawl and I could not stop, sounding the smothered grunts of a distressed, tongue-less idiot. She's still alive, right? She's not dead, right? I muttered under my breath.

I was informed that someone, a boy, was chasing her—

I shook my head. Words toppled out: I didn't do it...I didn't...I didn't—

Then why are you crying? Two girls this morning confirmed that a boy with a blue schoolbag was running after her. Jia Ming told me he had nothing to do with it. I didn't believe him at first because I know he's a big troublemaker, but someone else said that he was with Jia Ming yesterday and they walked home together.

That's a lie, I wanted to say, but did not say.

Go back to your seat and think about what I've said.

I saw Mandy in a full body cast made soggy by the tears of her grieving family. What would Ma think of all this? Would the jury find me guilty? Would I be crowned with a wet sponge? I was saddened that I might not be around to watch May grow up. What would I say to her? What brotherly advice would I give her before the gloved hand of the executioner pulled the lever? I could see the headlines in print, the letters bold and capitalized: BOY

RUNS GIRL INTO TRAFFIC...CAR ACCIDENT
LEAVES GIRL PARALYZED...ONE BOY DESTROYS
THE HOPES OF TWO FAMILIES...BOY IN PRISON,
GIRL IN GRAVE.

The cafeteria was a cauldron of cacophonous clamor: chairs clattered against tables, metal legs screeched on polished tile, steel pans clashed on counters in the kitchen, towers of foam trays squeaked when separated...above this amalgamation of noise, the grind of my teeth sounded loud and clear.

Jia Ming, being his usual self, egged some boys on to arm-wrestle. I watched him, his grinning lips, his white teeth, his shining plateau of a forehead where crushed capillaries once protested. I had lied to Ma—I ran after Mandy; that, I could no longer refute. But how had Jia Ming fallen completely out of blame? He was running, he was a faster runner, he had to be ahead, he had to be. Mrs. Song said there were witnesses...who? Did they not see him? Was he blocked from their view?

Mandy won't be with us for some time, said Mrs. Song after lunch. She was hit by a car yesterday. We received a call from her parents this morning. Her right leg was broken, and she's having surgery right now as we speak.

A duo of crystalline streams gushed from my eyes. Everyone turned to stare.

Leave him be, let him cry, said Mrs. Song. He has problems to work out.

Somewhere under a blue drape illuminated by three circular lights, an exposed patch of skin dyed brown by iodine was parted by three masked figures...muscles were cut, blood was suctioned, vessels were cauterized, and bone was filed, screwed, and hammered.

When I got home, Ma said, Everyone at work was

talking about the girl today. The story was on the local news last night. Did Jia Ming say anything today?

I shook my head.

I don't know...I can't understand...to laugh and say that she'd died...his mind is twisted...I don't want you around him, he's a bad influence.

When Aunt called Ma that night, she told her all about it. Since the accident, whenever the phone rang, my pulse would gallop. I was in constant fear that it would be Mrs. Song on the other line, the flapping of her vocal cords transformed into electrons flowing along the insulated spiral-wire through the socket and out onto a track of cables gently parabolic from the steady paws of a sole navigating squirrel or a multitude of defecating pigeons that sounded: Your son's a criminal, your son's going to jail....

How was Mandy doing? Did the doctors fix her leg? Would she be able to walk again? What would I say when I saw her again? Did she know that Jia Ming was also chasing her? Would she sympathize if I told her that Mrs. Song made my life a complete misery just for the sake of an answer? What did her mother and father think of all this? If I were to marry her someday, would her parents forgive me? Would she herself forgive me? Couldn't we just leave the States and go back to China? The flight's booked...pack your bags...we're leaving, and we're never coming back—was it so improbable for Ma to say those words? I began wishing for circumstances to bring about such an outcome: Grandfather winning the lottery and buying us a big house in our hometown...another country declaring war on the United States and forcing us to flee...I conjured a hundred different scenarios that would take me away from this place. My sleep was disjointed and laced with unpleasant dreams. I counted Ma's erratic snoring and I tapped my fingers to the pace of Ba's constant snoring. I wanted to wake them and confess the truth in the peace of our home, but I could not bring myself to do it.

I continued to sink into my quagmire of shame day after day, and I felt as if my whole being could disintegrate at any moment under Mrs. Song's cruelty. With the coldness of a premeditated killer, she subjected me to a daily barrage of questions. I started to wonder whether she was in fact deriving some pleasure from the psychological torture she was putting me through and not at all interested in exposing the truth. She pulled me out of the classroom every afternoon and asked, Are you ready to tell me what really happened?

And each time I rehearsed in my mind behind the farce of still lips: I ran, but I didn't cause the accident...I ran after her, but I didn't chase her...you see, we'd been doing this every day since...it was the first time that Jia Ming...and look what happened when...Jia Ming was ahead of me...Jia Ming was ahead, I'm sure...he said she might have died, he called her a stupid girl...it's Jia Ming who should be here, not me. Despite all of my mental preparation, nothing ever managed to come out of my mouth except, I...I...I was—

You were what? Out with it!

There was no possibility of voicing alternatives. Any admittance to running meant the act of chasing, and chasing was the ultimate catalyst of the crime. I had lied to Mrs. Song, and I had lied to Ma. And lies, being lies, once told, could not be untold. No, I said, I didn't chase her.

She shook her head. Why are you crying again? What's there to cry about?

Perhaps it was the intonation in her voice or the tear-

171

distorted scowl of her face, perhaps it was my over-burdened nerves, but I was certain at that moment of what to do. I could not deviate from the original story; I had to stand my ground. Yet the very next moment, I wanted to surrender, and I wanted to explain everything, but all I could do was stare at the reflections of myself in her eyes, an idiot of contradiction.

The drill became familiar: she would ask if I was ready to admit to what I had done, and I would shake my head. Then she would ask if that meant I was not ready to admit or if I took no part in the accident, and I would say I took no part. Like a skillful lawyer, she constructed a series of rhetorical questions to lead me toward an eventual betrayal of my act. There were times I wanted my lie revealed. I wanted shelter from the constant deluge of guilt, but I maintained my stand and denied all accusations. Whenever I felt I was losing the verbal battle, I resorted to the shake of the head, the unshakable no: No, I didn't chase her, I said, I kept saying, I would say, and I would keep saying.

Does your mother know?

Had I given away something? Had I twitched a brow? Blinked too fast? Opened my eyes too wide? I did not answer. My throat was searing and I felt sick to my stomach.

What I don't understand is why you insist on lying. In American schools, teachers can't hit students. You're lucky for that. Believe me, I would've beaten the answer out of you from the start. Do you think you're making your mother proud with this kind of behavior?

Something gave. A collapse of composure.

Maybe I should just call the police tonight and tell them about you. Did you know that punishment for those who don't confess is more severe than for those who do?

Mandy's in the hospital with a broken leg. Let me ask you again: Did you chase her?

I became desperate, so I blurted, My friend did it.

Your friend? she said with disbelief. Why didn't you tell me earlier? What's his name? This is an interesting twist. I want to know more. Who's this friend of yours?

His name is...his name is...his name—

You don't know his name?

I shook my head.

What school does he go to?

I don't know.

What grade is he in?

I don't know.

And why did he run after Mandy?

I don't—

Come with me! She pulled me out of the chair, held onto my sleeve, and dragged me back to the classroom. I've an announcement. We have here before us a liar, a rotten little liar! I've given this liar many chances to tell the truth, but he won't. Look how miserable he is. Let him be an example to all of you. Liars can cry all they want, but they'll *never* be forgiven!

The principal called me to her office the next day. I know you must be concerned about your friend Mandy, she said. Mrs. Song told me you two used to play a lot during recess. I spoke to Mandy's parents yesterday, and they told me she is recovering from her surgery and doing well. I heard that you may have been involved or that you may have witnessed something. Is there anything you wish to tell me? Do you know who was chasing her, or why she was being chased?

I wanted to cry, but I bit my lips and wrung my hands behind my back, forcing myself to remain as calm as I could. Then I shook my head.

If you think of anything, please come and let me know.

As I walked back to the classroom, I thought about Mandy, the curvature of her lips, her black hair that looked brown in the sun, the redness of her tongue that sculpted those first unconditional words of welcome, but I forgot how she looked. I could not remember her face no matter how hard I tried. After that day, Mrs. Song's brutal interrogations came to an end. Over the ensuing weeks, my guilt was gradually replaced with a sense of profound emptiness. I realized how much I had missed Mandy and how slowly each day was passing without her laughter and company. I did not fully appreciate how much joy our conversations brought me or how much I looked forward to spending time with her at recess. There were no more updates about her, no news regarding her recovery or when she would come back to school. With the approach of summer vacation, I did not know if I would ever see her again.

* * *

I see ceiling lights fly by like detached lane lines. I feel like I am riding in an upside-down car. Let me take one more breath of air, just one breath, I say.

They shake their heads and hold the mask over my face. The flavor of strawberry tickles the inside of my nostrils. I try to sneeze but my mouth will not open.

I am inside but I know it is raining outside. Ma is standing beside me. I thought you were out in the waiting room, I say drowsily.

To tell you the truth, I'm scared, Ma confesses. What if they put you to sleep and you don't wake up?

I'm already asleep yet I'm still awake so there's no

need to worry, I say.

She is reassured by my answer. I'm going to pray right now, she says. She falls on her knees with her palms together and begins to hum the chant of the Buddha, her tongue vibrating between her lips.

You're here to have your tonsils out? the surgeon asks.

I nod.

He reaches into my throat and pulls out two bulbous nodes that stain his fingernails violet. Now it's time for the real operation, he says.

I'm going back to work, Ma says. I'll come and take you home after.

They crank up the fumes and I fall asleep. When I wake up, my left leg is missing. Mrs. Song is standing beside me. She puts the sneaker onto my foot as I slide off the bed. You will go and apologize to Mandy now, she says.

Where are you taking him? asks the security guard outside my door.

Mrs. Song walks up to him and slices his mouth off with a knife. There is no blood, just a gaping hole in his face. He remains at his post, unable to talk, his eyes shifting back and forth with haste.

We make our way through a series of rotating doors and take an elevator up to a glass walkway that straddles across a two-way street. Skyscrapers in the distance are obscured by fog.

Two figures are standing at the other end. One is leaning along the banister taking small steps; the other is standing by in close observance. The smaller figure is Mandy, draped in a white hospital gown. She is learning to walk, one arm on a crutch, the other arm holding onto the railing; her face winces with each step. The larger figure is her mother.

As we approach them, I am overwhelmed with happiness. I want to run up and give Mandy a hug. I want to tell her how much I missed her, and I want to tell her simply that I love her. But my leg is missing so I cannot run.

He would like to say something, Mrs. Song announces.

The patter of a million raindrops against the glass is deafening.

I try to speak but my throat is stiff. I'm sorry, I finally say.

Mandy smiles. It's okay, I have yours now.

I reach for my leg but she backs away.

Come on out, it's time to go home, Ma says. Ma is on the other side of the revolving door with a big umbrella, its domed nylon crackling in the downpour. May is also waiting. She has grown older and more mature. She rests her hand on my shoulder and reassures me that I will one day get my leg back. A shard of lightning separates the sky. We pedal our feet like we are on bicycles. Ma's grip tightens over my wrist. A gust of wind flips the umbrella and yanks it out of her hand, a tremendous roar of thunder reverberates through the air, and the traffic light before us falls crashing to the ground.

5

ELBOWS ON THE METAL BARRICADE, chin in hands, marveling at the reflected pixels of neon billboards in the water, Lone Eye found himself in the company of two girls by Pearl River, a chance encounter on a warm summer night, one of those thick, humid nights when the smells of the afternoon were still discernible, the kind of night that drew young men and women out of their homes to stroll under the soft brush of rustling willows, tap their feet in karaoke clubs, and fill city buses with the stink of digested alcohol. He sparked conversation, awkwardly at first, until it turned comical after gentle persistence. They hid their giggles behind modest palms at his stories, which he told with suspense and art. He invited them to a midnight movie, and they agreed, unable to resist his boyish dimples, his quirky sense of humor, and his lustrous eyes.

On this particular night, a woman in red with salon-curled hair and cherry-hued lipstick strode into the same cinema with her husband, a partner of a prominent investment firm. He was a short, insecure man with a slight hunchback, a patch of eczema on his nape, and nostrils that caved from the weight of his glasses. He hated this kind of scene: a mishmash of young flirtatious couples boasting wealth with pretense or embracing poverty with vulgar pride, but his wife loved crowds, the kind that crackled with barbaric spontaneity. Living comfortably in the lap of luxury rendered life somewhat drab, and what could be more thrilling for her than to mix in the sweat and flesh of coarse commoners?

Lone Eye and the two girls found a couple of empty seats. The bond of friendship (or was it some kind of fate?) ordained that the girls would sit together, so Lone Eye planted himself to their left, disappointed at not having, contrary to his original hopes, a girl on each side. While they talked between themselves, he felt incredibly alone, and his thoughts drifted to his wife and her mahjong game back home...until the woman in red took the seat beside him. He watched as she sat down, accentuating the curvature of her buttocks before planting them firmly onto the seat. He felt that most lustful of tickles deep within his belly, and a cold sweat started to bead. He swallowed twice and smiled at her.

As if the movie were to take place in the audience instead, as if the conical beam of the projector were pointing down at those two seats, the woman in red sent her husband off to buy drinks and snacks—an appropriate opening scene. The moment he left, Lone Eye, having forgotten about the two girls, quickly assumed the role of charmer and gentleman, smooth with sweet talk and uninhibited compliments, overeager with contrived jokes and anecdotes. Perhaps through another dictation of fate, the husband, feeling a tug of his bladder, went first to join the long, boisterous line toward the restroom. He always felt queasy about having to urinate amongst strangers, having to stand atop a ledge and aim one's stream against a stained wall without dividers, its tiles perpetually coated with a thin curtain of water that cascaded onto a grated ditch. A group of rambunctious adolescents beside him reached over and shook each other's arms and hollered, Taking a piss on your hand again? Are you going to lick it afterwards? The line was long at the concession stand as well—a gift of crucial minutes. Back in the theater, the woman seemed to have taken an immediate liking to Lone Eye, laughing at all of his jokes as if they were old friends.

Could this really be happening? Could I get this lucky? Lone Eye thought.

As the husband struggled to navigate through the narrow space between rows, balancing soda and chips in his hands, she scribbled down a time, date, and place to meet on the back of a card printed only with a telephone number and handed it to Lone Eye. The lights dimmed and the movie started, as did the affair.

They saw each other several times a month when her husband stayed late at the office, surrounded by papers at his desk, his back to the view of the sleepy city. They met in parks, theaters, eateries, wherever it was convenient, whatever fit the mood. He was in perpetual amazement; he could not believe how lucky he was. She was quite a prize for any man chasing such thrills—she was the gorgeous wife of a rich and powerful yet physically inadequate man. It soon gave way to a new arrogance, an inevitable boost of his ego, he saw himself—how could he deny it?—as the savior of women. No matter their class or looks, no matter what they had or where they came from, they could not do without men like him.

She proved too easy to charm, but he did not care to wonder why. After several months of movies with formulaic plots, cheap hotel rooms with cigarette-burned sheets, and quiet strolls along Pearl River, he eventually learned that she was having other affairs and had been doing so for years.

Why?

Because I'm bored, and there's no good reason not to.

Does he know?

No...and yes.

Which is it?

What would he do about it? She took a drag off her cigarette and propelled a column of purple smoke toward the ceiling. All he cares about is work. He suspects it but he doesn't ask. That's how it's been.

How many others?

She placed a delicate finger over his lips and said, He doesn't ask.

Children?

None. I had an operation. That was one of his stipulations before we married. No kids, ever.

The affair lasted through the winter. The cold air was warmed by the breaths of their cyclic grunts, and perfumed by fermented burps and toasted tobacco. Ah San knew; she knew as surely as she felt the kicks in her belly, the morning nausea, the swelling in her feet, the nocturnal headaches—she knew, and he knew she knew, but what did it matter? He had done this for years, and she had never said a word. Love for him was the freedom to obey his lust, and love for her was the freedom to buy whatever she wanted. Love for her was money, wads of cash stuffed into her purse; that was love, and anyone who disagreed was tragically wrong. The theory of romance, the idea of commitment and loyalty, was an empty concept; those who followed it were living a lie. He provided her with sums that rendered her deaf, blind, and mute to his evenings of giggles and sighs, of tangled sheets on weakened bedsprings, of the itch of passion and false confessions of true love. He gave Ah San the means to embark on weekly shopping sprees that separated her from the working class: afternoons in air-conditioned retail space, the screech of sliding coat hangers, the tickle of dress hems on her calves and shins; she bought clothes that looked expensive, knockoff handbags, footwear for all seasons...the more to own, the merrier to be. On rare days, she felt an inkling of remorse, an iota of doubt, but it never progressed further; one look at the swarming crowds with crumpled bills in their hands fighting for their shares at the markets where whirlwinds of flies buzzed over pyramids of fruits and gutted fish were splayed out on melting ice beds gave her the pleasure of knowing she was not one of those who struggled to make ends meet on a daily basis, and would never be.

Spring arrived in bloom, then summer brought its typhoons. In a sequence of events as seemingly ordained as their first encounter, the affair came to an end. On a warm night, one week to the year of their first meeting, they walked out of that same movie theater onto the street and were approached by another couple, a woman in purple and a man blissfully smiling.

Look who it is...it's been a while!

You!

You're the last person I expected to see here, and at this time.

I was just going to say the same for you.

The woman in purple ogled Lone Eye for what felt like minutes; her eyes scanned him up and down, left and right, clockwise and counterclockwise, long enough for the other to notice. She forced a smile and asked, Who's this beautiful stranger?

Just a friend...we met a while back. He's handsome, isn't he?

He certainly is.

And who's this? I don't believe I've met him before.

Just a friend as well...you know how it is...we're on our

way to the movies.

We were just leaving.

Where to?

You're always so nosy.

Lone Eye looked at both women, one then the other then back to the one, a witness to their optical jabs, the subtle tensions and twitches of the skin around their eyes.

We need to be on our way. Call me sometime, and we'll catch up, said the woman in purple who suddenly jolted forward and bumped Lone Eye on the shoulder. She hung onto him for a moment and awkwardly brushed past his left thigh. I'm so sorry, she said. Nice to have met you. Goodbye for now.

When Lone Eye boarded the last bus home and reached for his wallet to pay the fare, he noticed something in his pocket, a card printed only with a telephone number.

Thus it began, another affair, another summer of humid nights on thousand-times-slumbered, thousand-times-washed, and thousand-times-dried sheets beside the woman who once wore a purple dress. On their second encounter, she told him to call the woman who once wore red.

Why?

I want you to end it.

What do you mean?

From now on, you won't be seeing her anymore, and I want you to tell her why.

Why's that?

Because you're with me now. Like a trade, one for another, old for new.

Right now?

Right now. She watched as he dialed.

What should I say?

182

Say it's over. Tell her she's no longer a part of your life. She put the bottle to his lips and made him take a full swig. Then she drank the rest, laughing her infectious, anarchic laugh.

She's not picking up.

Try again.

—Hello?...

She stifled her laugh and whispered loudly, Tell her! Tell her it's over!

—Hello...I...

She cupped her palms over her mouth, snorting furiously, her face flushed firecracker red, as he put the mouthpiece closer.

—I'm sorry...I...

You're *sorry*? That's great. Stick the knife in deeper with more apologies. Say you're sorry, say that to her again.

—Hello?...

What did she say?

Nothing, she just hung up.

She must have heard me. Did she hear me? That poor bitch.

He gradually learned the truth from this woman who could guzzle liquor and down whole bottles of wine like no one he had ever met. Tangled inside slurred words and hiccups, he learned that she belonged to a class of women trying to fend off the ennui of marrying rich by competing with each other: flaunting wardrobes, bank accounts, makeup cabinets, and most important of all, sexual conquests. That was how he understood it. Though he never gave it much thought, it made perfect sense now how he was able to woo her and the one before with minimal effort and why they had literally thrown themselves at him upon first encounter—he had always assumed it was his looks and charm. Now he understood why this woman carried around a stack of cards printed with her telephone number ready to hand out like coupons for a department store sale. He never imagined that such people existed and in large enough numbers that he would stumble into their midst. How many others like her would he never meet? How many opportunities forgone? How many secrets muted by a soft finger on the lips?

One rainy morning, she told him that he was her victory, for he was a stolen man, stolen from the woman in red who had done just that to her years ago.

Three weeks later, Ah San gave birth to Jia Ming.

As with all whims of the flesh, the affair, like its predecessor, skidded to an abrupt end on a night when Lone Eye met his mistress in a rundown hotel room. Groggy after a particularly passionate session of lovemaking, both fell into a dreamless sleep. The snap of a turning key cracked open his foggy eyelids. He was able to make out two figures in the doorway: a guard in uniform holding a large ring of keys, and another man who stepped in and looked around with utter dismay at the contours of their blanketed bodies, at her toenail-painted foot uncovered, and at the empty wine bottles on the nightstands. The air was thick with the mutual sweat of lust consummated. The guard quickly walked away after pocketing the money he had been given for facilitating this timely exposure; his footsteps sounded synchronously with the jingle of keys.

Lone Eye struggled to sit up as the stranger approached. With one quick swipe, the man yanked the sheets off the bed, unveiling, as if in an act of magic, two glistening bodies. Lone Eye immediately stood up and censored himself with a pillow; the woman, curled in a

184

fetal position, moaned, shifted, slowly woke, and let out a deafening shriek upon recognition of her husband.

I don't fucking believe this! She was right...some bitch rang tonight and told me I'd find you here...I didn't know what to make of it. Before she hung up, she said when I find you to tell you that she can play games over the telephone as well. I don't fucking know what's going on. I don't know why someone would call me up and leave a tip like that, and I for sure didn't expect to actually find you here. You worthless whore...to take *my* name and drag it through the mud!

Lone Eye started inching toward his clothes strewn on the floor. Before he could reach them, she stood up and willed a forceful retort, Yes! He's the one I've been sleeping with. He's one of many—

The sound of a crackling slap; her torso twisted around and collapsed onto the mattress, pulled down by the weight of her head rebounding from his vicious palm, a smudge of drool and blood leaked onto the sheets.

Lone Eye dropped his clutched pillow and confronted the man with a shove to the shoulder. Don't you hit her! What kind of a man—

Lone Eye's words trailed into nothingness. He toppled stiffly onto the ground, his blood flowing warm and thick over the tiny bristles of the carpet, while she, limp as a wilted flower, sobbed with her hands over her mouth. Broken glass shone like misshapen emeralds under the dim ceiling lamp.

He woke up in a white room with no windows. The inside of his head was throbbing. His right eye was covered with thick gauze, his scalp in bandages, his sole eyeball shifted hastily and sought comprehension, but met only the eyes of his wife sitting on a chair with their son in her arms sucking on a pacifier.

Awake finally? Where are your clothes? They told me you were found naked on the floor of a hotel room with your head smashed in by a bottle. What do you have to say for yourself?

He closed his eye, pretended to fall asleep, and fell asleep.

♦

—There's a new head waitress here...it hasn't been a month, and already she's telling lies, she's trying to get all the good workers fired by spreading rumors about them...I don't know, maybe she thinks she'll lose her job...no...she's in charge of all the waitstaff...all she does is spread rumors and gossip...what?...no, no...that's not like me, the Old Man raised me too well for that kind of thing...I'm just too stupid maybe, too honest, I'm not capable of backstabbing...I don't understand how they do it...how can people be so lacking in common decency?...she's been trying to trash my reputation ever since she stepped foot into the restaurant...who knows? I don't listen to stuff like that anymore, I don't let it affect me...she's trying to get me fired...complaining to the manager about this and that...she's been here for less than a month and she's already pitted all the waitresses against each other...enough about her, how's the Old Man doing?...he's still smoking, isn't he?...he needs to stop...what?...school's already out for the summer...did I tell you that we're moving again?...next week...yes...another building altogether in a different part of Chinatown, we'll be on the seventh floor this time...there're two bedrooms, so it's an upgrade for sure...yes, it's subsidized housing...the management office of that apartment complex told me the expected wait was five to seven years, the prior tenants found a new place so they left and the family ahead of us on the waiting list wasn't interested anymore so we got it...the bastard mentioned the other night that Wei Jian and Shorty are looking to move as well...who the hell knows where?...I'm sure they won't tell me and I'm not going to ask, we've all drifted so far apart, they're practically strangers to me at this point...I wonder if that bitch Ah San drove them out, I wouldn't be surprised...what?...don't worry about that, I've already booked one, I was hoping he'd have time before the actual move but his schedule was full, I couldn't get an earlier time...

* * *

The geomancer came dressed in a silken black robe stitched with old Chinese characters and tied at the waist with a long, red, braided rope. He wore black shoes which he refused to take off. In his suitcase were some small-print, thin-paged books and a large bronze compass carved with hundreds of symbols separated into columns by grooves like the spokes of a bicycle wheel. The contraption, mounted on a black velveteen board, was set on our table. I marveled at the miniscule etchings on the metal and the raised needle that was perpetually swinging, as if unable to make up its mind.

Don't touch that, boy.

Get away from that! Ma shouted, accompanied by her usual glare. Sorry, sir, sorry, I'll make sure he doesn't go near it.

While balancing the compass on an open palm, the man inspected all the rooms, flipping each light switch on and off, running his hand along the walls, and pulling the window shades up and down. As he made his tour of our apartment, he told Ma what to do in order to maximize harmony. The sofa should face north given the layout of this unit, he said. You should consider putting some potted plants in these two corners. Your son's desk should be moved to the southwest corner which will ensure high grades and test scores in school. Most importantly, no bed should be in line with the bedroom door unless you want spirits passing through in the night to meddle with your dreams. I see you already have an altar for the gods, that's good. Put the merciful bodhisattva Guanyin Pusa on the top tier and the general Guan Yu below, and remember to light twelve sticks of incense in the kitchen every evening for a fruitful bounty.

Ma followed him around with full attention and jotted down his instructions onto a piece of paper.

The geomancer then looked out from our living room window and pointed to the centerpiece of our view—the tallest building in the city, sixty-two stories of pristine, sharp-edged glass jutting into the infinite blue, designed by the architect who, too, fled our country, our very city—and said, That building there has too much glass, that's bad.

What do you mean?

Spirits travel in different mediums, some in the netherworld of mirrors. Such a large reflective surface directly opposing you means a lot of evil spirits will be reflected straight into this room.

What should I do?

You need to hang a small mirror in the window facing outward to reflect them back out.

I see. I can put it anywhere in the window?

Yes, just make sure it faces out.

I understand.

He started pacing back and forth by the door. Before

he left, he said, One more thing...I sense that you're experiencing some difficulties at work, is that right?

Yes, yes! A leap of her heart at the recognition of its troubles. She nodded with vigor.

Here's my advice. Pray on your knees to the bodhisattva every morning and every night. Let her know about your problems, let her know who's trying to harm you, then kowtow one hundred times. If you do that, your troubles will disappear.

Every word was welcomed by her eager ears. There's this one woman who was just hired, and she's been trying to find fault with me, Ma said. I don't understand...we're all simple-minded people trying to make a few dollars to put food on the table and she—

Just do as I say and things will get better. I need to leave for my next client.

Thank you very much. Ma went into her bedroom and returned with a red envelope. Thank you for all your help.

He pocketed the money without hesitation but stopped suddenly on the way out and said, I see you also have goldfish.

The fish were my contribution to the new apartment. I had won them at the Chinatown fair that took place every summer in celebration of the selfless queen who stole the tyrant king's immortal herb and floated up to the moon. For two whole days, the roads in Chinatown were blocked off to traffic so that local stores could set up tables in the streets to greet residents and hand out advertisements and discounts. After making our rounds and meeting some of the shop owners, Ma and I had found ourselves in a boisterous parking lot between two seafood restaurants where a man in swimming trunks sat on a plank above a tub of water. There was a line of children perpetually elongating and shrinking, all waiting for the opportunity to throw a ball toward the bull's-eye. Urged by Ma, I became one in that linear crowd. Don't be so shy, she said. How can you achieve great things in life if you can't even throw a ball in public? Go and give it a try. So I did. The ball left my hand with uncertainty and hit the target with absolute certainty. Down he went, a splash. While the shivering man climbed back up for the next throw, I was given a prize of two unblinking goldfish in a knotted bag of water.

What about them? Ma asked.

Separate them. Get another glass bowl and put one on each side of the window.

Why?

You want symmetry and you want odd numbers. Just do as I say and you'll have no regrets. Goodbye now.

* * *

—The boss is lowering our wages, he said the restaurant's not making enough money...not enough...does he think we're stupid?...what he means to say is that he wants more profit for himself...let me tell you something worth a laugh...our lunch break has been cut for almost two weeks now, he doesn't want us eating lunch on his time...he has money, what's there to understand?...money's the only value in this country...some customers had complained there weren't enough servers around noontime...the problem was that the waitstaff was sitting down to eat right in front of the boss, I've enough common sense to stuff food down in five minutes and go back to work, but they'll sit around and chat and say, That table wants something, someone go help them...so the boss took away our lunch break and told us to eat a full breakfast in the morning...to be honest, I'm fine with it, I don't eat much anyway, but it's funny, some of these

190

women complain so much, after the second or third day, they started whining about how hungry they were, that they'd faint if...remember when we used to work in the countryside? Now that was hunger, starving for an entire day in the fields, but the way these people...no, it just made me laugh...here's the best part: One of them stood in the middle—I mean, literally in the middle of the dining area—and downed an entire dish of shrimp dumplings...she just stood there, reached into her cart, and plucked the dumplings off the plate right into her mouth...I was watching, counting, one, two, three, four, in less than a minute...she's a recent immigrant...she's got that thick-tongued country accent...on her first day at work, she gave a customer the wrong dish, and he said, No, that's not what I want, so she got him something else and he told her again, No, that's not what I want, and she said to him, I don't understand what you're asking for, so he repeated his order, and then she said, What did you just say?...it was like a chicken talking to a duck, even the customer started laughing...so anyway, one of the other workers walked up to her, pulled her aside and said, Don't eat in front of everyone, don't be so stupid, and she retorted, I was hungry, I was hungry, and the other woman said, Then eat in the kitchen away from view, you'll get fired if the manager catches you, and she just kept saying, I was hungry, I was hungry...the boss saw her and she was gone within the hour...what?...no, it's not the spiteful head waitress who got fired...she's dumb but not that dumb, it was someone else...speaking of that bitch, you won't believe what she did the other day, she told the kitchen to make more dim sum at the close of lunch, the manager hates it when there's anything left over, he yells at us when there's even half a cart of food left, I said it wasn't a good

191

idea and you know what she did?...no, much worse, she told me to mind my own business and not to meddle with her important duties, can you believe she said that?...I kept telling her, The customers are on their way out, we don't need more food...twenty minutes later, the kitchen comes out with three whole carts filled...the manager had a fit, and that spineless bitch blamed it all on me, she told the manager I gave the order without consulting her which isn't even possible, I don't have that authority, all requests for orders go through her first...I stood my ground, I argued back, I wasn't going to be blamed for her mistake, but she insisted that I was responsible...the manager's an idiot if I've ever seen one, he didn't know what to think, he turned away and told us to sort it out ourselves and said if it ever happens again, we'd both lose our jobs...this bitch wants me gone because she thinks I'm going to take her spot, she knows I'm capable of working harder, she doesn't want to get demoted to my position, I guess the extra hundred dollars a month and the added authority make a big difference for some people...I don't know why he hired her in the first place...I'm genuinely trying to help the business out, I do everything to make sure food gets sold, and I treat the customers well and I try to make sure nothing's wasted...it's not my restaurant so I shouldn't care, but I still try to do a decent job...this manager has his head burrowed so far up his ass that he has no idea who the honest reliable workers are...you wouldn't believe how stingy he is, just the other day, this couple came in for lunch and left without paying, they told the cashier they didn't like the food and that the service was hostile, the manager fell into a rage, it was literally a transformation, his face got red, he started shaking all over, and he actually ran after them...I'm not kidding, it was like a cartoon...the couple flagged down a taxi and was already driving away, but he sprinted after them...of course he came back empty-handed, gasping for air...once he caught his breath, he yelled at us for not helping him chase them down, is he insane or what?...every job's as bad as the next, anyone who's rich here treats the poor like dogs...the drama never ends, I've got new stories every day...another busboy got caught stealing...whenever they go clean up a table, sometimes they pocket some of the tip, it's always happened, but it's gotten out of control lately, they're doing it at every other table or every third table, when they dump dirty plates and cups into the bins, they'll slip the bills from beneath the teapot into their pockets when no one's looking, so at the end of the day all the cart waitresses get less money...I've seen it many times, but I can't do anything about it, and I'm not going to say anything, I've no objective proof, it'll just start more conflicts...a few of them were fired earlier this year, they got caught by the manager himself...most of the workers here emigrated from the countryside, from rural China, they've no courtesy or manners and they'll trample over you to get ahead...how *did* I end up here?...all the signs told me everything was wrong all along, ever since the wedding, even before that...any weaker woman would've left—no, any smarter woman would've left—but I'm too stubborn and all the more an idiot for it...every night I think, Tomorrow I'm going to pack my bags and buy some plane tickets and I'm going to fly home with my children and leave him here...every morning I wake up and I know in my heart there's nothing here for me, I'm doing this for my children, for their education, their futures, but not for me...I don't want to think about it...just the other night, I was telling him how the bitch at work was starting all these

193

rumors, and you know what he said? He told me to mind my own business and just do my job, that's what he said, that's all he ever says, he's memorized his lines now, they just slide right off his tongue, he'll say, There's nothing more I can do, and I'll say, Tell me where the other part of your salary is, I know Hu's paying you some in cash and you're keeping it for yourself...all anyone ever thinks about in this whole country is money...he feels secure at his own job, his brother's the boss, he has no idea the pressures of working under someone who hovers around every minute and every day telling you what to do and trying to spot each little mistake, he knows nothing of the competition here, the wicked things people are capable of...he rambles on about how many hours he has to stand before the wok, how hot the kitchen is, how exhausted he gets, it makes me sick...at the end of the day, no one's a threat to his job...it's all backwards here, if I work hard, someone thinks I'm a threat and tries to get me fired, if I slack off, out the door I go, and if I work just right, then it all depends on the whim of the boss...to be an honest woman trying to raise a family here is impossible...I've told myself to stop thinking about all this but I keep thinking and it gets me nowhere...when I find myself thinking too much, I just turn on the cassette player and sing...

Beside the window that framed the city's pixilated skyline, Ma sat every night with a telephone pressed warm to her ear while her words sounded on the sunny side of the world, fragmented with sporadic sniffs, echoing the verities of her heart across the ocean in the form of electrical currents toward a place once called home, her voice speaking the truth of human despair as cold as the pale moon's reflection off a cracked window, yearning for a happiness as elusive as the unseen stars behind the

194

intangible impenetrable dome of city lights....

* * *

A glint of sun bouncing off petite scales cast transient slivers of light against the side of the bowl, a display of silent serpentine fireworks; the other in the opposite corner forever in shade knew no such warmth.

Do the fish ever get bored? I asked Ba one day.

He sat on the couch, legs crossed, reading a newspaper.

Wouldn't it be nice if they had company?

He looked up but said nothing. A few days later, he came home with two new goldfish and placed one in each bowl.

♦

My wife's been home for many months now, and she has no intention of finding work, Lone Eye said, breathing deeply and shaking his head. When she gets hired, she also gets herself fired, it's all a farce.

She's just having a hard time adjusting to—

It's been two years.

Maybe she's—

It's easy to make up explanations. Brother, your wife doesn't spend money the way mine does. Let me tell you what my wife is going to do today: She'll go downtown and come back home with bags of new clothes.

Ah San came out of the restroom. A shake of the head from Wei Jian halted the conversation. Waitresses were pacing about, shouting out the contents of their carts. Jia Ming filled his puffed cheeks with tea until drops started leaking out from his puckered lips.

I heard you got another raise, is that true? asked Ah

195

San after she sat down.

Wei Jian nodded.

That's twice in the same year.

Yes, said Shorty, smiling at her husband with admiration. He's learned some English and that's helping a lot.

Jia Ming was trying to stand his chopsticks upright, but they kept falling over and hitting the edge of his plate, the chime of his mischief unheard amidst the bustling chaos. He knocked his cup over twice, soaking the pink tablecloth with two spreading stains to the disappointment of his father, who looked at him with a disciplinary stare that went unperceived. A plate of egg tarts arrived at the table, delivered by the wrinkled hands of an old waitress. Jia Ming put one on his plate and crushed it to a yellow pulp with the bottom of his spoon. Voices swirled without distinction, a cesspool of audible oscillations, a static of organic radios tuned to insignificant frequencies—above all was the call: *Ha gau siu mai!*

Shrimp and pork dumplings…like four proverbial characters to be printed in gold on red rectangles and pasted on immigrant walls to remind them of why they came, of their gratitude at its chanting to fill their tip buckets with dollar bills.

Xia jiao shao mai!—advertised, raspy-voiced, sing-song, accented, melodically monotone, heard and heeded, desperate and exhausted—a wailing of idiots.

Ha gau siu mai!

Jia Ming drizzled chili oil into his soda and stirred it with a straw.

Mei Lan had an attentive look on her face, as if she were sitting in a classroom, fascinated as always by conversations between adults. She smiled at the memory of all those nights when her father sat with her under the conical illumination of a desk lamp and worked, she at her math problems and Wei Jian at his grammar, to the soulful hums of a summer breeze, the white noise of raindrops, or the muted kiss of snowflakes on the pane. What we're doing is moving forward, climbing up step by step, always remember that and be proud, Mei Lan told Jia Ming and me many times because her mother had told her.

Jia Ming jumped up suddenly, knocking over his soda, and said, I want to go to the bathroom.

Sit down! shouted Lone Eye.

He sat down and pouted.

Don't yell at him like that, said Ah San, waving down a waitress for another soda into which Jia Ming dropped bits of torn napkin.

Stop that! The bass of his father's voice reverberated through the distracted air. In the rage of Lone Eye's eye was the reflection of Mei Lan who had been smiling all along, the kind of soft, obedient smile that made other mothers and fathers envious.

Boys are always a little mischievous, it's just harmless fun, said Shorty.

Let him be, don't scream at him like that...you're his father, not some stranger, said Ah San.

Lone Eye stared straight at his brother, his eyeball jerking about in its socket, the other perpetually hidden behind a drooped eyelid.

Fried green peppers, fried tofu, fried eggplant! Fried green peppers, fried tofu...I didn't see you all...how long have you been here? Ma asked as she neared their table. It's very hectic today, a few workers are out sick...can I get you all any food?

Nothing fried for me, I've a sore throat.

I'll have a plate of green peppers, said Shorty.

A sizzle of smooth green shell, the ground fish paste browned, and oil flecks flicked up in parabolas. Here you are, enjoy. I'd chat for a bit, but we're really busy. Ma walked away chanting, Fried green pepper, fried tofu, fried eggplant!

Lone Eye watched Ma as she slowly maneuvered her cart between tables. Turning to Shorty, he said, You working women, I admire you all so much. It's hard to find a good job here.

You have to take whatever you can get, Shorty said.

What do you do at the hotel? Lone Eye asked.

Shorty gave an abridged description of her job. My hands have gotten coarse from the chemicals, I never have to cut my nails anymore, she exaggerated. They just constantly get worn down.

Mei Lan picked up the teapot and struggled to fill Ah San's empty cup, one hand grasping the handle, the other guarding the lid, a grand gesture of politeness.

You'll scald yourself...let the grown-ups do that, you just sit and eat the food, said Ah San, who took hold of the vessel and filled all the cups to the brim.

I don't want any tea, said Jia Ming. It tastes like pee.

That's enough! A heavy hand smacked across his head.

Don't hit your son like that! You're his father...and we're in public, said Ah San.

Why don't you make yourself useful and get a job? Lone Eye snapped.

Jia Ming watched his father intensely while rubbing the back of his head with his fingers.

Why are you bringing that up now? We've talked about this...it's hard to find good work if you aren't lucky—

198

Luck? Do you think Shorty's lucky? She's a hotel maid. She makes beds, scrubs toilets, and washes other people's dirty towels—do you think that's lucky? She works hard so she doesn't get fired.

Brother, please calm down, said Wei Jian.

I stand in front of a fryer for ten hours a day. I get blisters from the splattering oil. Do you think that's lucky? You still think we're in China? Do you have any idea...the paycheck I bring home every month...to watch you waste it all on the latest line of fashion...am I lucky for that? This is America. You work here. You work for what you want, you don't sit around and have it handed to you! Take a look around...do you see all these women? They're pushing carts around to sell dim sum so they don't have to rely on their husbands' paychecks. Why don't you try that for once?

I—

Don't give me excuses, I've heard enough. Some of these women have babies at home, they have children who aren't in school yet, they have mouths to feed...but you? You can barely take care of our son. Look at his behavior, his total lack of manners...if you mess him up, guess what? There's no second chance. I'm sure you remember what the doctor said!

Two salted crescents crystallized over Ah San's eyes. Such things were never spoken about even behind closed doors, let alone in public. Wei Jian and Shorty both ignored the statement as if it had never been uttered. Ah San excused herself and headed for the restroom. With uneasy hands, Shorty lifted the teapot and tried to make peace by filling Lone Eye's teacup and the one of his absent wife.

Let's not argue...I'm sure Ah San works very hard...if you're not a woman, you won't understand, Shorty said. It's hard to be a woman in a foreign country raising a

199

family...give her some time to—

You think it's hard because you work. She doesn't. She just shops.

She's taking good care of Jia Ming...it's not easy, especially with boys. You're at the restaurant all day...you've no idea how draining it can be at home, cooking, cleaning, all that housework—

If you think she does any housework, you're giving her too much credit.

They saw Ma approaching and immediately hushed up. Can I get you all any more food?

No, we'll be leaving soon, thank you, said Wei Jian.

Lone Eye shook his head. I'm sorry...I didn't mean to ruin lunch.

It's okay. Give her some more time. She's not used to this lifestyle.

When Ah San returned, her eyes were bloodshot. The rest of their time passed in silence. Shorty waved down the suited man for the bill. The remainder of the food was packed away in white boxes printed with red pagodas—in went the last egg tart, a small mound of rice noodles, the last shrimp and chive dumpling. The flaps were folded along their pre-creased lines; the handle of metal wire was bent at a right angle. Dollar bills were placed under the teapot. The cries of *'ha gau siu mai'* grew soft, softer, and finally inaudible as the door closed behind them.

Your husband didn't mean what he said, Shorty consoled Ah San on the way out.

As if the tone and timing of those words had affirmed some notion brewing in her mind, she said, I understand...go on ahead, I left something inside. She ascended back up the steps with hustling feet.

What the hell did she forget? asked Lone Eye.

She didn't say.

What the hell could she possibly have forgotten?

Brother, calm your nerves.

The sun became a glowing smudge behind a white clump of cloud. A significant period of time transpired.

What's taking so long? I'm going in to look for her, said Jia Ming, who sprinted up the steps.

When you get home, apologize to her and cheer her up. She's your wife. Just let it go. It's not worth the headache, said Wei Jian.

The ball of cloud passed; the sun resumed its blinding intensity and illuminated the street without shyness.

Here she comes.

What were you talking to that man about? asked Jia Ming.

What man?

The one in the suit. You were pointing fingers. What were you talking about?

Nothing, that's none of your business. I was asking him where my purse was.

No, you weren't. You had your purse with you. You're lying!

Little boys should mind their own business.

But—

But nothing.

And what was that other woman saying?

That's none of your business.

◆

—If not for them, I would leave in a heartbeat...

* * *

—That head waitress got what she wanted, that

goddamn bitch, she finally got me out...I don't know the details, I don't want to think about it...some customer filed a complaint against me last weekend, someone told the manager that I wasn't doing my job at all and said I was being rude and disrespectful, the bitch overheard and chimed right in, she fanned the hell out of that fire, she told the boss that several customers had already complained to her about the same problem, can you believe it?...I've more ability to work in my pinky finger than her whole damn body...she made the whole thing up, it was all made up...that manager is an idiot, he thought about what she'd said for a few days and decided to fire me today, he said he couldn't take any more chances with me causing so much customer dissatisfaction...that geomancer predicted this...

* * *

—In one ear and out the other, that's what I think whenever someone tells me to take language classes, You'll find a better job if you can speak English, people always say...talk about the obvious...I can't sit in a classroom, in one ear and out the other...you can ask me the same question a minute after it's been answered, and I won't remember the answer...the fates have set out for me a life of physical labor, I can outperform anyone when it comes to manual work, but ask me to use a pen, and I'd sooner fly...I'm here to work, I'm not here to go to school...do you remember what our teachers did under the new policies?...remember how we had to teach ourselves four years of grammar and math in one week? I still remember what the teacher said, If you don't pass this test, you'll be in trouble with the principal and the government...what did that even mean? Expulsion? Time in jail? Torture?...of course we all passed, a copy of the answers appeared on test day, and everyone copied from each other, we all graduated and then we got shipped out to the countryside to work on fields and farms...

* * *

—Old Man, you've been coughing a lot lately, are you sick?...what?...who said?...she heard wrong, I'm looking for work now...you need to take better care of yourself...take some deep breaths, go get a glass of water, you don't sound well...put her on...hello...is he sick?...did you tell him that I lost my job?...how did you say it?...I told you to wait...is that him still coughing?...tell him to stop smoking, it's bad for his health, put him back on the phone...the boy says you need to stop smoking, it's terrible for your health...

* * *

—Don't tell me you've forgotten...I know you remember...he hid money from me, he trusted his damn brothers with it...I got sick of his lies, only a fool like me would've believed him for so long...I was a seamstress then, and I was making more than a culinary school graduate, have you heard of such absurdity?...I told myself he wasn't lying, It's just the times, just the times, I kept saying...and then one day, Ah San stopped me in the street and asked, Why does your husband leave money with us? Is your house not safe? Why not put it in a bank? I hope you know we're not responsible for it...I still remember that afternoon, I was in total disbelief—and this was *after* the motorcycle! I didn't ask him directly, but I gave him many chances to come clean, and he pretended like he didn't know what I was talking about...he should've been an actor, such wasted talent...why be a chef when you've got such great acting skills? I thought he had changed after the motorcycle, I really thought he had changed, he kept pretending like he didn't know what I was hinting at, I got tired of it and just asked him, Are you hiding money from me again?...of course he denied it...it's not about money, it's really not, it's about trust, there's no trust in this marriage, none...who knows what he's thinking?...there's no shame in being poor as long as you can be happy together...every word of his is a lie, and that's no exaggeration...maybe he wants to line his coffin with cash, I don't know...it's a prison here, a cell of four white walls...leave Chinatown?...go where?...they cluck, and I quack...he'll never change, I'm used to it and getting more used to it every day...when he wants sex, he'll attempt conversation, but the moment we're done, he'll turn his back to me and start snoring, it's worse than sleeping next to a rock...do you remember how hard he persuaded me to leave China?...it made sense then...it doesn't matter now, when I catch myself thinking too much, I play the cassettes, I play them loud and sing even louder...

* * *

—I got another cart waitress position at a different restaurant...I'm very relieved, I didn't think I'd get hired again so soon, I was starting to get nervous, I kept thinking what would happen if I were to remain unemployed for the next few months...the owner's a local, they say he bought out the old restaurant and closed it down for renovations...who knows?...maybe he wants to try his luck with a new name, clearly he has enough money to throw around...how's the Old Man? I haven't talked to him in a while, how's he doing?...tell him there's nothing to worry about, tell him the children are well...

* * *

—It's fine until he's home and then I get angry, I don't even know why, it just comes out, I can't control it, it's
204

automatic, like a reflex, it's the same each time: He yells for divorce and I scream the hell back at him, I have so much hatred towards him, I never thought I could hate anyone so much...every time I see his face, I think about all his lies, and that look he gives me, it's in his eyes, his eyes are asking why I'm here ruining his life...I dare him to touch me one more time, I'd have the cops drag him straight to jail...he's got a steady job and his brothers are all here, his whole family is here, and I'm here by myself an ocean away, my night's your day...Let's get a divorce!—that's all he says, he knows I won't get a lawyer, he knows I care too much about the children...you can't imagine what it's like here, waking up to a job you're scared of losing because you're working too little or too hard and everyone below you is trying to take your spot and everyone above thinks you're out for theirs, we're all here to make a few dollars...any other woman would've dumped him...I ask myself every day, What the hell is he good for? I've yet to find an answer...I know he's thinking, There's not a damn place for you to go...and he's right...one day, I'm going to say yes...I'll say, Let's get a divorce...I'm going to look him straight in the eyes and say yes...he can yell all he wants right now because he knows I can't go anywhere, I've no family here, I can't speak English, and I can't support the children on my own, he knows that, he knows I won't do anything to jeopardize the family...I can't leave, I dream about it all the time, but I know that I can't leave, not now, I wouldn't forgive myself, I can't do that to my children...America's a very revealing country, if you're not rich or you're not smart, then you're just going to suffer, it's that simple...come the day, he'll regret being so arrogant...what does he have to brag about?...he's a cook at his brother's restaurant, he makes fake Chinese food, is that something

205

to be so proud of?...there's no use getting all worked up about it, I just turn on the cassette player or the television if...it never bothers him, he can study through anything, his concentration doesn't break, sometimes I'll be singing and I'll just watch him...he picked that calligraphy brush for a reason...

* * *

Ma's voice fell nightly upon my ears tuned to harsh screams, an angelic sound above the muted humdrum of glowing windows, bright and shining apertures darkened by silhouettes engaged in the struggle of life against the billboard of evening sky bruised neon purple. Her voice imitated those of dead singers immortalized on film to be broadcasted at the tap of buttons from a convex glass screen buzzing with snowy static...those singers who sparkled in the glitter of defunct fashion, their necks embellished with pearls, their bodies cloaked in light-shattering single-toned dresses, their slender ivory arms veiled in satin caressing the microphone into which flowed without flooding invisible waterfalls of sadness. Must be nice, I'm sure, the money and the attention, but surely they've miseries of their own...and if they're in troubled marriages, they could sing about it, and the world would listen and sympathize, or they could run off, and half the world would pursue—that was what Ma said once. Her voice in song brought back nostalgia for the hot and humid nights filled with the buzzing of frenzied mosquitoes, nostalgia for the yellowed wallpaper under which crawled a canvas of centipedes and termites, nostalgia for the empty space between wood-planked steps giving a view with repetitive linear hindrance of the hunchbacked grandmother below who swept up every morning the dust that fell from the bottoms of our shoes. That same voice in argument was the antithesis of song, a wild and untamed shriek that made ears wince: it squeaked like fingernails on polished slate (a feedback of misplaced microphones) and studded the skin of anyone in range with innumerable goose bumps, each little hair at attention. She sang low and she sang high, she sang duets and dropped octaves to sing male lines, she sang with a resonance that filled the sky, and in the warmth of my blanket, I hummed softly alongside....

* * *

The granules released at the separation of thumb and forefinger fell into the water. The bottle slipped out of my grasp and fell to the ground, spilling its contents.

What mess are you making now? Ma asked.

I swept the crumbs back into the container. I'm just feeding the fish.

Why are there two of them?

What?

Her voice escalated, Why are there two fish in each bowl?

Ba bought them.

She cursed his name out loud and cursed again.

There was yelling that night, their voices harsh and grating like Chinese operas sung by actors and actresses in dazzling robes with faces painted white and eyes outlined black and cheeks dabbed pink, the incomprehensible high-pitched dialogue accompanied by sporadic clangs and bangs of percussion. It's a form of art, Ma said once. They're singing about love.

Ba told me to toss the goldfish into the garbage the next morning before school.

But they'll die, I protested.

Then flush them down the toilet, they'll go to the ocean where they belong. He handed me a small net with which I scooped them up one by one, their small, slick bodies bouncing about in my closed palm. Flush them down the toilet.

But—

Just do what I say.

I looked at the last goldfish in my palm. I looked at its unblinking eye and wondered, for reasons unknown, for reasons primitive and impulsive, what its insides looked like. If it had to go, it might as well go, I thought, and without hesitation, without giving myself the possibility of thinking twice, I pressed on its belly with my thumb. The skin cracked, and its viscera squirted out like miniature toothpaste, a roll of clear yellowish jelly. Three goldfish in the toilet bowl, swimming, and one in the cup of my palm, dead. A depression of the lever would, I imagined, drain them through swerving pipes to an underground tank where human waste from the entire city was collected and mixed by spinning blades. Could fish smell? If so, that would be unfortunate. I pressed the lever. Their scales shimmered for the last time in the bathroom light as they swirled down the white gullet, circling, gurgling...I thought back to that first day of our arrival when my cousins and I formed a line before the toilet and took turns flushing down bits of polystyrene foam from the packaging of a new portable stereo.

* * *

—I can't leave, not now...but come the day, he'll regret it...I know with all my heart he will regret it.

6

UNDER THE CEILING checkered with phosphorescent squares, thin crescent moon shadows formed beneath our eyes. The flag of stars and stripes dangled half-folded on itself. The principal appeared with a tall, scrawny boy who was wringing his hands behind his back. Good morning, Mrs. Pam, the principal said. Here's your new student.

Mrs. Pam was our third grade teacher; she was wide-nosed and square-faced, and her lips, unable to close all the way, revealed a hint of buck teeth. Her lessons, delivered with neither passion nor strictness, were ideal catalysts for daydreaming. To the luck of all daydreamers, she was completely incompetent when it came to discipline.

Come on in. This will be your seat.

The sharp-cornered, communal U-shape of our desks remained unchanged as we shifted to make room for a chair that she hastily inserted.

Please make him feel welcomed.

Jia Ming leaned over and said, Who's this idiot? He smells like a farmer.

Summer had confined his mischief to the apartment and rendered his mother its sole recipient. On the first day of school, Jia Ming had sensed Mrs. Pam's perfect lack of authority and asserted his role as class clown. We had all become dependent on his outbursts and antics to urge forward the slug-paced revolution of the clock, to soften the resonant tick of each unwilling second. For his services, he was sent to the principal's office several times a week.

I just go to the bathroom and draw on the walls, he confided one day to me and Mei Lan.

You never go to the principal's office?

I've been there a few times. She just calls up my mom, that's all. My mom doesn't care...when I get home, I tell her it wasn't my fault.

We opened our reading texts to the story of the week: a family picnicking in the woods finds a lost baby bear whom they adopt until its mother, after weeks of exhaustive searching, reclaims him and repays the family with a gleaming jar of honey collected over years of raiding beehives.

What kind of a family eats in the middle of a forest?

They're picnicking, explained Mrs. Pam. They have a house in the countryside.

That's stupid. Country folk are retards.

Jia Ming, don't use that word! I've told you many times—

I bet the bear cave smells like poop.

Jia Ming!

I have another question. How come the mother bear didn't just eat the family? I saw this show once where a wild bear ripped off someone's scalp.

That's enough.

Lunch was time for even greater calamities, and on this day, he was the instigator behind an overcooked stalk of broccoli being thrown at the loser of a thumb-wrestling match, the dousing of a distracted girl's peaches with milk, a deep belch that brought up a bolus of part-digested food promptly spat out onto the table to cries of disgust, a cursing at the lunch lady who told him to calm down...and his crowning achievement, with a snicker turned guffaw turned breathless gasping: the dropping of a peach wedge down the new boy's shirt. His antics were prematurely cut short when, from the corner of his eye, he caught a glimpse of two boys trading cards. He quickly sprinted over to join them.

I'll give you these three for that one, said one to the other.

I don't want those.

What about—

You're both idiots, Jia Ming said, snatching away and thumbing through their stacks. I can buy these in packs of twelve for a dollar. Neither of you have anything valuable. Get them out of my sight. He tossed the cards back onto the table.

Not unlike the televised numbered balls that tumbled in the transparent globe every night and made an addict of every degenerate immigrant—the gambling dens in Chinatown were filled with unshaven restaurant workers whose faces were wrinkled beyond recognition, who propelled mucus and saliva from their raspy throats to briefly stain the pavement like dogs marking territory...they were addicted to the lottery, they were consumers of an industry that consumed them and thrived on their ignorance and greed-distorted perception of probability, yet they persisted without hesitation because of the possibility, however slim, of immediate attainment of that which had beckoned them across oceans and continents; not unheard of were those who lost their entire paychecks in one day trying to match the numbers that rolled out of the colossal gumball machine or finding the one-million-dollar scratch ticket in the brightly colored reels obscured by cigarette smoke, wafts of which escaped with each ring of the bell hanging above the door to signal every eager

211

entrance and every dejected exit—these cards, much like what the lottery was to our fathers, became an obsession: laminated rectangles issued by licensed manufacturers of costumed crusaders flaunting fiery fists, gargantuan guns, sculpted six-packs, bulging biceps, and specialized superpowers. These were tokens to the top of the boys' social ladder. Trades took place every day, some spectator-less, others in full view of the envious eyes of those who could not afford the cards. Jia Ming wasted no time learning the hierarchy of value behind each card and with seemingly limitless cash bought each week's new releases.

I just take it right out of my mom's wallet, he boasted whenever anyone inquired into the source of his wealth. She doesn't keep count, so I just take whatever I need. You should try it. Who cares if your mom finds out? Just pretend you don't know what she's talking about when she asks, it's so easy.

*　*　*

The start of the third grade marked Mei Lan's transformation into an effusive extrovert who took every opportunity to share her personal life with anyone willing to listen. Her younger brother, born around the same time as May, became an inexhaustible topic of conversation.

During his checkup, the doctor said that he's above average in everything, she told me. My mom always jokes that he might eat us into bankruptcy. His brain needs all the energy it can get. The nurses at the clinic all said he'll grow up to be very smart, possibly smarter than me, and definitely smarter than anyone else I know. He might even be one of those kids who'll go to college when they're sixteen. One time, I dropped my eraser and spent all afternoon trying to find it, I was looking under the bed and through my backpack and between the pages of my books, and when I finally gave up, my brother, who was only a few months old, started waving his arms around and gestured toward the floor lamp. The eraser had fallen and landed behind the lamp. He was actually trying to tell me where it was, would you believe it? Did I ever tell you that he spoke my name before he said anything else? I told my parents, and they thought I made it up. I'm pretty sure that he knew how to talk before he actually started talking. I think he doesn't want everyone to know how smart he is, so he's holding a lot of things back and only revealing his capabilities when the time is right...by the way, how's your sister doing?

She's fine.

I think when our siblings grow up, they'll be good friends.

Maybe.

Wouldn't it be fun if Jia Ming also had a younger brother or sister? In a few years, they could all go to school together the way we're doing now. But I don't know if that can happen. Sometimes I hear Jia Ming's parents argue at home, she said with an intensity in her eyes as if she had been harboring this secret for a long time and had been waiting to tell someone. Whenever they fight, his dad always tells his mom that Jia Ming is the only chance they have, so she needs to raise him properly. He always says something like, You can't have another child so if you don't take good care of Jia Ming, you won't have anything later in life to be proud of. I don't know what that really means, but their arguments always sound harsh. I don't like to eavesdrop—my mom says it's not polite to pry into other people's affairs. And besides, that's not what I want to tell you about. I'm *really* excited today...can you guess why?

No, I said, shaking my head.

213

She told me that her mother had officially assigned her a title in the family: the older sister, not just of her brother, but of the household. It was the most important role she had ever been given. Her mother said it was her duty to do whatever she could to help her little brother reach his full potential. I'm going to be responsible for making sure that he grows up to be the best and smartest little brother ever, she said. I can take charge of him as much as I want...I've already started brushing his teeth at night. The pediatrician said that he has the best teeth of any toddler he's ever seen, so I'm going to keep them perfect and clean. Do you help take care of your sister, too?

Sure, when my mom needs me to, I said.

Well, I'm going to be helping all the time, even when it's not needed. When he's older, he'll thank me for all that I did for him. My mom said that nurturing someone you love so that they achieve great things later on brings the best kind of happiness.

* * *

Show me, said Mrs. Pam. I know it's the new craze, but you can't do this in my class. It's distracting.

Do what? I wasn't doing anything, said Jia Ming.

Show me what's in your pocket.

I don't want to. You can't search me. You're not the police!

She did not know how to discipline him; all she could do was shake her head, turn away, and resume her lesson.

The commotion on the way home was at an all-time high. The hype of those cards left every boy and even some girls in a perpetual state of hyperactivity. Those with the best cards struggled to stay ahead, those with mediocre sets orchestrated trades to try and catch up, and those

214

without turned to voyeurism. The objective was to boast as extensive a collection as possible and to acquire all the rare and special releases. Deals were struck behind the backs of others, dramas of hurt feelings and betrayal became commonplace, and their collective enthusiasm over these tireless tirades of trades, repressed in class, burst out in full fury at lunch, at recess, and on the bus.

* * *

Nobody was spared from Mei Lan's gloating over her brother's intelligence. Early on, we all marveled over this prodigy, this child whose name and legacy we would know one day. Some of Mei Lan's friends felt lucky just to know her; the chance to associate with the sibling of a future genius was a special privilege. We were captivated by her anecdotes of his feats and abilities that sounded impressive for a boy not yet one-and-a-half years old. Jia Ming was the first to tire of hearing her brag; his doubts quickly turned into rebuttals before degenerating into blatant mockery. His ridicule, whether intended or not, gradually made us all aware just how excessively embellished her stories were, to the point where, little by little, her friends began to ignore her. At her persistence of declaring her brother a savant, Jia Ming told her during recess one afternoon in front of some classmates that her brother must in fact be a dunce, an actual idiot. That's how people are, he said. When they don't have something or when they want to believe in something that's not true, they tell everyone about it nonstop. My mom does it all the time.

* * *

Come to the back! Jia Ming has new cards!

They all rushed over, maintaining their balance as the bus rattled down the road. The new student watched from a short distance the unveiling of two packs mummified in gold and black foil stretched taut as if freshly ironed. With the calculated movements of an expert mime, Jia Ming slowly tore apart the wrappers and revealed a few cards from the first pack. He thumbed through the second and flashed two more cards before the circle of hungry eyes.

No one's allowed to touch these, he said.

You're so lucky.

How did you get so many rare ones?

Where did you buy those?

Can I see them? I promise I won't drop any.

Jia Ming, will you trade with me? I'll give you everything I have.

The voice, meek at first, came out of nowhere: How come you don't protect your cards?

The crowd turned.

The new boy, whose fierce eyes betrayed none of his reticence, quickly dug into his pockets and pulled out some cards of his own, snug within plastic sleeves. I have sleeves for all of mine...see? Realizing that he now held their attention, his voice escalated. They protect the cards from fingerprints and scratches...and you have to put the expensive cards in hard cases so they don't get bent. If a card gets bent, it's no good.

Jia Ming has a lot of bent cards, someone said.

That's because he doesn't know what he's doing, the boy responded with sudden confidence.

What's that one you're holding? I've never seen it before.

This is the most expensive card I have. It's worth twenty-five dollars.

Jaws dropped, gasps ran amok, and the whole of their focus shifted onto the new boy, who in the span of a minute had dethroned Jia Ming from the spotlight. It was all the more impressive for he had been at the head of the collecting game all along yet made no indication of it. They swarmed around him and demanded turns to view the encased rectangle of light, an illusion of three dimensions on two, a false sense of action. The tempestuous fire of the hologram danced in their black pupils unhidden by lids stretched maximal. With the appropriate tilt of hand, one could see a raising of arms, a downward swipe of the sword, a twirling of the cape, and a decapitation of the monster's head, whose vicious angry face turned into a grimace of agony as it rolled onto the ground.

Who cares about that? I've more cards than you, way more, Jia Ming said. He brought out his entire collection, stacks upon stacks, and began offering trades aloud so as to regain his audience. Who wants to trade for these? He held out the two gold-foiled cards that came in the second pack.

I hope you know those are fake, the new boy said.

Fake? What do you mean? someone asked.

Jia Ming's lips flattened bloodless. What do you mean fake?

Your cards aren't from the official maker. They're from a dud company, so they're not worth anything. That's why you get so many special ones in each pack. Look at the logo on the back, it's different...and besides, the real cards come in a green and blue wrapper.

Jia Ming wasted all his money on garbage!

Who wants to trade with him now? Not me!

Jia Ming flushed red—with humiliation? Anger? Or was it a coincidental turning of the bus for the sun to reveal the folly on his face? The clown, the rebel of authority who was always right even when he was wrong, was finally wrong. There were suppressed chuckles

217

escaping from palm-covered nostrils as staccato snorts, from pinhole breaks in sealed lips as vocal flatulence, from the creases between fingers as a dry-leaf rustle. They were all laughing at him. He would remember it, every syllable of that encounter.

The new boy brought all of his cards to school some days later in a black plastic box. Jia Ming watched from a few seats away, his knees digging into the green vinyl, elbows and chin propped on the back of the seat, eyes fixated and out for the kill. In the undefined flicker of an instant, he knew what he would do, he saw it clear as the act itself: he saw each step of the timed collision, a smack of bodies to be made all the more convincing with an exaggerated cry of one caught in surprise. He stood with knees bent and ready. When the cards were taken out of their box, he counted to four: One, two, three, four...you stupid kid, he thought. If it weren't for those cards, you'd be nothing. He sprinted forth and screamed a loud greeting. A momentous crash knocked the box onto the ground, freeing the plastic-sheathed cards to cartwheel across the dusted floor like a small explosion of celebratory firecrackers; the covers became scratched with fine lines as if etched on by a mermaid's fingernails. Jia Ming, bending over to pick them up, sarcastically apologized, I'm so sorry...but they're fine, they're all protected, isn't that right? Don't worry, nothing lost—what's that word you use?—value...nothing lost value. Crouched with hands hidden from view, he stuffed some cards into his hind pocket before standing up to pat the new boy on the shoulder three affirmative times. I'm so sorry, he repeated, in rhythm with that tap, one, two, three.

The new boy confronted Jia Ming the next day. You took some of my cards!

A smile flashed across Jia Ming's face. What are you talking about?

Don't pretend you don't know. Tears formed in the boy's eyes. He sniffed erratically and held in what would have been an unrestrained bawl with the tightening of palatal muscles.

Why are you crying? Are you a little girl?

Give my cards back!

I don't know what you're talking about.

You took some when they fell, I know you did. Just give them back to me.

I didn't take anything.

A crowd formed to watch.

I know you took them. Just give them back. They're not yours!

You have no proof that I stole them.

Give them back!

Prove that I stole them, and I'll give them back to you.

His lips quivered, and his tongue was paralyzed by the weight of the words crumbling in translation from emotion to audible sound. He had lost his cards and his spotlight, and there was nothing he could say or do. Maroon spider webs crisscrossed the whites of his eyes as Jia Ming waved him off with a smirk of dismissal, exiling him back to anonymity.

♦

It was that time again when temperatures dropped, when leaves turned brown and left branches naked, thousand-splintered, stiffly-frazzled, and bird-less.

Each day was a repeat of the one before, forged from the same mold with mild alterations, spat out from the assembly line to pile up as weeks and months, the gears of the great machine in perpetual motion fueled by the mirage of progress.

Each morning started with a breakfast of assorted pastries or two hard-boiled eggs or sticky rice wrapped in banana leaf and a bowl of milk, that vile bovine secretion. The bus picked us up and wove its way through Chinatown before burrowing down into the tunnel and emerging loud and beastly on the elevated motorway straddling over the piers and wharfs near the city's financial district where thousands of suited professionals sauntered to their glass cells. I had the seat to myself; Mandy was no longer around. The last I heard, her family had moved out to a suburban town and she was enrolled into a new school. Many rides I sat through recalling a recurring dream of mine: her faceless parents on a ferry across Pearl River—its waters bright yellow, almost fluorescent—singing to the rhythm of the waves. Where's Mandy? I ask. They point to an old woman with bulging fish-eyes swimming in the river. I scream, Watch out! The boat's going to hit you. Mandy sings in response: I know, I kno-oo-ow...

The bus raced across the suspension bridge and parked before the brick complex of education where numbers were added and subtracted, words were pronounced and spelled, worksheets were assigned and graded, and chalkboards were written on and erased. The pinnacle of the day was the forty-five minutes of freedom during which we ran and squealed without restraint, playing games of freeze-tag, dodge ball, kickball, and soccer. Our cries of excitement rose skyward like smoke from the smokestacks of distant factories. Each afternoon, we closed our textbooks and placed them into the plastic bins beneath our chairs along with notebooks and workbooks, the physical weight of which was to be transformed into the ethereal substance of knowledge, the sole reason for their sleepless flight, so that we too could fly on illusory wings.

Winter's chill stilled the streets' patter and made our teeth chatter, blanching the days gray and cold with the atmosphere of idle dreams and empty rooms. Blizzards entombed cornices in ice, hung icicles from fire escapes, and awakened herds of snowplows from their summer hibernation. Sleet glassed the streets for cars to slide and feet to slip, sidewalks were sanded and salted, and snowplowed heaps were eroded under the struggles of soles and the forces of leaps.

* * *

We'll be moving to a new place, Mei Lan said. My parents want to leave Chinatown because it's too crowded and full of immigrants. Chinatown isn't the best neighborhood to live in because the streets are smelly and everyone spits on the ground and there's garbage overflowing everywhere. You and Jia Ming should come over to visit after we move. Do you know what the best part is? We got a new car!

I had heard from Ba that Wei Jian recently bought a used car, but Mei Lan told us it was brand new.

You don't know how good it feels to ride in your own car, she said. My dad has driven me to school a few times. I can sprawl out in the back seat and turn on the radio and listen to music. It's so much better than being on that loud, dirty bus. She said she felt sorry that neither Jia Ming nor I had that kind of privilege and hoped that our families could afford cars of our own in the future.

When are you moving? I asked.

I don't know, but it'll be soon. We went to make final inspections of the new place this past weekend. She talked about how spacious it was, how each room was equipped with a radiator that would keep them warm in the winter, how the floor tiles were so polished that she could see her reflection clearly, and how there was a designated parking spot for their car.

She took my inclination to reverie for undivided attention. The details that she provided about her new home, while thorough and concrete, were also perfectly vague. I could not tell if it was a house like Uncle Hu's, or just another apartment. I thought back to the time we visited Uncle Hu. I thought back to the lush lawns and the playground set and the myriad of rooms and hallways, how I got lost around every corner and how every doorway seemed to lead to a space where one could live an entire life, where the walls (unlike those of a prison cell) felt expansive instead of confining. I recalled the kitchen with its modern appliances and granite countertops and lacquered cabinets, the bathrooms with their glossy sheen and immaculate whiteness, and the bedrooms and offices filled with ornate furniture. I wondered if Mei Lan would be living in a similar setting. She spoke about her relocation so favorably that I felt occasional pangs of envy. I thought to myself how comforting it would be to escape to my own soundproof space away from my parents' frequent arguments. This temptation provided ample fodder for daydreams during the commute to and from school, on insomniac nights, or sometimes even in the middle of a conversation with Mei Lan. It was something that I had always wanted: a place of retreat where I could close the door and shut out the world. More often than not, I tuned out what Mei Lan was saying and thought instead about the perfect room, one that I did not have to share with May, one that I could call entirely my own—it would have a window overlooking a spectacular view, a soft springy bed, perhaps some posters of wild animals on the wall, a clock to keep time, a desk with drawers, a dresser to compartmentalize all of my clothes; in short, it would be a flawlessly organized enclosure with every item in its designated place. I thought about the decorations and furnishings I would want, but I knew that Ma would encroach and set it up the way she saw fit. Maybe I would house a pet, not a cat or a dog, but something exotic, like a bird of prey. Maybe I would win a bedroom makeover contest on a game show—even Ma would not stand in the way of so much free money—and I would ask for an arcade, a basketball hoop, a miniature train set, maybe even some carnival attractions to be set up so that my friends could visit and win prizes. My daydreams inevitably veered into absolute nonsense, scenarios far beyond the absurd.

* * *

—Hello?...it's five in the afternoon here...what are you calling so early for?...what?...I'm cooking now, I can call you back after dinner...what?...hold on, let me turn off the stove...I can hear you...who?...the Old Man?...when?...what did the doctor say?...I should've known, he hasn't sounded like himself lately, his cough was getting worse...he's been in the hospital already for how long?...why are you just telling me now?!...why didn't you tell me earlier?...how's he doing?...what did the doctors say?...how can they say nothing?...did you ask them?...how much has he been smoking?...I keep telling him but he's so stubborn, it can't be good for his lungs...did he tell you not to tell me?...don't bring that up, it's different...as if I don't have enough to worry about...have they given him any medicine?...I don't know why I left, I really don't know...every day I just

223

feel...it's not like there's gold to be picked up off the streets here, there's gold all right, deep in the greedy pockets of managers, and let me tell you: It's not ours to pick, you scrape for every penny you earn, you work like a dog, and at the end of the day, you stick out your hand and if you're lucky, you'll get a few morsels...it's my fault, there's no one to blame, if I had any intelligence, I wouldn't be in this situation...are you going to see him today?...how long do you think he'll be there?...hospitals make people sicker, being confined in bed all day with other sick people and all those germs floating around...do they let him go outside?...you should prepare his meals and make him some soup, hospital food is not good...I want to sponsor him over one day, Western medicine is so advanced, the doctors here are the best in the world, not to mention the air isn't as polluted, I want to put you two on a plane and fly you both over...it's boring as hell here, so you'd die of boredom, but at least you won't die of illness—

A snap of mechanical viscera suddenly sounded. A rotation of the wrist, a squeak of the hinges, and in wafted the smell of kitchen grease.

—I'll call you back later...yes, yes...goodbye.

Ba came in and placed his dinner packed in two takeout boxes on the table. He sat on the couch and breathed a heavy sigh.

Why are you home so early?

Restaurant got hit with a power outage. The whole town's affected so we closed early, he said.

Ma took a seat on the couch. The television was off, its convex screen reflecting with slight distortion the silence and inertia between them that seemed almost tangible. My sister just called. The Old Man's sick...he's in the hospital...it's probably nothing, but I don't know whether she's telling me everything. It's one more thing for me to worry about.

Ba was staring straight ahead at nothing in particular, eyes diverged, a distant focus.

I haven't talked to him much over the past month. She always told me he was out of the house or something...I should've suspected...I think he's been sick for a while now. I know he's stubborn, always insisting that nothing's wrong especially when it comes to his health—

Why are you telling me? What do you want me to do about it?

You don't have to do anything. My father's in the hospital, and I'm concerned about him. They don't know what's wrong with him.

You can't go back to see him, that's for sure.

I never said I would do that.

There's really nothing you can do.

You think I don't know that? I wish I could get the hell out of this place—

I'm sick of coming home to nonsense like this! You want to go back to China? Do you have any idea how much a plane ticket costs?

That's not what I—

Let's just get a divorce if you're so miserable here.

Divorce, divorce, divorce...don't you get tired of saying that?

My back's killing me, standing in that kitchen for twelve hours—

Because I'm doing so great myself! You make it sound like you're the only one suffering.

This is about money, isn't it?

What money?

The money you want me to give you to go back and

see your father.

I never said that.

You implied it.

The last thing I would do is ask you for money. I make almost as much as what's printed on your paycheck, and I'm a lowly waitress. I know that you're earning more than you admit. Your entire side of the family is in on it, and you've left me in the dark. But I know, I'm not that stupid. Don't bring up money, this isn't about money. My father is halfway across the world and he's sick. I can't visit him, I can't help him, I can't do anything.

Do you want me to pay for the medical bills? Is that what this is about? I already give you everything I make—

For the last time, I don't care about your money! You can hide as much of it as you want, you can go waste it on lottery tickets and whores, you can save it up to line your coffin, I don't care—

Let's get a—

I'm tired of hearing that! When words have no meaning, there's no point in repeating them. Why don't *you* find a lawyer? Go ahead. You never back up anything you say. Find the lawyer and *I'll* sign the papers. I was talking about my father and you started yelling about money. I don't think I've ever met a more selfish man. I don't know how I ended up in a marriage like this—

I give you all of my wages at the end of each month—

You don't have to keep up the act. I've already told you many times that your brother's wife, Shorty, revealed your lie when she came by for tea and mentioned your promotion. That was two years ago!

And I've already told you many times I don't know where Shorty heard that from...it's completely ungrounded...it's pointless to keep talking about it if you won't believe me.

I don't believe you because you're lying. You lie once and dig yourself into a hole, and instead of getting out, you keep digging deeper, covering lies with more lies.

Ramble all you want. I have no money to spare for your father's illness. My whole paycheck goes to you, and that's that. If you think I'm hiding money, where is it? Show me!

You know I can't do that, and I don't need to. People say things for a reason. They don't just make it up out of nothing. Who the hell knows where you're hiding the money?

I—

And one more thing: Stop complaining about how hard your job is. Your brother's the boss! Try working under some stranger, try working at a place where everyone's out to get you. You think it's easy to raise a family off the money you give me? You think your paycheck's all you need to provide? Let me make one thing clear, go clean the oil out of your ears so you can hear me, let me say this loud enough so it goes through that thick head of yours: It's *not* about the money, it never was. It's about trust...and you can't speak a single goddamn truth!

Let's just get a divorce, we won't miss each other—there's some truth for you.

I don't know what I did in my previous life to deserve this, I was just talking about the Old Man and the conversation turns into—

To hell with the Old Man.

Get out! I don't want to see your bastard face! She wiped away her tears. Get out, you bastard, get out!

What do you think now that Mei Lan's moved out? I asked Jia Ming.

I'm glad, he said. I have the whole apartment to myself. Her room is no longer off limits. I can stay up late and watch all the television I want. She used to complain that the volume was too loud, but that's not a problem anymore. Things are so much better without her and her annoying little brother around.

You don't miss her company?

Why would anyone miss her? She's just a know-it-all. Her brother used to cry a lot and wake us all up in the middle of the night. I'm glad they're gone. I get the whole apartment to myself. I can do whatever I want in her room because now it's *my* room. You should come over to play some time. My mom won't care how rowdy we get.

Have you been to their new place?

No.

Do you think Mei Lan is living in a big house like Uncle Hu's?

Who knows? Maybe they're living in the city dump, he said, snorting his obnoxious, infectious cackle.

* * *

I've an idea for a fun project, Mrs. Pam said. I want you each to tell your own story, something unique about you or your family or your siblings or where you grew up, whatever you want. That way, during the week before winter vacation, we can all learn something about each other.

When it came time for the presentations, many students stood before the class telling all-too-brief anecdotes before sheepishly sitting back down. Others looked pale and dumbfounded with nothing to say. A few broke down in tears from stage fright, and two boys—Jia Ming was the first, the other followed in his example— improvised an absurd story on the spot much to our delight. At the end of it all, Mrs. Pam was thoroughly disappointed; she shook her head and sighed. I wanted you all to do what Mei Lan did, she said. That was what I wanted.

In a flawless tongue unmarred by stutter or hesitation, a fearless Mei Lan stood before the class dressed in a matching shirt and skirt before a collage of photographs, some yellowed black-and-whites and others fading in color, of her parents before they met, their wedding, herself as an infant, and her younger brother. When I saw the pictures of her brother, I could not remember whether or not I had ever met him in person.

Shorty must have said to her daughter the night before, Do you understand the importance of leaving a good impression? This is a chance to hold your head high before everyone and let them know who you are and how proud you are.

For what seemed like hours, Mei Lan talked about her family and her ambitions, speaking with an incredible fluency and sophistication that was rehearsed and perfected every night before her mother, who must have listened and reminisced about a time and place before any of us were born, a time when her mind floated with endless dreams of the future ever changing like cumulus clouds on a clear day.

♦

Under four bright rooftop windows over chlorinated waves made with slapping arms and kicking feet, surrounded by tiled walls agleam with luminescent tentacles that seemed to ensnare the whole interior in a neon net, they met. On this blistering day, he came with his friends and she came with hers—one in each group knew the other—to the new indoor swimming pool, just built, the largest in the city. They met for the first time: the young gentleman in blue trunks, the ridges of his ribs faintly visible with each breath, and the young lady with her hair in a bun, short with stocky legs, nervously wringing her swimming cap. After the informal introductions, they dispersed amidst the amebic gurgles, splashes, shouts, and echoes. The boys dived in, kicking, wrestling, and threw water into each other's faces until the screech of the lifeguard's whistle calmed them for a brief period. Three of the girls, who were competitive synchronized swimmers, turned upside down in the middle of the pool and made a floral formation with their legs, each envisioned the distant medals, the applause and publicity and attention, their faces on national newspapers that all would recognize, faces of youth and vigor and talent, radiant faces touching billions of empty hearts to be filled with the dreams of others. The young woman with her hair in a bun cheered loudly and clapped gently, while the young man in the blue shorts watched with playful awe and made shrill whistling sounds with his thumb and index finger between his lips. The day thus advanced until their skin was wrinkled and their eyes were tinged red. They got out of the pool and headed for the lockers; the creak of diving boards grew softer as they walked past the bleachers scattered with plastic bags of shampoo and soap and hair brushes and slippers. The young man and young woman parted, having forgotten each other's names....

* * *

They met on another day around a felt table illuminated by two light bulbs under green shades. I'm Wei Jian, he said, What's your name again? She smiled demurely, and looked away. The air, plush with tobacco smoke, sounded with the arrhythmic clatter of resin balls like an amplified cracking of arthritic spines. All around them, players bent over with cues on a bridge of thumb and index finger struck the flawless white spheres with strokes smooth and silent as the pulse of a butterfly's wings. Pockets bulged as the table was cleared, the crisscrossed fibers stretched until the sinking of the eight ball relieved the burden of the nets into the wooden triangle, a resurrection of the pyramidal intimacy to be shattered by the forceful propulsion of the one left alone. They stood beside each other and spun strands of whispered conversation, watched their friends play, and inhaled the curlicues of smoke ascending from cigarettes wedged into the nicks of ashtrays. They left early with years of pool hall stink clinging to the fibers of their clothes and stopped somewhere for sodas. As the fizzing cola stung their tongues, each one was finding a stunning symmetry in the other. Before long, they were sharing opinions on life and love, all the while, unbeknownst to them, building the foundation for something beautiful. They were like abstract reflections of each other, finding more agreements than not in all matters moral and personal. They spent countless evenings walking along Pearl River, the breeze tickling their toes, their soles blackened by the dust that seeped into their sandals....

* * *

The beverage shop where they sipped coffee—he in a pressed shirt and brown corduroys, she with straight hair that gave way to frazzled curls—was filled with the aromas of imported cocoa beans and exotic tea leaves. The steam of the bittersweet elixir rose slowly from their mugs as they looked onto a busy street blurred in the smoke of roaring city buses tailed by hundreds of bicycles and motorcycles, loud with the collective sputter of motors and tinkling of bells. The sun shone on the parched faces of senile couples in straw hats and plastic sunglasses, working men shuffling about in haste, children dazzling in bright clothes, siblings holding hands, red taxis impatiently honking, vans loading and unloading cargo, such bustling movements of life, motions from left to right, right to left, going, going, everything caught in the smoke-storm of progress and the halitosis of industry. Rows of haggard bums in tatters held out grimy palms, pickpockets operated in pairs, and a policeman stood on an island in the middle of the intersection, the epicenter of order, directing both traffic and pedestrians with rotating arms, guiding the motions of vehicles that briskly halted or lunged forward at the shriek of his whistle, damming rivers of passersby that flowed in segregated segments at the wave of his gloved hand. He was thinking about how lucky they were, sitting there in the prime of their lives watching through the vapor of their drinks the intricate watch-work of progress that they were a part of, the rush headlong toward the unknown, and she with her eyes staring at a vague point without fixation on any object, with a slight curl of the corners of her lips, was silently thinking the same thing....

* * *

Her hair fluttered madly, the soft lashings of a hundred thousand serpentine filaments. The trees swished with repetition and the smoke of chugging ferries blossomed and dispersed. Gray clouds galloped across the sky and obscured the yellow orb. The white bridge glimmered in the distance, straddling the brown, murky water, the shores of which were filled with hundreds of cyclists, their flames of youth long extinguished, the impending hush of senility fast approaching, but still they pedaled on, baskets laden with water spinach, bok choy, bitter squash, pork bellies, and chicken thighs. Amidst this moving collage of life, they paced along Pearl River, fingers in delicate entanglement; he told her of all the things he aspired to be, his wish for his children to be learned and proud, and he wanted her to help him make that happen. She listened, inwardly smiling. Their exchange was interrupted by a loud crash. They turned around to witness the outcome of an inauspicious meeting of two bicycles: one with a bundle of sugar canes strapped to the back and jutting out from the sides, the other with a sack of firewood and a loosely draped fishing net. This tangled crossing of paths caused double jerks of surprise that flung each rider off the triangular seat; each turned his neck to witness the other's fall. They watched for a moment as both bicycles crashed to the ground before continuing on with their conversation, the witnessed accident a mere line in the novel of their lives, insignificant, affecting neither plot nor moral, unlike the visions of their future dually projected....

* * *

The groom wore a black suit, a shine in his hair and shoes; the bride in a red dress, her face powdered to a shade of budding carnations. She was his first and he hers. Despite all the gossip over the difficulty of maintaining a marriage, the delicate balance of power and submission, and the discrepancy between theory and practice, everyone said they were a perfect fit, not out of politeness but out of truth. On the night of their wedding, they kissed before the flashing cameras while the inebriated crowd applauded and whistled. The waiters came out bearing plates of whole marinated chickens, jellyfish with pickled daikon radish, steamed bass, roast pork garnished with shrimp chips, vegetables wok-fried in garlic and oil, a soup of crab and yellow chives....The first sip of wine was bittersweet, and slowly the feeling arose, an effervescence of the spirit. She had one more glass, and another, until it was just sweet and no longer bitter. She did not remember how they got home. He carried her up the stairs, both laughing, and collapsed eagerly onto the mattress. She felt the cool reed mat of the new bed and the raised stitching of the dragon-and-phoenix patchwork against her bare back. She shivered in his arms and her skin became taut and studded at the moment she felt warmest....

* * *

They woke up the next morning and brushed their teeth with new toothbrushes and new toothpaste. She combed her hair with a new comb and yanked out stray strands while he straightened out the sheets scrunched and wrinkled from yester-night's spiraling pleasures. They headed down the street, arms around each other, she with a small metal canteen in hand, its shining surface reflecting in curved lines the cobblestone pattern of the street, the bare yellow wall of the building on the left, the cracked brick wall on the right, and some birds overhead in the rectangle of sky. The canteen swayed from its handle and squeaked softly as they joined the line of assorted ages and heights toward the cart from which rose columns of steam infused with the smell of fresh congee and fried dough, the aromas electrifying salivary glands to drown the tongue in

234

anticipation. They approached the lady in an apron constantly drying her forehead with shirtsleeves who scooped ladles of dripping white congee to fill the canteens and packed in a brown paper bag one, two, or three sticks of fried dough. Beside her, another woman was cutting strips of pork and rolling it into flat planes of rice noodle to be steamed and served with peanut sauce. He wrapped his arm around her waist on the way home while the flutter of her blue dress tickled the bare skin of his leg. After breakfast, they went for a ride on his motorcycle through the city, zipping through the discordant honks of taxis, horns that in ten years would be silenced in certain districts, hefty fines for disrupting the upper class tenants of the condominiums to be built. A car crash had stopped traffic, but it did not affect him. Revving a series of leonine roars, he raced between the halted cars, and she giggled with fear and closed her eyes and wrapped her arms around his waist. As he sped up and took sharper turns, the grip of her arms grew tighter, almost desperate, loosening not one bit....

* * *

They were both in bed, looking at the reflections of themselves in each other's eyes. He flashed his warm cozy smile, showing the dimples she found so nice, and put his ear next to her belly to listen. There was a kick, a rumble deep within the visceral labyrinth of amniotic fluid, a knock of acknowledgment from a growing consciousness, a gesture from the unborn. He remembered the itch that burst under sweat-soaked sheets and their gasps sweet as the first breaths on a spring morning. Nine months in the womb, a replica of both into the uniqueness of one: his hands, her eyes, his hair, her skin, his smile, her nose, their hopes, their visions, their dreams. The pangs of contraction. The sound of her first cry. The grasp of her tiny hand. She held the baby in her arms while the crescent pools of tears remained stagnant in her eyes. Then came the sleepless nights filled with cries and the bittersweet hangover of night to day to night without distinction. He came home one night after work and when he saw both his wife and daughter sleeping so serenely, snoring so softly, his lips curled into a smile of profound gratitude before he slipped into his pajamas and fell into a slumber of kings....

* * *

They used to sit, the three of them, on short-legged stools around a plastic tub with a bundle of sugar canes boring holes through the weak translucency of plastic bags at their feet. They chomped on the canes in silence, tearing off chunks with clamped teeth, extracting the syrup to glaze over their tongues with the mechanical grind of jaws, then spat out the fibrous pulp into the tub. It was a summertime treat in the hot sticky hours between sundown and star-rise, in the soggy living room where the yellowed wallpaper bubbled from humidity amidst the mewing of stray cats. Uninvited flies hovered about and landed on the pile of chewed fibers, scampering about on delicately brittle legs before taking flight to avoid swatting hands. On other nights, she stood by the kitchen sink, a continuous trickle from the faucet, with a small bin of strawberries, an expensive and rare import. With knife in hand, she cut off the crowns of leaves and stems, and sliced away all parts bruised, crushed, or molding, transforming their teardrop shapes into deformed rhomboids, trapezoidal cones, and lopsided tetrahedrons. They were collected in a metal sieve, thoroughly rinsed, and savored as an after-dinner treat. Regardless of season, he always brought home a pineapple and left it on the

236

kitchen counter to ripen. When the fruit was suffused with hues of gold, he snapped off its green wig with a twist of muscular arms, and with a cleaver in hand, he skimmed off the armor-like skin until it stood naked on the chopping block, its flesh studded with brown hairy holes which he excised with a smaller blade. The fruit, glistening yellow, carved with diagonal scars, was cut into pieces, and dunked into a bowl of salt water. The acid left their tongues tasteless, bleached their gums, and spawned archipelagos of canker sores on the underside of their lips....

* * *

It was the day after the telephone call affirming the completion of all paperwork with the final stamp of governmental approval obtained. His wife had received the news with uncertainty, but in the span of a few hours, leaving China became a decision of utmost certainty. They found themselves that afternoon in a bookstore, confined between two shelves spanning floor to ceiling, browsing travel guides to America. They were awed by its majestic landscapes and urban skylines. When they read about the brightest manmade spot in the world, they heard the clatter of roulette wheels and the melodies of slot machines as if they had already been there. When they saw a two-page spread of the four-headed mountain, they envisioned for a moment the addition of a fifth face, that of their daughter. And how fortunate that they would be in close proximity to the university known to every Chinese household—a letter of acceptance typed on paper watermarked with the shield of truth was a universal dream of all Chinese parents for their children. They marveled at the photographs of its lecture halls shrouded in ivy, the bronze statue of its founder, the multi-columned façade of the library, and the white-steepled church in the center of the quadrangle. On the night before departure, having sold off their furniture, having visited old friends and spoken tearful goodbyes and received congratulatory farewells, having packed their remaining possessions within zipped zippers and buckled buckles, while both his wife and daughter were asleep on the floor, he sat in the bare room and glided a rag dabbed with polish over his shoes, back and forth, back and forth, until they reflected the token of moon shining through the curtain-less window....

♦

—Hello?...good morning...I'm sorry to hear that...I understand...please get some rest...goodbye.

The babysitter is sick, Ma said, turning to me.

She picked up the phone and dialed.

—Good morning...yes, sorry for calling so early...my sitter is sick...I was hoping to...that's not...I see...I'll be there...goodbye.

Ma hung up the phone and remained quiet for a moment, watching the flakes collide against our window and slowly slide down the glass onto the unmarred white incline that had accumulated on the ledge overnight.

At least they cancelled school for you, she said. You're coming to work with me today.

What about—

She's going, too. You can look after her there.

Why can't I just stay home with her?

Look at the snow outside.

So?

If something bad were to happen, I would never forgive myself.

Nothing bad will—

You're coming with me, and that's final. I just have a

feeling today, a bad feeling. I can't describe it. Go pack some books.

We arrived at the restaurant with thick clumps of snow on our boots that melted upon contact with the carpet. Ma settled us into a corner table. The blinding whiteness of the blizzard made insignificant the artificial light of the hanging glass lamps. The heat was on full; a transparent film of wavy distortion rose from the radiators by the windowsills. I watched a few senile customers waddle in with small steps, crooked at the union of pelvis and spine as if blown by a lifetime's worth of wind from behind, blown forward, urged and goaded onwards toward the unknowable; their feeble but constant will to remain upright left them all submissively stooped. They came in to eat, converse, and take refuge from the storm.

It's you. Hello, come over, have a seat here. This is my son, and this is my daughter. Say hello. This is one of our frequent patrons, he has become a good friend of mine. This man came here many years before us, Ma said.

Your mom has told me a lot about you, about how well-behaved you are, the elderly man said.

I forced my lips to arc a smile. Under Ma's scrutiny, I had to engage the stranger.

The babysitter called in sick. The boss said I absolutely had to come in. Two of the other waitresses are sick as well, so we're short-staffed. I had no choice but to bring them with me.

The stranger turned to me. See how hard of a worker your mom is? he asked.

I nodded.

What grade are you in? he asked after Ma left us alone. Third.

Do you know English? Are you in a bilingual class?

Yes.

Your mom told me how you used to sit on the balcony for hours listening to those lessons on the cassettes and how you learned to write the number one. You must be very disciplined. When did you come here?

When I was five.

And you're how old now?

Eight.

You're lucky to have come so young. The possibilities before you are endless. They call this country the land of opportunities, but that's only true for young people. You get to learn English in school, do you know how important that is? You can't go anywhere if you don't speak the language. You don't want to grow up and work in a place like this, do you?

I shook my head.

Of course not. Do you know what you want to be when you grow up?

No.

Any ideas?

I don't know, maybe I'll study animals—

Good! Science is the way of the future...

I wondered what my classmates were doing. They always bragged about their escapades whenever school got cancelled, claiming they spent the day sledding on trashcan lids, building snowmen, and bombarding civilians below from rooftops above. What fun that must be!

...you'll get money and respect. It's a good choice. If you lose interest, go into engineering. The world will always need scientists and engineers. My son's friend is an engineer, and he owns a big house. Chinese people make good engineers because we're good at math and logical thinking. And business, let's not forget that, especially here in America. Any interest in business? It's probably too early for you to know but consider that as well. No country can do without scientists, engineers, and businessmen. They're the people who move the world forward...and doctors. Everything else is a waste of time, believe me. I wanted to be an engineer when I was younger, but I didn't have the opportunity. That's why it's so important that you're here at a young age. Your future hasn't been written yet. The old generation here, they're practically useless, people like me are better off back in China, it's our home, that's where we belong, there's nothing here for us. It's like your mom says: We're just stuck inside four walls. The best part of my day is to come out here, have dim sum, and meet some people. I can't leave Chinatown, there's nowhere for me to go, and besides, I don't have a car. Even if I did, I wouldn't know where to go. Now your mom has reasons to be here. She's got you and your sister, she has children to provide for. She makes more money in a month here than she would a year in China, but she's in a dead end, too. She's counting on you to get her out. You and your sister, you two are her future. She's got very little else to look forward to. Imagine coming here to push that cart around day after day, can you imagine? What's the point? But she's got to put food on the table, isn't that right? You can't go to school on an empty stomach, am I right? Do you understand what I'm saying?

I nodded, staring at the motion of his lips, the wrinkles on his face, and the mole on his right temple out of which grew a thick, solitary hair. I saw the glimmer of his yellowed teeth, and one of a different color, silver perhaps, blackened silver.

I'm sure your mom has told you how poorly the boss treats everyone, and I can back her up. I've seen this manager yell at the workers for no good reason. Some people get a little bit of power, and it goes right to their heads. They think they can trample over everyone else.

I nodded again. Out of the corner of my eye, I saw a shadow without distinction, a mere haze swelling at the periphery. It was Ma approaching with a large plate of fried noodles. Her face seemed to glow; perhaps it was due to a change in the lighting, a thinning of clouds, or a trick of the eyes—whatever it was, she came toward us looking ages younger.

I'm glad you guys are talking. Here's something to eat. I'm so glad you're taking time to talk to my son.

He's got a good head on his shoulders. I see you've a lot to look forward to. He told me he wants to be a scientist. That warms my heart. That's a fantastic thing for an old man like me to hear. And your daughter, she's so adorable and so well-behaved. You must be very proud of your children.

Thank you for such kind words, Ma said. She placed a glass of cola on the table with thousands of bubbles studding the inside of the glass that floated to the top and gathered on the surface like miniature frog eggs. Then she left to tend to another patron.

What does your dad do? Your mom doesn't talk about him much.

He's a cook.

Your dad must be proud of you, too. It makes me happy to see a young boy like you with your head in the right direction. It takes years to stay on the right track and just minutes to stray from it. You make friends with the wrong people, and before you know it, you've thrown away all that you've worked for. But you won't stray, I know it, I can tell. He paused for some time before continuing, You probably have homework to do...and here I am rambling away. I should get going. When your mom comes by, tell her I said goodbye.

I nodded.

He stood up, patted me on the back, put on his hat, and left.

* * *

The snow came down and left no distinction between sidewalk and street. The streetlamps turned on and suffused the empty roads with a hue of clementine. After dinner, Ma thumbed through a box of cassettes and inserted one into the player. Dual stumps gripped by circumferential teeth reeled the film from one spool to the other, freeing the dead voice that Ma sung along to.

* * *

The colossus roared with turbulent momentum, a battalion ship plowing ahead through the darkness, intruding over white lane lines, spitting up slush from all ten tires to splatter against the windows of vehicles it passed, its cargo rumbled, its rusted frame shook with violent jolts, its radio was turned on to maximum volume...there sounded the sudden smack of metal on metal, a side mirror went airborne, the car swerved, and all within held their breaths as the metal barrier dividing asphalt and dirt, dividing landscape and artifice, seemed to approach and then recede, the silhouettes of leafless trees and scarred rocks became vertiginous, a slam of brakes led to a desperate deceleration and all within were tossed around as if on a malfunctioning carousel, rebounding off seat cushions, the confusion of a pillow fight, the thrill of a mass riot, the tightening of the heart before a steep descent...the car spun and crashed into the barricade...there was a burst of glass, hundreds of thousands of glittering pellets fell on the ground and camouflaged in the snow...he was the only one hurt, he felt the triple crunch of bone between his own weight and the door, he felt the searing sparks of metal on metal sting his face...they moved him away from the wreck, laid him on a jacket, and covered him with another jacket...Don't move me! Don't move me! Don't touch me! he screamed...the paramedics came and cut off all his clothes and strapped him down onto a stretcher which was transported through the rear doors of an ambulance where bright phosphorescent lights revealed in visceral vibrancy the red gelatinous blood on his head, the purple discoloration over his right biceps, and the taut skin of his naked body lashed pale by the cold winds...they took him to the nearest hospital, parting traffic with a wailing siren and a set of rotating lights that dyed the snowflakes red then blue then red then blue....

* * *

Ma was dancing with an invisible partner, arms levitated in midair, twirling delicately on her feet. From her cavernous vocal cords rose a perfect pitch in synchrony with the voice from the cassette player. She swayed across the living room while I sat by the window watching the snow drift down into the streets devoid of cars and people. It felt like we were the only ones in the entire city, the entire world for that matter.

The telephone rang.

—Hello?...yes...who is this?...yes, I'm his wife...he's where?!

7

COME ON IN.

His eyes were bloodshot, his head was patched with gauze, and his arm was in a cast. The air was stagnant; the room smelled sour and fungal. Ma stayed by the door with Uncle Hu and his wife.

Don't be scared.

I'm not, I wanted to say. I walked right up to him without hesitation to show him that fear was not on my mind, that my imagination had led me to worse places, and that I was old enough to deal with the reality of things. I stood by the bed and looked him right in the face, but I could not recognize him. He appeared not as my father but as a stranger, a bodiless apparition, a bloodied and bandaged head atop a pile of sheets. My back was to the window and its view of barren trees against a sky of flat clouds, the fine lines of branches appeared as if drawn from the tip of a calligrapher's pen. He lifted his arm from under the covers and ran his hand through my hair; his fingers felt warm and coarse, like moist sandpaper. There was a bag of fluid hanging over his bed, dripping a drop thirty times a minute; I wondered what it tasted like: salty like ocean brine? Sweet as cotton candy? Or was it plain tap water?

I'm okay.

My nostrils twitched at his rancid breath.

I'm okay, he repeated.

Ma came into the room, her fingers over her lips; the

whites of her eyes appeared opaline. He tried to turn and groaned in pain. Buried under three blankets, the topology of his limbs shifted with each adjustment; only the triangular mass of his right arm remained stationary. She sat at the foot of the bed, placed her hand on his leg, and asked, What happened?

He said nothing but continued to stroke my face, muttering, I'm okay, I'm okay.

How are you feeling? Ma asked.

How do you think I'm feeling? What does it look like? he snapped, jerking violently.

Hu's wife peered in from the doorway, but Hu drew her back. Ma got up and walked over to the rocking chair in the corner. Come over here, she said. Sit down with me. I went over and placed myself on her lap as instructed and watched both of their faces, their eyes vacant and devoid of connection. She stared at the monitor flashing colored spikes, and he stared out the window. I rested my gaze on the light above us, the yellow bulb casting its illumined cone behind frosted glass until circles and triangles and cubes fluctuated in a fluid dance and melded into sheets of sparkles like kaleidoscopes gutted, until the walls turned yellow, the window orange, and the snow pink, until all colors lost their identity and blended into one unrecognizable hue. Then I looked at him and saw that blood had covered his whole face; I blinked and it was gone.

A nurse in pink scrubs came in. Hello, she said. I'm here to check his vitals. She looked at her watch as she held two fingers over his wrist. She removed the blood pressure cuff from the wall, wrapped it around his arm, snaked the diaphragm of her stethoscope underneath, and inflated the cuff with repetitive squeezes. Hu entered the room and asked for an update. She started to explain, pausing frequently for him to translate for my father. Hu's struggle with English was noticeable, but she remained patient and courteous. The car had hit the railing on the highway. Ba's right arm, the humerus, broke into four pieces. The surgeons repaired it with metal screws and stapled up the incision. The operation had gone well.

Ba said, Ask her how long before I can go back to work.

How much time until he recovers?

It's hard to say. He'll need to be rehabilitated and learn exercises to regain his strength.

Ask her if I'll be as strong as before. Ask her if my arm will be weak.

She doesn't know for sure, Hu said. She'll page the doctor to come talk to you.

Useless, absolutely fucking useless! cursed Ba after she left.

It's okay, Ma consoled.

That's easy for you to say! You're not the one with a broken arm. They've got me on painkillers and I can still feel the goddamn pangs.

I'm just trying to—

You're not doing anything but aggravating me. I know what you're thinking. You're hoping I don't get any better so—

That's preposterous! You're my husband, why wouldn't I want you to get better?

Don't start arguing!

Please calm down—

I know where this is going...somehow you'll bring up money. I'm telling you right now I won't be working for a few months so don't expect any—

I wasn't—

There was a knock at the door. The nurse came back with the doctor, the same questions were asked, and the same answers were given, the same uncertainty merely repeated with greater authority. They wished us well and shook hands with everyone before leaving.

Sit on this side, my leg's getting numb, Ma said. I shifted over to the other side of her lap and noticed then that she was crying.

* * *

—He's recovering at the hospital right now, they took him to surgery yesterday...a broken arm, no other injuries...they spent hours picking bits of glass from his scalp and ear...I don't know what happened...I brought the boy with me but I left the girl home, I paid the babysitter extra...he was lying there, his head was wrapped up, he was lying there in so much pain and yet he was ready to fight, it wrenched my heart to have felt such distance...Hu drove us there...who knows? He doesn't actually care, it's all a farce, why should he? He's not personally affected...I'm right, I know I am, you don't know these people...that wouldn't matter to him, he could go hire someone else for a few months, it doesn't matter to him, there are so many people in need of jobs, everyone here is mad for money, I can see it in their eyes, I can hear it in their voices...I just asked him what happened and that was all it took to start an argument...in his twisted head, he thinks I'm worried about the loss of his paycheck...I held my tears back...No, not in front of these people, I told myself...I'll never forget the way he flung the door open for his whole side of the family to watch, he wanted to show them how big of a man he was, how much control he had, that night I told myself I would leave him, and today I was thinking the
248

same thing...I felt so pathetic...I hated him, but in that condition I wanted to forgive him, forgive him for every lie he's ever told, I just wanted to forgive him...his first words made me realize how much of a fool I was...I thought there might be a new start, that we'd become closer...I thought maybe we'd leave the past behind and learn to love each other and grow old together and watch the children grow up, you've no idea the emotions I felt those first five minutes, I was shaking...Maybe a new start, I thought...and then he opened his mouth...imagine your husband in bandages and a cast telling you that you're just aggravating him by being there, accusing you of worrying about his lost wages over his health...there's no hope, there's no...you don't know what it feels like...fate's hard to ignore when it's so apparent...what have I done to deserve this?...Hu and his wife must've been laughing hard inside, standing in the corner watching everything...when we were leaving, I turned around and went back in...a second chance, I wanted to give him a second chance, maybe it was the medication, maybe the anesthesia...I poured him a cup of water, but he looked at me and said, You're sorry for me, I can tell, do you feel sorry for me? I don't need your pity, get out, get the hell out, I don't want your fucking pity...then he slapped the cup right out of my hand...his brother stood by the door and saw the whole thing...

* * *

The next day at school, Mei Lan put her hand on my shoulder and said, I'm sorry to hear about your father, I hope he's doing well. There are many difficulties in life and this is just one of them. You and your family will get through this, I'm sure.

It was in her eyes, the pretension, the prime of falseness, all in her eyes. I could almost see the rehearsal she had with her mother the night before.

If you need to talk to anyone, I'm always here, she assured me.

During lunch, Jia Ming sat beside me and said, I heard your dad broke his arm.

So?

That is so cool! Does he have a cast?

Yes.

He pulled his arm into his sleeve so that his elbow protruded like an amputated stump, and shouted, Look! Can you feed me? I'm a cripple! Feed me!

* * *

—The nurse said he could shower, so I helped scrub him down, I dried him up with a towel and got him into his clothes and you know what he said to me? He said, Do you want a divorce instead? I thought it was a joke at first, but then he said, If you don't want to do this, then go and find a lawyer, I'll sign the papers...he's in the hospital with a broken arm, and he's threatening me again with a divorce...I thought back to that day, how I wiped up the water he'd knocked out of my hand while his brother looked on, how foolish I was, how stupid to think there could be a new start...if you weren't my sister, you'd think I was crazy, these stories I tell you, you've got to think I'm stretching the truth...Let's get a divorce and end the misery for both of us—that's what my husband says to me after I wash the shit from his asshole...I could've strangled him right then and there, I'd go to prison, but at least he'd be dead, there'd be one less bastard in the world...

* * *

Ba left the hospital with his arm in a sling and some prescriptions. When he got home, he rolled up his sleeve and showed me the eight-inch cut sealed with a line of twenty-five staples, a row of metal fangs that resembled a zipper. After the staples were removed, he showed me the residual holes and the blood-scabbed incision. Three afternoons a week, I accompanied him after school to a rehabilitation center where a therapist brought out a box of toys and gadgets—rubber balls, malleable putty, coiled springs—to help him regain his grip strength. The other afternoons he was either asleep or watching television or reading a newspaper in his recliner.

Where did this come from? Ma asked upon first encounter with the new piece of furniture.

It's a gift from Hu.

For what?

To help with my recovery.

Really? Or is it a discounted reimbursement?

It's always about money with you.

Don't twist things around. I'm just looking out for you. It's a work-related injury, isn't it? A four-hundred-dollar recliner sounds a lot cheaper than a couple months of salary. Are you getting any compensation for your time off?

How could they pay me if I'm not working?

There are laws for things like this. I'm just trying to look out for you.

* * *

—Today?...that's great news! I'm so glad to hear it, one less thing for me to worry about...did they tell you what was wrong?...I've been so caught up in...is he back home already?...I see...tell him that we're fine, everyone's in good health, did you tell him about the accident?...good, don't mention it, he'll worry, and what he needs is rest...the important thing is that he's better now...did they ever say what was wrong?...you're right, I should be relieved...call me once he gets home, no matter the time, and tell him to stop smoking...what?...the bastard's making improvements...the doctor didn't say for sure but at least a few months of therapy, that's all I know...I can't think about it anymore, over the last few weeks, I've been stuck in the past, obsessively going over all the decisions that got me here, it doesn't help that he yells for a divorce every day...if I had a choice, I'd go and undo everything, that'd be my choice...you don't have to remind me, I know it's for the children, but how much better is it in the end? There are more opportunities and resources here, but does that really matter? There are a billion Chinese families that would sacrifice everything to be where I am, but at the end of the day, are we really better off?...I know I could be happier, I know what's wrong, and there's nothing I can do about it...I make his breakfast and lunch before I leave for work, I come home and make his dinner, I help him shower every night, I help him dress, and after all that, we still manage to fight...it's a matter of time, one day I'll be gone, and he'll wake up to an empty house, I promise you...

* * *

How many?

Seven, said Wei Jian. Six plus a young one.

This way, please, said the suited man with a walkie-talkie in hand. We're quite busy today now that the snow's stopped.

The busboys were clearing the table, collecting in large plastic tubs the grease-smeared ceramic plates, empty bamboo baskets, and half-filled teacups, balling up the white tablecloth and wrapping in its folds a scattering of chicken bones, strips of rice noodle, splotches of spilled sauces, tea stains, bread-crusted rice paper, used toothpicks, and napkins smudged with the imprints of oily lips. A fresh tablecloth was spread and seven new sets were laid out. A raised seat was brought over for Mei Lan's little brother.

What kind of tea would you like?

Oolong, please.

The moment he sat down, Jia Ming began to drum on his cup with a pair of chopsticks, singing with exaggerated discordance and swaying his head from side to side. A few people turned to stare. Having decided that he was not tolerating any foolishness today, Lone Eye smacked his son across the head with a stiff palm. Ah San immediately chastised her husband for hitting him in public. Even Mei Lan found the situation comical and turned away to chuckle behind four fingers, her thumb resting intimately against her right nostril.

Ma saw them and walked over. Can I get you all anything?

We'll just see what comes by, said Shorty.

I haven't seen your son in a while. It's been more than a year. He's not a baby anymore, he's grown so much, he looks just like his dad.

Wei Jian smiled. He's quite the troublemaker already...if he turns out to be half as well-behaved as your son, we'll be proud.

You always know what to say. Let me know if you want anything in particular, and I can get it fresh from the kitchen. She left to circle the tables, yelling out the contents of her cart.

Jia Ming, seeing that Mei Lan was amused by the slap and not wanting to disappoint, embarked on a series of outlandish acts: sticking chopsticks up his nose, dipping his finger into the tea then picking his ear, drinking his tea then spitting it back into the cup, trying to chew as much food

253

as possible, ducking under the table to untie his father's shoelaces....

When Ma looped back, Ah San waved her over. How fresh are the pork buns?

They just came out of the oven.

We'll take two orders.

Ma lifted two baskets from the steaming pit with insulated tongs and placed them in the middle of the table.

Is it true that your husband was in a car accident? Ah San asked suddenly.

Ma felt as if time had just hiccupped. Yes, luckily it was nothing too severe.

Not severe? That wasn't what I heard.

What do you mean?

I heard he broke his arm in multiple places, said Ah San, reaching for one of the buns.

Ma swallowed the illusory lumps in her throat. What are you getting at?

Nothing in particular...people talk when big things happen, and I'd heard that—

I don't know who you're hearing things from, but you know how people are. They talk, but they have no idea what they're talking about. He's at home recovering and he's doing fine.

I was very worried when I heard the news. I thought: How terrible, how absolutely terrible if her husband got seriously hurt...how could one woman with two kids in a foreign country possibly make it without the man of the house? I'm so glad to hear he's doing well. That takes a great burden off my heart. Did the doctor say if there would be any permanent damage?

Ah San, what the hell are you trying to say?

I'm just happy for you that everything will be okay. I

254

got quite a scare when I found out. I couldn't stop thinking what would've happened if they hadn't swapped days, if my husband had gone to work that day instead—would he have been as lucky? It terrifies me to think about how little control we have over things…to think it could've been my husband in that wreck. It's as if the fates intended otherwise.

* * *

You never told me you traded an off-day with him.

What?

You never said you swapped with Lone Eye. You just said that Hu wanted you to go into work that day. You said you didn't know why, but you did.

What are you talking about?

Why did you lie to me?

Lie about what?

You told me you had to work that day because Hu told you to. Why didn't you just tell me you had switched days off with Lone Eye? Why do you need to be so secretive?

What difference does it make? Why are you making such a big deal out of this?

Because his bitch of a wife gloated in front of me about how lucky she is that it isn't her husband lying at home like a cripple!

I would've been in that accident regardless of whether I told you or not.

That's not the issue.

I don't have time for this nonsense—

Nonsense? I want you to be truthful, and you think that's nonsense? Your brothers would love nothing more than to see this family fall apart!

* * *

—He's learning to use chopsticks again, I was nervous at first, the first few times he tried, he couldn't do it, he got so frustrated I thought I saw tears in his eyes...he's getting better now, he can hold them, but he has trouble manipulating them...he tried cooking last weekend, he wanted to make dinner, so I let him, I told him not to do anything bold and just take it step by step, and of course he didn't listen, he tried lifting the wok from the stove to the sink and just dropped the whole damn thing...

* * *

—They came by the restaurant again...it shows how far apart we've drifted, I don't remember the last time all three families got together...I know that Wei Jian and Shorty moved across town a few months ago, I heard they even bought a used car...they never told me and I never asked...I'm sure they did some kind of housewarming get-together, I'm glad they never invited me because then I would've been forced to show up with gifts...Wei Jian and Shorty are tolerable, they can be haughty and pretentious at times but they're not bad people...Ah San and Lone Eye, on the other hand, I want to be as far away from as possible, I hope I never cross paths with them again...they're still living in the old apartment, the one we all moved into at first...I wouldn't be surprised if Ah San drove Wei Jian and Shorty out with her schemes...Jia Ming's a little monster, his mother must have done something awful in a previous life to get him this time around, Ah San has no idea how to manage him...what?...you met him a few times back in China, even then he was mischievous, but the older he's gotten, the more out of control he's become...his behavior in public is downright shameful, I would never let my kids act that way...it's sad and funny at the same time, his mother lets him get away with everything, you wouldn't believe the things he says, the mouth on that boy, he insults her to her face, and she just laughs it off...he's scared of Lone Eye, but she softens all of his attempts at discipline...some waitresses came up to me the other day and asked if those were relatives, so I said, His relatives, yes, but not mine, I've no ties to those people...they kept saying how different Jia Ming was compared to my son, so I told them I've enough sense to teach my children manners...I didn't see it, but someone said he was trying to pick into another lady's purse, can you imagine?...only in the third grade and already starting to steal...what?...Mei Lan's very well-behaved, they've taught her to be courteous and polite but she'll turn out like the rest of them, all smiles outside to hide a rotten core inside...amongst his whole kin, there's not a speck of good intention to be found...

* * *

—The other workers, even the customers, everyone keeps saying that we should be getting money for his accident, they say that's how insurance works...I have no idea what any of it means but...you're asking me?...he hasn't said a word...I really don't know...we don't have a life insurance plan if that's what they're talking about...I don't know then...someone said something about the employer having to compensate...someone else mentioned something about the penalty the truck driver has to pay...I don't know...all I know is that multiple people have said that we should be getting money from the accident...he hasn't mentioned anything...do you really think he'd volunteer that information? I mean, he can't even tell me he switched days with his brother, you think he'd tell me some insurance company is giving him money? I'm not going to ask anymore...as if we don't fight enough...it wouldn't matter either way, he's not going to tell me...or he'll play dumb, you're exactly right, the last thing I need is for him to think I'm after his money again...

* * *

—He lounges around and sulks like the whole world should feel pity for him...do you know how much he exaggerates his pain? I walk into the room, and immediately he'll start to wince and sigh, he has so much pain just lying there, yet he has the fire to argue with me every night...

* * *

—Ah San's been talking about Lone Eye like he's escaped some terrible fate, like the whole accident was preordained and her husband avoided it, she's spreading it all over town about how her husband averted disaster because of all the good things he's done, do you believe it?...there are customers repeating her words verbatim back to me: Things like that don't happen to people who don't deserve it...she's been going around saying that, it's sickening, I don't ever wish harm and misfortune upon others but for her I think I'll make an exception...

* * *

—I haven't heard anything...I don't know how it works, America's a very legal country, unlike China where it's all about bribes and corruption...they said that the insurance company pays for the medical expenses and the government compensates the employer to pay the worker, something like that, I don't know, it's too complicated...

* * *

—How's the Old Man doing?...that's good to hear...I know it takes time...I was talking to him just yesterday, maybe I'm thinking too much, but I keep feeling like he's not the same, something's missing from his voice, a vitality...I know he's fine but I still worry...have you told him about the car accident?...are you sure?...I think he knows that something's not right...he asked me how the bastard was doing the other day, he never does that, are you sure you didn't say anything?...I've always been truthful and I feel bad hiding this from him...if I were in his place, I'd want to know, but he'll just worry, and it won't help anything, I'll tell him myself later...

* * *

—What sense does it make that someone would pay you for a chance injury?...I know the surgery's paid for and the damage to the car is covered, at least that was what he said, but beyond that I'm in the dark...it doesn't make sense, it's as if someone comes to you and says, Here's some money for your misfortunes...a few days ago, one of the customers asked if I'd heard anything from anyone, phone calls or letters about reparations, and I said I hadn't, and he said, I don't want to pry into your affairs but your husband works for his brother and funds always go through the employer...maybe he got paid already and he's just not telling me, or maybe his brother Hu just pocketed the money...

* * *

—A coworker asked if we were pressing charges, something about suing the other driver for negligence...the other driver was in a truck, that's all I know...they don't have the license plate, and there's no identity, so I can't see how it's even possible...Chinatown is too small, gossip and news spread fast, everyone's got something to say...I'm not going to ask him about it, he'll think I'm after his money again...I used to be stupid enough to tell him exactly how much I was making and where I kept it...maybe he's already been paid and he's keeping the reimbursement to himself, that wouldn't surprise me at all, who the hell knows?...ever since the motorcycle affair back in China, I've not trusted a single word of his...

◆

Hu stepped onto the platform in a coffee brown, shoulder-sharp suit, an ivory shirt, and a dazzling tie, the kind that labeled its wearer a seeker of luxury. He took in one deep breath and said, Back in the motherland, I can always recognize her by her stink. Hu stood beside his wife, whose mascara-thickened lashes arched like tiny fish hooks and whose pores were concealed with powder. Their daughter stood timidly between them in a frilled dress and tailored jacket, her shoes black, black like her hair lightly waving in the warm winds gushing from the shadowy gullet from which their train had emerged, decelerated, and stopped to regurgitate passengers from its connected bowels into the maddening swarm where pickpockets surveyed their prey with sharpened scissors hidden in sleeves ready to snip away loose handbags in search of jewelry, passports, and cash, while others exchanged winks, lifted brows, flashed fingers, or twitched noses, meanings disguised in seemingly meaningless gestures, the silent language of elaborate diversions and setups under a thousand whirring fans, under billboards perpetually buzzing with the white noise of numbered tabs forever in flux. His brothers were waiting for him at the main entrance and, while waiting, witnessed two expert muggings.

How much? asked Lone Eye. How much do you think they make doing that?

Enough to keep at it, Ba replied.

Let's say you get caught, what do you do?

You bribe off the cops. If you get caught again, maybe you go somewhere else.

Maybe they're stealing for the thrill. The money might be secondary.

You don't actually think that, do you?

It's not impossible.

Do you think they have families? Do you think that, after a day of stealing, they go home and have dinner with their wives and children? Wei Jian asked.

It doesn't matter. You have to eat regardless. Steal to live, live to steal, and in the end, what of it?

By that logic, what of anything?

Well, they must make more money than we do, Lone Eye concluded.

The familiar face of the oldest brother appeared out of the crowd, smarmy with self-satisfaction, escorted by his wife and daughter, time-skewed renditions of each other. After some hugs and handshakes, they accompanied Hu to his hotel. After Hu dropped off his belongings, phone calls were made to all the wives and a time was set for dinner. There was a feast that night; no degree of fatigue could halt Hu's desire to boast about the fortune he had made in America. At an appointed restaurant, they sat around a table with a rotating circle of glass crowded with plates of marinated chicken garnished with stalks of cilantro, cuts of roast pork belly on a bed of shrimp chips, scallops with garlic and vermicelli, shark fin soup, steamed sea bass in ginger- and scallion-flecked soy sauce, four pounds of boiled live shrimp, clams wok-fried with peapods and squash, frog legs and garlic in a clay pot....Each dish was carried out by a suited waiter to overfill the table. Most plates were left unfinished; some were barely touched. In an absurd show of wealth, Hu waved down the waiter and placed several more orders. He was a one-man show in the spotlight of capitalism; he talked about his new house in the suburbs with ample green space, a wine cellar, granite top kitchen counters, a surplus of bedrooms, a private driveway, remote-controlled garage doors, and how every morning he woke to the sound of an electric alarm, to the smell of fresh soap and shampoo, to the warming mist of hot water at the twist of a rust-free knob....

I was sitting beside Ma who ate very little, her eyes looking at nothing in particular. The men drank their beer and spoke about American economics and government, about the power and glory of the dollar.

Coming back to this country, I feel like a millionaire, Uncle Hu said. With the living standards here, my bank account's practically grown tenfold...and don't think I came back empty-handed. I have things for you all, I'll unpack them soon...what good is a brother who doesn't come bearing gifts?

The air became thick with the musty odor of inebriation after several rounds of drinks. The self-congratulatory tone of Hu's words became even more overt.

I have gifts for all of you...they cost a hefty sum...I brought things from America that cost twenty, no, thirty times more than the most expensive brands here, and they're not even top of the line...imagine if you had the money to...

Not a word was spoken to the wives during dinner,

and they in turn said nothing. Ah San broke the silence and asked her husband not to drink so much. He laughed and dismissed her with a wave of his flushed hand. This is a day of celebration! he said.

After another round, Wei Jian said, Brother, your daughter's very tired, she's fallen asleep and drooling on the table...why don't we get together another night?

Yes, and it'll be just us boys next time!

* * *

At their next gathering, none of the women were invited.

They love my food and they keep coming back for more. It's loaded with grease and salt but they keep coming back for more...when in doubt, I tell the cooks to throw it in the deep fryer. That's how Americans like their food. You make something that people want and you can sit back and watch the cash flow in, Hu said.

Is it that easy? Ba asked.

Sure. If you make a good product, the market will reward you—that's the sheer beauty of capitalism. Of course I'm simplifying, but that's the gist of it. All you need is a good work ethic and some patience...if you have that, you won't starve. Anyway, I wanted to ask...I've been thinking lately...I'm the oldest of the four of us...as the oldest brother, I have a responsibility to...how shall I put this?...I've found quite a bit of success and...how should I say this?

Just say what's on your mind.

I'm thinking of sponsoring all of you over to America. What do you think?

Do you mean it?!

It'd take some time. There's a lot of bureaucracy there.

These endeavors require money and time...and connections, let's not forget about connections. But, you see, I have all those things.

I can't imagine a better place to live, Lone Eye said.

I can't guarantee it, but I'll see what I can do. I've been thinking about it for some time.

Hu, you're really not joking?

No, I've given it serious thought.

Entranced by this proposition, each saw himself in Hu's place, returning in some distant future to scoff at the homeland, to walk into restaurants, hotels, high-end retailers, and turn frivolous purchases into status-affirming statements.

Your wives will come along and they can find work. Your children will go to school. You can all come work for me...I'm opening a third restaurant and I'll need help.

In his beer-swooned state, Ba laughed and burst into applause. What an opportunity...the four of us there together...this is the best thing I've heard!

I'm glad you like the idea. When I get back to the States, I'll have all the paperwork sent to the appropriate agencies. The kids will be there young enough to learn English. Look at my daughter, she speaks just like an American. No accent. And the economy is just superb right now. Everyone's hiring. The markets are thriving. There's no reason not to go now. Rent is cheap, food is cheap, and the market is booming.

We'll have to talk more about this, said Wei Jian.

Yes, we will. And don't forget, I have things for you all.

The matter was discussed in greater detail over the subsequent week. Hu had already taken definite steps toward the sponsorship. It soon became obvious that this was the main reason for his sudden visit.

* * *

The sky was neon purple and deep sea cobalt and citrus orange all at once as the sun plunged toward the polluted horizon. Hu waved down a taxi and took the front seat. His three brothers squeezed into the back. Each pothole along the roundabout route made the cheap vinyl seat covers squeak.

Where the hell do you think you're going?

This is a faster way to the hotel—

We're from here!

He's trying to scam us.

It's faster this way...with the traffic...and the time.

When they arrived, Lone Eye handed him a quarter of the sum owed and walked away, laughing at the driver's empty threats.

Up in the hotel room, Hu said, My wife's out to dinner with her friends. Perfect timing. Last thing I need is her bickering about being too drunk...women and their damn complaints.

That's right, Lone Eye proclaimed, slapping Hu on the shoulder. My wife only knows how to complain and spend my money.

Hu took a bottle out of his suitcase and poured out four glasses. Try some, it's French cognac, I brought it from the States.

They toasted, drank, and refilled their glasses. Before long, they were all talking at once about the prospect of immigrating to America. Their voices all seemed interchangeable, dizzily echoing a storm of merriment, flashing the luminous fire of dreams that run from their dreamers and chart their own paths.

Hu staggered to the closet and swung the doors open.

Before I forget, I brought these back for you, my brothers!

He took out three rectangular boxes, each containing a stack of shirts with matching ties folded around stiff cardboard and wrapped in a translucent kind of plastic. They looked at the shirts—algae green, cotton candy pink, glacial blue, whipped egg yellow—and the matching ties that dazzled with kaleidoscopic intricacies: interlocking circles, alternating stripes, and checkered diamonds.

You won't find anything like this here. My gift to you is a taste of high society.

I hope you don't mind, said Wei Jian, unwrapping the shirt and collecting the pins in the cup of his palm. I'm going to try this on right now.

Go right ahead. Men of class need to look the part.

How do I look?

Pretty good...it'd be better if you had some nice pants to go with it.

A glance at the clock reminded them of the time. They packed up their shirts and headed downstairs. Thank you for bringing us this taste of the West, said Wei Jian.

While they were waiting for a taxi, Hu put his arm on Ba's shoulder, his voice intimate but loud enough for the others to hear. I want to talk to you about something, I've said this many times, I've found success and wealth, I have the means...that's why I can afford to open a third restaurant...I've earned far more than what I need...the shirts, they're expensive, that's for sure, but they don't really mean much. I want to help. I know that, out of all my brothers, you're struggling the most. Tell me, are you still working at the same restaurant?

Ba nodded.

How do you get there? On bicycle?

Yes.

That's what? An hour each way? More? Maybe that kind of time is better spent with family. Let me make things easier for you. How does a motorcycle sound? What do you think of that?

I can't accept—

Then what can I help you with? Listen, we're family, we look out for each other. How about a motorcycle? If you want one, just say so.

It would reduce the commute time for sure but—

It's settled then. Hu patted Ba on the arm. Just think of it as a gift for now.

Ba watched as Hu headed back into the hotel, his figure a shrinking silhouette in the rectangle of shining doors. Lone Eye and Wei Jian got into the taxi and called for him, but he waved them to go on ahead. He decided to walk home that night and embarked on the kind of contemplative daydreaming that flourished in the repetition of steps. His mind, lifted by alcohol, found itself in a new state of wakefulness as he strode along Pearl River afloat with watermelon rinds, plastic bottles, aluminum cans, and plastic bags; its gurgling waters sparkled, like his black hopeful pupils, with the undulant shimmer of neon rooftop billboards. The dream of the future burned in his mind with the intensity of those neon advertisements. For a moment, the lights across the river assumed the enormity of a metropolitan skyline, and the river before him stretched into an ocean—he stared at those twinkling lights, and in their brilliance, he saw the good life that was his to claim on the other side of the world. He saw himself amassing a fortune, cashing monthly checks at the bank, and he heard, as if it were next to his ear (perhaps it was a trick of the wind), the musical screech of the machine printing out his deposit slip under the single-eyed camera.

267

He walked under the starless sky breathing in the air faintly smelling of smoke and grinned at the beauty of his vision, at the prospect of settling into a big suburban house or a lakeside mansion complete with butler, maid, and a few fancy cars in the garage. He laughed aloud, he clapped, and he made imaginary toasts to the wind. He stepped over manhole covers embedded in the pavement, he passed clusters of white lights on metal poles that shone like miniature moons, he bought two colas at a drink stand to quench his parched throat, and then he urinated into the river to ease his stretched bladder, the sound of the trickle rendered almost mute by the lapping of tiny waves. He sauntered past the rustling trees that would rustle on through the morning, empty amusement rides that would flash colors and play music, and stone stools and tables that would fill up with old men playing chess or admiring their caged birds. He passed the place where some time ago, he made a kite out of rice paper, wooden sticks, and glue, and I shouted with delight as we ran, trying to get it to fly. I remembered the breeze in my face, my hair blowing wildly, the clatter of our feet on the ground, the spool spinning in my hand, the thread unraveling into the growing distance between the kite and us—it reminded me then of the spool that spun upright on a metal rod atop Ma's sewing machine, and with each press of the pedal, the spool became thinner, its thread stitched along a designated path through the eye of the needle that punctured a sheet of fabric hundreds of times per minute, guided by her steady fingers...her fingers that peeled Grandfather's apples with a knife, the skin descending in one continuous strip...on the night of marriage, she told me once, at midnight, if a woman could peel an apple before her bedroom mirror from start to finish without breaking the peel, the marriage would be a lasting one; so, I asked if she—and the wind grew forceful, and the kite fluttered erratically in the air and began its epileptic descent, zigzagging down like an oversized autumn leaf right into the river. Ba chuckled all the way home, applauding spontaneously, and bade premature farewells to the sleeping silence all around him.

I thought you went to dinner, Ma said when he got back.

I did.

Until now? Do you know what time it is?

Hu took us back to his hotel.

For what?

He gave us some shirts and ties, they're very expensive. He's a made man now. He's more successful than we'll ever be if we stay here. We're going to America someday—soon, maybe.

What? What are you talking about?

He said he'd sponsor us for immigration.

When?

Whenever the paperwork is done. Can you imagine?

And what am I going to do? What about your son?

You're both coming with me.

Are you drunk?

Not drunk, happy. Listen, this is a real blessing. He's going to get us there. We're all going, all three families—that's what he said.

What?!

He'll get approval from the American government. There's so much money there to be made.

What are you saying? You're going to America?

No, *we're* going to America, we're leaving for a fresh start, do you understand? A new start in life—

How much did you have to drink? You have work in a

few hours.

You're not listening to me, but you'll see—
Go to sleep, you have work in a few hours.

* * *

Ba donned his new shirt and tie, the knot lopsided, but it sufficed, along with a fresh pair of black pants and an old pair of shoes. Ma rummaged through the drawers and pulled out some clothes for me. She combed my hair and smoothed the wrinkles from my shirt, plucking off bits of lint with her fingers. The summer air outside was thick and humid as if saturated with oils from the great frying pan of the city. By the time we boarded the ferry that reeked of armpits and feet and sour breath, Ba had sweated through his shirt, soaking the fabric with the stuff falling in beads from all of our foreheads. I sat beside Ma, and together we watched the foaming crests and troughs as we approached the dock on the other side. The necklace of rubber tires around the boat collided with those lining the pier, and the olive waters splashed up to darken the moss-covered logs. After rounding some corners and crossing some streets, we arrived at the restaurant and took the elevator to the fifth floor (in actuality the fourth—four in Chinese is homophonic with death, so fourth floors do not exist) and approached the designated table to occupy the three remaining seats. There were chicken bones on their plates, paper squares peeled from the base of barbecue pork buns, empty bamboo baskets on the rotating glass, fresh tea stains on the tablecloth, and circles stamped on the gridded card.

Ferry was late, Ba said.

We've already started eating, said Lone Eye.

The women remained quiet as usual; there seemed no place for them in the flurry of brotherly chat. A beam of sunlight shone through the window directly onto my face, a blinding white nova reflected off a distant pane, its bleaching tentacles birthed from an ocean of fire eight light-minutes away. As conversation waned, Hu turned to Ba and said, I got you the motorcycle, we can pick it up next week.

What motorcycle? Ma asked.

Didn't he tell you? Your husband's getting a motorcycle, Lone Eye said.

It's okay, Ba said. I'll tell my wife what she ought to know.

What motorcycle? Ma asked again.

To delay answering, Ba waved down a waitress for a plate of tripe, poured himself another cup of tea, and raised the small cup to his lips. His tongue was scalded by the hot liquid but he did not spit it out. Yes, it'll help a great deal, he said.

What are you talking about? Ma whispered into his ear.

Ah San overheard and chimed in, Don't you know? Hu's buying your husband a motorcycle.

We'll talk about it later, Ba said.

When did this—

I said we'll talk about it later!

There was a looming silence on the way home, the kind that made everything else louder. We walked ahead past houses with opened doors, dirt-caked windows, grandfathers on stools fanning themselves, grandmothers peeling squash and apples and tearing up vegetable stems and leaves to be washed, and mothers bathing toddlers in tubs of warm water and calling after children whose echoes invoked in the old a mix of nostalgia and envy.

What is this about a motorcycle?

Hu offered to buy me one.

When did this happen?

Last week.

Were you going to tell me?

I'm telling you now.

You should've said something before we left. Everyone there knew except for me.

What does it matter?

It matters because it makes me feel like I've no part in this family.

Hu offered to buy me a motorcycle to shorten my commute to work.

And you accepted?

I didn't really...he just bought it.

How did everyone else know?

He made the offer when we were out together last week.

How much did it cost?

He didn't say.

Do you have to pay him back? It's a very expensive thing to just give away. I don't think you should accept it. It's not a good idea. Is he expecting the money back?

He didn't say.

What do you mean? What did he say last week?

He said to think of it as a gift for now.

Does that mean you have to pay him back later?

I don't know.

You need to ask if he wants the money back or not. You need to get a straight answer from him. This is too big of an expense to take lightly.

* * *

You washed it? How?

What do you mean how? I washed it with the rest

of—

Why would you do that?

You left it out on the couch.

I didn't mean for you to wash it. I left it out to bring to the cleaners!

Don't raise your voice.

Hu brought them back all the way from America...they never wrinkle. You can't just wash them like everything else. I have to get them dry-cleaned. Don't wash these shirts again. They cost more than the furniture in this house.

Your brother gives you a few shirts and you start to worship him—

I don't want you touching these. They're more expensive than—

More expensive than the furniture in this house, I heard you the first time. Let me ask you: Who bought the furniture? I did, with my money and my father's money. Who paid for the wedding? I did. Aside from the bed, what else did you contribute? Nothing. Not one thing! Now your brother throws you some rags out of charity, and you're ready to turn your entire home upside down!

It was a gesture. He flew halfway across the world...he's going to give us a different future—

You had no money for the wedding and no money to start our life together. It was *my* family who made all of this possible. Don't ever come in here and act like none of this is worth anything!

It was your father's own choice to help. I never asked him. Maybe he felt sorry that his daughter had the misfortune of marrying a poor man.

He helped because he knew it was important for you to save face, not because you deserved it. Who are you to undermine what my father has done for us?

And who are you to undermine my brother's success?

A few shirts and you're ready to turn this house upside down—who would've known? A proud man like you so easily won over by—

He's my brother, he doesn't need to win me over with anything.

Apparently he does, I've never heard you talk so much about him.

That's because he's back to visit—

And handed you some rags!

* * *

Who else are we waiting for?

My wife, Ba said. She's on her way.

Why bother? asked Lone Eye, his lips curled, a smirk in passing.

I told her to meet us here. She's dropping the boy off at her father's.

Let's hope she gets here soon, Hu said. I have places to be later on.

Does your wife know where we're meeting? Are you sure you told her? Lone Eye asked.

Ba nodded. I told her the exact address and time, so she knows.

Hu, how much longer are you staying for? asked Wei Jian.

Don't know yet, another week or two maybe. We'll stop by some other cities before we leave. I'm my own boss, so I make my own schedule.

A free man.

That's right. The higher you go, the freer you become.

Enough waiting around, let's just get a table, I'm starving. Come up when she gets here, we'll be on the third floor. Let's go. Lone Eye led the way.

Ba waited for a while and, after some impatient moments, crossed the street to buy a newspaper. What's taking her so long? I know I told her this teahouse and this time, he muttered to himself. He paced around to calm a rising anger and then lost himself in a sea of printed characters while leaning against a stone column in the lobby. Had he not been reading behind the pillar, he might have seen her head, one in the crowd outside, eyes searching, scanning, looking through the revolving door and then turning around and retreating, not once but twice. He finished one article, then another, then another.

Still waiting?

Ba looked up. It was Wei Jian.

I told her not to be late. I told her that Hu's got a busy day. Don't wait for me, you guys should start eating.

Start eating? Did you lose all track of time? We're almost done. What do you want to do if she doesn't show?

We'll just go.

I'll let them know.

He went back up and reappeared later with the others.

Still not here yet?

I don't know where she is.

I'm in a rush. We need to go, said Hu.

Let's just go then.

As they exited the building and turned the corner, Ma waved from a distance. Her voice rang high. There you are! I've been waiting for almost an hour and a half. Where were you?

Where were *you*? I told you the exact time and place. I've been in the lobby waiting like an idiot. They finished eating already. Don't you understand that Hu's got important things to do?

I would never let my wife be so....Lone Eye let the sentence trail off; its meaning required no further words.

You said to meet by the side entrance. I was there early just to make sure...I even circled around—

I said the front doors, not the side entrance. You didn't listen. Let's go, you've already wasted enough time.

Ma's face was blank like the facade of glaciers as she came to a realization, a slow lifting of a transparent curtain.

I told you to be here at twelve, and it's already past one. You can't even follow a simple direction.

They walked over to the bus stop together—a unified force of four brothers—and headed for the motorcycle shop with Ma trailing behind them.

* * *

The motorcycle stood slanted on its kickstand under our balcony. Its brilliant ruby shell was covered by a brown tarp.

How could you talk to me like that?

Ba ignored her and opened a can of beer, which he tilted over his mouth, diagonally, then vertically, imbibing the bittersweet brew that transformed impossible ambitions for a few fanciful moments into real possibilities.

How could you talk to me like that in front of your brothers?

I was sitting out on the balcony reciting poems I had memorized from yellowed pages between graying covers, the spine of the volume loose and fraying, the glued fabric torn to reveal a hardened meshwork of thread. The characters conveyed a beauty of rhythm (the beauty of their imagery would come much later), the familiar rhyming gallop that for unknown reasons made me think of clouds metamorphosing in the wind, a kind of thought set free, an answer for its own sake to break the infinite cycle of questions.

I was there early, Ma said. You said to wait by the side entrance. Don't deny it. I circled the block a few times and passed the front doors but I didn't see anybody. I almost wanted to go up but I didn't know which floor. I don't need to explain anything right now. Your brothers all made condescending remarks at me and you joined right in.

Another crack, another hiss of escaping gas, the sharp detachment of aluminum. He was watching his dreams fly high while she rattled off an incessant barrage of words. He saw visions of a utopia within grasp; he saw himself rising up the societal ladder, amassing wealth and power. Her voice to him was a sandstorm blown by aimless winds, a meaningless verbal entropy.

Is that how you act when you're around them? Am I just some fool tagging along? I'm happy you got the motorcycle. I know you wanted it...I don't want to argue over this...I really don't want to argue. Ma was unaware that doubt had taken root, that its ultimate fruit two decades later would be a last goodbye not uttered.

I don't want to argue either, Ba said. Today should be a happy day for both of us.

Ma shook her head and took a deep breath. It's a very nice motorcycle. Did you ask Hu if you need to pay him back?

Ba shook his head.

You need to ask. There's too much money involved.

*   *   *

We were invited to Wei Jian's house for dinner the week of Hu's departure. We stood before their door and knocked three times. There sounded a metallic clatter of pans, a backdrop of indistinct chatter, and the shrill laughter of Jia Ming whose steps culminated in a twist of the doorknob. Shorty appeared behind him in an apron and invited us in. Dinner will be ready in a little while, she said. Everyone else is already here.

Do you need help? asked Ma. You're making food for four families.

No, just have a seat. I'm almost done.

I can't believe you're hosting all of us.

Just sit down and relax.

It smells delicious, let me help, this is too much work for one person.

A room of audible discordance: the firecracker pop of damp vegetables in heated oil, the bang of folding stools unfolded, the theme song of a television drama unwatched, the honk of rush-hour traffic flowing in from the open window, the talk of adults and the play of children, the hum of ceiling fans, the scrape of spatula on wok, the clanging of lids....Ma and Shorty shuffled out of the kitchen with steam-billowing plates in hand.

To your health, Hu!

A clink of glasses.

And to our future wealth! said Ba.

We'll toast to that again once the plan is set. These things can be unpredictable.

With your money and status, surely you can get us there.

I should think so. We'll be one big family. Hu cleared his throat. Let me do this the right way. Let me take this time to formally invite all of you to the United States of America where even the poor can get rich. You'd have to be backwards to turn that down, am I right?

We can drink to that, said Lone Eye.

If anyone's got questions, speak up now. No? Good.

I'm sure you'll all be happier there. China's too corrupted. There's no future here. Look at my daughter—she speaks English with no accent, she's got American friends, she'll get a real education, and she won't be snatched away to the countryside to learn from farmers, that's for sure...not to mention all the stories of people who spend their entire life savings to be crammed onto a boat for months eating only canned food. They risk their lives getting there and they're not even assured a green card. Then there are all those fake marriages that get orchestrated. It's incredible how much people will risk for something they want...and don't forget about the ones who fall victim to scams. I've heard stories of government officials waiting at the dock to turn the ship back. What a nightmare! Imagine giving up your whole fortune to go on a boat and brace natural disasters and starvation and disease. You arrive, but you can't get into the country, and you're forced to come back here where you've nothing left. The few that make it can't always find a place to settle down. They can't find work. I will have jobs for all of you and a place to live. I'm giving you everything legally. I'm giving you all fresh starts in life!

It sounds like a paradise, said Shorty. But there must be poor and even homeless people there...or am I wrong?

People there who are poor have no ambition. Because of government aid, they get away with being lazy. If you have any work ethic at all, you can be sure that you won't starve.

Let me propose a toast: To the wealth awaiting us! Ba said.

To the future! shouted Jia Ming, who picked up his cup of water and extended his arm.

Even the boy understands! said Hu.

To America! Jia Ming yelled.

Once you're all there, I'll have to take you on a tour of my house. I've got more rooms than I know what to do with. I've got the most modern heating and cooling system. I have a private yard and my own garage and driveway. It's pointless for me to describe it. Once you see it, you'll understand why I'm so proud to call it my home. There's no feeling like waking up in a house that you've purchased with your own hard-earned money. There're so many ways to make a good living in America because of the emphasis on education. It's no doubt the best place in the world to live for anyone willing to work hard.

Brother, do you think China will ever catch up? asked Wei Jian.

The West is so far ahead in terms of technology and their bureaucratic systems are in order...China's got none of that.

You think that'll change in the near future?

Not likely, everyone in power here is so corrupted.

The solution then is to get out, said Lone Eye.

That's right! It's been great seeing you all. Hu turned to Ba and said, By the way, how's the motorcycle working out for you?

I save two hours each day, I'm not as tired, and it rides very smoothly.

That's what I want to hear. More time to spend with family. Seems like it's already made a difference.

Sometimes I don't even hear it start up...and the mileage is incredible. The other cooks keep asking where I got the money for it. I just shrug and say I've got people looking out for me.

That's what I'm here for!

Are we talking about the motorcycle? asked Ah San. I heard that Hu bought you a motorcycle, is that right? My husband only brought home some shirts and ties the other night...too bad you don't need a motorcycle or Hu could get you one, too.

A silence clung to the air, thick and inert.

Hu cleared his throat and said, If things keep up for me as they do now, a little help here and there is no problem.

Would you mind me asking how much that motorcycle cost? Ah San asked. I heard it was brand new. Motorcycles nowadays are so expensive.

It cost a good sum, said Hu. He can drive down any street, and I guarantee he'd have the best one, top of the line.

When are you coming back to visit again? I can't help but wonder what you'd buy us next time, perhaps some cars.

Next time we see each other, hopefully it'll be on my side of the world. Ah San, you sure know how to joke, I hope I haven't come off looking like a millionaire. I wouldn't want to steal the thunder from my future millionaire self.

Of course not, we'd all expect houses when you're a millionaire, not just some shirts and ties, she said.

Ah San, your attitude would fit right in with the American mentality, Hu said, trying to change the subject. The women there have careers of their own. Brothers, when you get to the States, you'll have to keep an eye on your wives. They might make three times your salary while working only a third of your hours.

Is that right? said Shorty. How progressive!

In the States, everyone's got opportunities. Girls go to school and compete with the boys, and both end up—

What does your daughter think of her father buying

such a big gift? interrupted Ah San. Did you buy her something as well? Every time I come back from shopping, the first thing that Jia Ming asks is what I got for him.

Hu took a prolonged glance at his watch. It was obvious where the conversation was heading. I haven't had such good home-cooked food in a long time, but we need to get going. It's getting late, he said.

Stay for dessert, said Shorty.

I'm meeting an old business partner. I don't want to keep him waiting.

Did you have enough to eat?

Plenty, I'm very full.

The food was excellent, said Hu's wife.

I hope to see you all in the States sooner than later. I'll be in touch once more before I leave China. Thank you again for the wonderful meal.

With an unexpected suddenness, they departed. We saw them out the door and waved goodbye as they got into a taxi that happened to be waiting by roadside.

It's strange how some people are luckier than others, said Ah San back at the table.

Hu's lucky, sure, but he's worked hard to get where he is now. He has two successful restaurants and is about to open a third. That can't just be luck, said Wei Jian.

I wasn't talking about Hu. Luck isn't the right word...maybe some people are just—I don't know—greedy? Greed sounds a bit harsh, that's not what I'm trying to say. I can't think of the word now. I'm sure you know what I mean...some people just want other people's things—

Should I get dessert ready? Shorty asked abruptly, hoping to divert the course of the conversation.

Receiving such a generous gift...I guess some of us

just aren't so—how did my wife put it?—greedy?...no, no...lucky, that's it, lucky, Lone Eye said.

I'm curious...how much of the motorcycle did he pay for? Half of it? All of it? Ah San asked.

All of it, every last *fen*! Ba said loudly.

All of it, said Ah San. He must favor you...but then again, your family *is* struggling the most, so I suppose that's fair...the rest of us aren't quite so poor—

Ma slammed her chopsticks down on the table. What are you trying to say?

Look who's finally spoken up! I should've known...thieves don't like being put in the spotlight.

Let me go and heat up the sweet red bean soup, said Wei Jian who quickly headed for the kitchen, accompanied by his wife.

What are you trying to say? Ma asked again.

I'm sure you know.

I don't.

Let me take care of this, Ba said.

I guess greed really *is* the right word. Some people want things so much that—

Why don't you look me in the face and say what—

Mind your business! Ba shouted at Ma. I said I'll take care of this.

Ma held in the rest of her words. The intensity in her eyes spoke volumes louder. She bit her lip and reached for my hand. The tension of her grasp told me to stand up, but a subsequent tug of her hand—she thought better of it—sat me back down.

Some people are very calculating, Ah San continued. Hu's leaving in a few days, I guess you could always send the money you owe him overseas, but with that kind of distance, isn't it easy to delay it until it's forgotten?

What are you trying to say? Ma asked.

I said I'll take care of this! Ba shouted again.

Seems to be quite a show they're putting on, right? They're just playing opposites.

I don't mean any disrespect, Ah San, but what the hell are you implying? Ba asked.

You know perfectly well, you're not stupid. I have to admit, I could never sink to your level, Ah San said, turning to Ma. Teaching your husband not to pay for something, teaching him to steal...no, that I could never do.

* * *

Did you hear her at the dinner?

Ba said nothing.

I don't understand. They all knew about it. They knew it was Hu who offered to buy the motorcycle, but somehow *we've* become thieves—

What do you want me to do?

I've never been invited to a dinner and insulted like that. Ah San tiptoed around the subject and then called us thieves in front of everyone. What did she say? That I taught you not to pay? That I taught you to steal? People speculate others' incentives by what they want themselves.

She wasn't trying to—

Don't defend her! You were there, you heard exactly what she said. And what did you do? Nothing. You screamed at me to mind my own business! I was going to insult the hell out of her, but you yelled at me, you yelled at *me* instead of her—

I—

They must be laughing now at how much we fight...and they're right. I can't believe you just sat there. I have enough self-respect to not let others speak ill of my family. Give the motorcycle back to him!

284

What?!

It wasn't yours to begin with.

I won't do that.

Can you really keep it after what they said? And your brother Hu is so obnoxious: I'll take you all to America, I'm wealthy, I'm my own boss…it's so transparent the act he puts on, can't you see through it? Or has his money blinded you? It's all just childish narcissism. He wants us to worship him. He makes it seem like he's giving away his money, going on and on about his success. Do you really think he cares about you? It's all an act. He's thinking: Here you go, this is how rich I am, this is what I can afford, here's something for you all to fight over. Either you return the motorcycle, or we pay Hu back, there's no third option.

* * *

Thanks for coming out on such short notice. I know you're leaving in two days. You've helped us out so much. This is the least we could do, Ma said.

Don't be so formal, Hu replied. I'm just happy that we can all get together for dim sum one more time.

How often do you take a long vacation like this? asked Wei Jian.

As often as I want, Hu said with a smirk. I'm my own boss.

Do you travel within the States a lot? Are there nice places to visit? asked Shorty.

There are landmarks in every part of the country. All the famous colleges are in the Northeast, which is where I live. You'd be surprised at how many tourists visit the campuses. And the cities there are full of history. In the Southwest, you can drive through the desert, which is supposed to be very scenic. On the West Coast, there are national parks with thousand-year-old trees and snow-capped mountains for skiing...and let's not forget about the city of sin, the biggest gambling pit in the world...astronomers say it's the brightest spot on the planet when viewed from outer space.

What was that about colleges? Wei Jian asked.

America's oldest and most prestigious colleges are—

Do you mean—

Yes, yes, I know what you're going to ask. That one's actually in my state. I've heard that regional students have a higher acceptance rate, so I think my daughter will have a good shot. Everything they say about that university is true. If you get in, you're set for life. Every major company will want to hire you. You can be assured of a job for the rest of your life regardless of the state of the economy.

Is it really like that?

Of course. Education is one of the foundations of capitalism. It gives you the ability to differentiate yourself from others, to specialize in a skill and give back to society in a way that others can't. When you can offer services that other people demand, it generates income. Education is crucial. Think about it: China's got a billion people, but it's so backwards here that nobody knows anything and everyone's in the same ditch, everyone's a pawn to someone higher.

That's true, said Lone Eye.

When I get you all there, you'll see why America holds so much promise. You've got to experience it. There's no limit to the opportunities there. You can always reach higher, you can always do better...capitalism works because of the inherent human drive to be better than everyone else...it's a positive cycle—the more you push yourself, the more doors open. They call America a free country for a reason...with enough status, you don't need to answer to anyone.

How's the school system structured? Shorty asked.

There's elementary, middle, and high school for the first twelve years starting at age six. Before you graduate high school, you take exams and apply for college and pick the best place that accepts you.

Is it all free?

Of course not, why would it be free? It's the road to being a productive citizen. Why would that be free?

What if you can't afford it?

There's help, there's always help. Money is floating around somewhere. In fact, if you're at the top of your class with the best test scores, the college will pay your tuition and—

Do you have to pay them back? Shorty asked.

It depends. Sometimes you don't.

Will they really pay for it? asked Wei Jian.

If your kid's good enough, sure...and if not, there are other ways. Like I said, money's always floating around somewhere—

Is your daughter in school yet? Ah San interrupted.

She's in an advanced daycare. The instructors teach basic math and English and social skills.

Does that cost anything? asked Shorty.

Of course! It's expensive, but if you're going to spend money on something, education's the best investment, wouldn't you agree?

The conversation came to a gradual end; the silence was filled by extraneous exchanges, the muted mashing of molars, and mumblings over dumplings. Both Wei Jian and Shorty embarked on daydreams of the future and imagined their daughter walking across a stage in a robe and tasseled square hat to receive a diploma and a firm handshake.

The dim sum here is delicious, said Hu.

I'm glad you like it, Ba said. The main reason I...we...invited you out...is because—

Just tell him, Ma said firmly. There's no need to talk around it.

Ba took out a thick envelope from the inside pocket of his vest and placed it on the table before Hu.

What's this?

It's money for the motorcycle.

You didn't have to...where did you—

I'm grateful that you're looking out for me, but I can't accept the motorcycle as a gift. This is for the best...I don't want my brothers to think that...I don't want any resentment over this.

Now I understand why you invited all of us out, said Ah San, rolling her eyes.

It's all there for you, Ma said. I checked with the original receipt.

I won't take it.

Please, it's for the best, Ma said. If you don't accept this money, I will take it as a personal offense.

The ferocity in her eyes left Hu no choice.

* * *

A turn of the key, a revving of handlebars...purple smoke escaped from a telescoping muffler, the air shook with sound, the sound of sputtering ferries, the sound of a smoker's cough...his accelerations made her heart drop...she wrapped her arms around his waist and buried her face in the billows of his jacket, she could hear the thud of his beating heart above the engine's cry, she gazed all around at the dizzying collage of architecture that housed wandering millions...the ditch had been dug overnight at the sharp
288

familiar turn turned unfamiliar with orange and silver cones; he swerved, the front wheel dipped; he tried to turn but could not, so he pressed on the brakes as mud and sand splattered up...they skidded sideways into the soft soil with wild wheels, their bodies were rent apart, and for a moment, both were airborne before making craters in the soft earth...he scrambled to his feet and brushed the dirt from her face—the motorcycle was on its side, its wheels still spinning—but she shoved him away, cursing him for almost killing them both...he looked at her and started to laugh, and she kept cursing at him, and he kept laughing, a big grin on his face...she was breathing hard and trying to slow her pulse; she looked at him, ready to curse again, but she saw for the first time how he was laughing with such life and such freedom that she too began to laugh....

When they got home from their joyride, Ba asked, Where did you get the money to pay—

I would've made you return the motorcycle to the dealer if I'd known you were such a bad driver.

Who knew they'd barred off that road?

Look at this rip in my jeans! I'm just thankful neither of us got hurt.

Where did you get the money?

My savings. I told you I wasn't going to stand by and let your scum brothers look down on us. Don't get me started—I still get mad thinking back to how Ah San accused us in front of everyone...why would you say something like that unless you thought it yourself? She was the one desperate, bringing up houses and cars. She wanted Hu to say, Sure, I'll buy you a house the next time I come back.

I can't believe you paid him back in full.

It's okay. I know how much you wanted it. Now it's

yours. No debts or favors owed. It's all yours.

She went into the kitchen and scooped rice out of the cooker. A plate of vegetables and a large bowl of soup were set out on the table. At the tap of chopsticks on ceramic bowls, the cat came running into the living room. Ma lit twelve sticks of incense and planted three before Guan Yu, three before Guanyin Pusa, three for the kitchen gods, and three for the sky, before sitting down to eat.

How did you—

It came out of my savings...and I sold off the pearl necklace...and I had some help from my sister—

You sold the necklace?! I had no idea you went through so much trouble to—

I want to see what those bastards have to say now.

I—

It was worth it. Now you can ride that motorcycle with complete freedom.

Ba stopped eating and looked straight at Ma. There was a slight twitch in his brow, followed by the ghost of a smile, and then he clamped his lips tight until they were blanched near-white.

It's not about money, Ma continued. I've always said that family comes first...I want to see what those bastards have to say now.

Do you have any money left?

I still have a pair of gold earrings and two bracelets...it'll be hard for a few months but—

I...I have—

We'll be fine, we just have to be more frugal for a while. It was my decision and I stand by it. If we need emergency cash for any reason, I can take the rest of the jewelry to—

You won't have to do that, Ba said with sudden

assertion.

I don't think so either. We'll manage just fine.

If we need money on short notice, I'll take care of it...

I won't let anyone look down on our family and think of us as thieves...

...I have money saved up.

...I won't let anyone insult...what? What did you just say?

I have money saved up.

What money? This is the first time I've heard you mention it.

At Lone Eye's...I...I keep...I've been keeping my money with him.

What do you mean?

I've been keeping my money at his house.

The mashed rice bolus remained in Ma's throat, unable to be swallowed.

I...I'm sorry...I never told you...

It was the only apology she ever heard from him...words so soft like a kiss of bullets on glass.

I'LL MAKE IT FOR YOU, she said.

* * *

The store was tucked in the recess of a secluded alley where dumpsters overflowed with empty cardboard boxes and plastic wrapping. The basement, stocked full, smelled musty; the cramped walking space was cluttered with stools and stepladders; the owner's gray cat was perched high and motionless like a sentry at the clouded window.

Can I help you?

She ignored him and began browsing through the spools of fabric, some leaning upright against the walls, others stacked on rickety shelves of ailing wood. Her hand brushed away the pale, silvery layers of lint and dust that had settled like moss on tree trunks. She unraveled the textiles, draped them over her bare forearm, and scrutinized their shades under the incandescent bulbs.

What are you looking for?

She pulled out various rolls and set them on a nearby shelf for closer inspection.

Young lady, you're going to rearrange my entire store this way. What are you looking for? he asked, his glasses slipping off his nose as he squinted in the dim lamplight. He nudged the bridge of his spectacles back up. Here, feel this, is this what you want?

She shook her head.

What are you making?

A suit.

For what?

A wedding.

Why didn't you say so?

I like this, she said, pointing to the first roll she had picked out.

That's a good choice. If you're going to make a suit, there's no point using cheap material. With a pair of scissors in hand, he let glide its parted blades across the tautly-pulled fabric, emitting a sound like the muffled tearing of paper. Can I show you some grays? Are you looking for gray as well? What about the lining? I've got an assortment of polyester and rayon and...here, let me show you.

She followed him to another corner, feeling as if she might get lost in the narrow, circular track of this little shop with so many textures and patterns and colors.

Take a look at these. I've some more in the back. Let me go get them.

He returned with more textiles under his arm, maneuvering awkwardly around the tight space.

She had already picked out what she wanted. I'll have two yards of this and one and a half of this, she said.

You're not interested in these?

No, she answered, rummaging for a set of black buttons and a small black zipper from a termite-gnawed wooden bin.

Under the white light diffused by the conical lampshade hanging from the ceiling to cast its glow over the counter and make temporarily visible the dust floating about like plankton in the sea, she counted out her money and paid the shopkeeper.

Can I help you find anything else?

I'm all set.

I got a shipment of satins in the other day, are you interested?

I'm all set.

I've also got some fine silks over there.

I have everything I need, thanks for your help.

He moistened the tip of his finger with the tip of his tongue and yanked free a plastic bag into which her purchase—wrapped in translucent rice paper then wrapped in newspaper—was placed and the handles of the bag tied into a tight knot.

Come back any time.

She stepped out of the store and opened her umbrella, the downpour crackling on its domed nylon. A chilly gust dotted her pants with rain as she rushed home with a sense of urgency and palpitations in her heart.

* * *

Keep still. Straighten your back. With a measuring tape in hand, she spanned the length across his shoulders, the circumference of his chest and waist, the height from his heel to waist, the distance from his shoulder to the base of his thumb. You'll look the sharpest, she said, unable to curb her smile.

In the early hours when the streets were empty and peaceful, she traced with blue chalk the outline of the jacket and the pants, she demarcated pockets and partitioned the lining, and she cut out the various pieces and brought them to work with her. At the end of the day when she was sure that nobody was around, she loaded her sewing machine with a new spool of black thread and, under the light of a single bulb, began to sew together the pieces.

When she first saw him in the suit, the shoulders angled, the waist tucked in, the pants flowing yet fitted, her heart raced with a familiar sense of urgency.

Walk around, she said.

He glided across the slick tiles, the stillness of the room shaken only by the voice of the junk man making his rounds on the street in search of metal and wood, a melodically discordant echo ringing through the soft sizzle of a summery rain: Buying scraps! Buying scraps! Buying scraps!

Turn around, walk back here. She adjusted his collar, brushed the dust off the lapel, and straightened out his sleeves. This is a good fit. Once it's all done, you'll look like a movie star. She tugged at the waistline of his pants. Maybe two centimeters less...yes, two centimeters, and then it'll be perfect—not too tight, not too loose—you won't even need a belt. How does it feel?

He nodded.

After some adjustments and finishing touches, he wore it one more time, walking around the living room as she watched in focused silence.

How do you like it?

It's perfect.

She made sure that the seams were sewn tightly, that the symmetry was flawless, the buttons aligned, all stray threads clipped, the pockets leveled, and the belt straps an exact distance apart. She brought the suit to the dry cleaners to have the chalk marks removed and afterwards hung it under a plastic sheath in the closet until the one and only day it would appear.

* * *

Ma wore a traditional red dress inlaid with gold thread stitched into flowers. A string of lustrous little moons, a gift from the Old Man, glistened modestly around her neck. It was the first time she had ever received something so expensive and exquisite. She put on makeup, another first in her life, a dab of pink blush over the cheeks, a hint of dark blue over the eyes, and her lips accented in maroon. The congregation gathered at the Old Man's house. The men, suited, mingled with drinks in hand, and exchanged handshakes, laughs, and congratulatory words. Ba grabbed Ma by the hand, and they posed in the living room as husband and wife, an inert epicenter around which everyone else revolved for a moment in the flashing light, stepping in and out of frame, laughing into the camera. After the photographs, a maddening flurry of hands from all directions stuffed the newlyweds' pockets and open palms full of red envelopes until they overflowed onto the ground and everyone cheered and applauded.

Ma, seeing the Old Man with a rare smile, broke from the crowd. Let's get some pictures of us, she said.

My girl's grown up, she's about to run off with another man.

What do you mean? I'm still going to be here.

We'll see about that, he said, chuckling. Things will be different, you're married now, you're someone's special girl.

Everything will be just the way it was.

I hope you're right...I don't care how it all turns out as long as you're happy.

You're saying strange things...is something on your mind?

It must be the alcohol. I'm very happy for you.

Aunt sauntered over, her face flushed red, her eyes staggering within their sockets. Sister, that pearl necklace looks sensational on you! Old Man, you better give me something just as beautiful on my wedding or else I'm going to be jealous. This is a day of true celebration. I can't believe you're married. It feels unreal. By the way, I wanted to ask you something: Who is *that*? Do I know her? Aunt pointed to the most conspicuous person in the room: a woman in a yellow dress.

A friend of one of his brothers, Ma said.

Who the hell does she think she is coming to a wedding like that? If I didn't know better, I'd have thought she was the bride. If this was my wedding, I'd go right up to her and—

It doesn't bother me. I just think it's funny watching her hold down the ruffles of her dress. It's like the dress is wearing her instead.

They stood together for a moment, the three of them in the corner of their house, its tiles warmed by the friction of strangers' soles. Most in attendance were his family and friends, people she had never met; she wanted to keep the wedding small, but invitations were informal and had spread through word of mouth.

Your husband looks like a celebrity. I can't believe you made his suit from scratch. That's real talent, and I'm not just saying that.

Ma watched as he wove through the crowd, greeting and entertaining all the guests like a suave showman, his hair gelled, a drink in hand; she had never seen him like this before.

What a happy day for us, the Old Man finally said. I couldn't wish a greater joy for you. You'll remember us, though. You won't be the kind of girl who forgets about her old family. I've raised you too well for that.

Father, is something on your mind? You're saying silly things.

Like the swapping of masks between acts of an opera, the contours of his face subtly changed. It must be the drink, he continued. You two will make a beautiful family. Don't mind me, I'm just talking nonsense. It's hard to...it's hard for me to let my daughter go, he said, almost tearful.

But I'm not going anywhere, I'm staying right here in the city, I'm going to be right here and we'll see each other just as much.

Enough of this gloom, Old Man, you should be happy for her. You should be celebrating like everyone else, Aunt said.

I'm very happy...to think I have one more to marry off...I don't know if I can handle another night like this.

Now you're *really* talking nonsense. I'm not even dating right now.

They stood together, the three of them, as cameras flickered all around like tiny bursts of lightning and more drinks were poured to fuel the communal merriment.

Things like this are always bittersweet. You lose something but you get something in return, the Old Man said.

As far as I know, nothing's going to change. I'm staying right here.

Of course you are. I don't know what I'm thinking. Go enjoy yourself, it's your night.

It is, isn't it? Ma's face shone with a profound smile.

Yes, it is.

No more brooding, Aunt interjected. I'm going to go light some incense.

With a depression of her thumb, the ridged wheel of the lighter clicked and a haloed flame rose to sear the scented tips. She held its red roots against her forehead, prayed for health and fortune and children for the new family, and planted the golden bouquet firmly into the ash of the bronze urn. At the moment the incense was wedged into the ash, a shrill pitch rang above the general commotion, a taut piercing scream: There's a gecko!

Aunt's sudden turn caused a few sticks to topple; their burning tips were extinguished and smoldered black upon contact with the wood of the altar. A lizard had intruded upon the party, having scrambled out from under a chair and across the floor. It darted past leathered soles and pointed heels, disappearing under the dresses of various women before reappearing, causing all in attendance to flinch and spill their drinks and jerk their feet like stringed puppets enacting an epileptic dance.

Ma looked on, unaffected, as the creature scampered under the dress of the woman in yellow.

It's on me! It's on me! Get if off! She kept her balance on one leg while the other flapped about like a fish yanked from briny depths. Her arms clawed for the hem. She thought she felt its moist skin on the inside of her thigh and, having lost her balance on one high-heeled leg, she toppled over. Some of the men struggled to keep her upright while others tried to lower her to the ground. Caught in this bipolar pull, she became completely helpless, a mere object of amusement that could do nothing but scream, and each one of her desperate cries provoked a reflex of cacophonous laughter.

Aunt looked on, unable to resist a smirk. How deserved, she thought, for coming to a wedding in such an outrageous dress?

Ba set his drink down and rushed over to help. He thrashed the billowing folds of her dress, his arms lost in its cascading drapes. He grabbed and shook the various folds, his hands submerged in the ebb and flow of fabric. He looked like a little boy playing on the shore, digging for treasure in the sand while the foamy crests of the

299

oncoming tide splashed up and down.

The lizard soon reappeared. With one resounding stomp, Ba tore off its tail and one of its hind legs. The others joined in and stamped their feet. The walls shook, the windows clattered, the furniture shuddered, the door clapped against its frame, the statues of the bodhisattva Guanyin Pusa and the warrior Guan Yu trembled, and a few more sticks of incense fell over. They trampled until its gelatinous viscera was smeared across the floor. The woman in yellow was on the verge of collapse. Ba asked if she was okay. The woman wiped the sweat from her pale forehead, smiled at him with an awkward familiarity, and thanked him for his help. It was he who first laughed, and then she laughed, and then they laughed together, their gaiety indiscernible from that of the merry crowd. Ba merged back into the group, slapping shoulders, shaking hands, drinking liquor.

Those things are impossible to catch. It must be a sign of good luck, someone said.

I propose a drink! someone else exclaimed, raising a toast to the carnage.

Glasses clinked and rose to lips, the meniscus of liquor dropped in some the depth of a sip, in others that of a gulp.

Ma remained in the corner, having watched his dive into that woman's gown. Her mind stumbled in retreat from an emotion she could not identify. She remembered the voice of the persistent shopkeeper, the texture of the polyesters she did not buy, the faded color of the bills she paid with, and all those lonely nights before the machine, pressing and releasing the pedal to join together pieces once disparate. She looked on now as he walked around to mingle, her new husband who seemed like such a different man today, a stranger in a black fitted suit amongst strangers. In a paradoxical moment of sorrow, desperately holding on to something that seemed to be vanishing for reasons unknown, she reminded herself that it was she who made that suit, that with her own two hands she guided its seams toward the pulsating sting of the threaded needle under the light of a single bulb while seasonal rains overflowed sewers to spread a soup of refuse all over the city.

The Old Man had been watching, too. He was going to say something to his daughter, but instead he took a long drag off his cigarette and spread the fiery sting of liquor over his tongue.

♦

It was a crisp and light morning, the air cool as the night that spawned it. Familiar faces congregated at the bus stop. Somewhere in my schoolbag, packed by Ma two nights prior, was the letter printed with the name of my new teacher: Mrs. Wu. The rumors were already spreading.

She's a total bitch.

A fifth-grader told me that if you don't do your homework, she gives you twice as much the next day.

I heard some kid failed a test, and she went to his house and yelled at him in front of his parents.

I heard she expelled a kid for chewing gum.

That can't be true, who did you hear that from?

Another fifth-grader.

Jia Ming was in hysterics, telling us of his latest pranks, and throwing his arm buddy-buddy over the shoulders of old friends. He boasted that he had been working out, doing a hundred push-ups every day, and to show off his strength, he opened some windows on the bus, a feat reserved for the strongest as the accumulation of dust and grime in the frames had rendered most of the panes immobile. He climbed over my lap and said, Watch this. A loud grunt. A sudden snap. The wind rushed against my face and reminded me of the bicycle rides that summer after a tightening of loose bolts, an oiling of the chain, and removal of the training wheels.

Long time no see, he said, proudly cracking his knuckles, and patted me on the back, three resonant taps. How's my little cousin doing?

Are you in Mrs. Wu's class?

He nodded. I've heard all the rumors.

Do you think they're true?

She doesn't scare me. Teachers are all stupid anyway.

A large rift in the asphalt sent a crashing shudder through the vehicle, causing a few to scream in fear and others in excitement. From a recess of my mind, a memory was catapulted forth, a memory of reality or perhaps of dream, a memory of Ma asking: Did you feel it last night? We were at the edge of an earthquake! It was news across front pages all over the world: SEVERE EARTHQUAKE IN CENTRAL CHINA. Towns had crumbled, skyscrapers had tumbled, civilians had been crushed to death, and children had been buried alive. The furthest vibrations had reached us. Our ground must have shaken, our house must have jumped, sofas must have shifted, table legs shivered, refrigerators toppled, unsteady walls collapsed, and televisions must have shattered. Did you feel it? Did you feel it? she kept asking. To the repeats of her question, I saw myself the night before standing on the balcony when suddenly the floor threw me several feet into the air, the distant horizon dividing dark sky from darker earth jerked upward as if viciously yanked....

The chaos of the first day of school had become a familiar thing. The lobby was packed with anxious kindergarteners and first-graders clinging to their parents. It was impossible for us to look upon the younger classes without a sense of superiority; through the confidence in our eyes, we were trying to tell them that we had been through it already. Then I saw Mrs. Lin in a black dress of yellow and white flowers, brown plastic-framed glasses, and parted short hair. She was shorter than I remembered. I wanted to call out and say hello, but shyness prevailed. She gathered her class and led them up the stairs. Two of her students held hands and bounced up the steps as if there were springs in their shoes; it made me think of the little red man sprinting to save the princess in the castle. Over the summer, Ba had bought me a game console, a gray box with some rectangular buttons and some colored wires that attached to the television and had a slot for the insertion of a cassette which at times had to be blown with a warm breath or cleaned with a cotton swab soaked in isopropyl alcohol before it came to life on screen—a wondrous world of crawling mushrooms, fire-spitting plants, shiny question-marked boxes, angry-faced bullets, lava-pooled castles, and flagpoles at the end of each above-ground stage. Once I ran up those steps and leaped way over the flagpole. I expected a miracle—a secret level unlocked, a million lives perhaps—but nothing happened; the music progressed, and the timer kept keeping time.

I heard Mrs. Wu's children ran away from her because she was too strict.

I heard she killed her husband and chopped up his body.

There sounded a click of high heels, a staccato

downward force; its rhythm was not that of a walk but something more precise. She came down the steps, daunting and tall; her black hair, neck-length, bounced uniformly like a wig. She had a square face the shape of a shield, a prominent jaw line, and her nose was a perfect isosceles triangle.

Fourth-graders, follow me!

Her classroom was pristine, the blackboard was the blackest I had ever seen, the books on the shelves were in perfect order, the desks were spotless—nothing was out of place. She made us stand by the entrance and called us in one by one to our assigned seats.

We have two new students joining us, so make them feel welcomed, she said.

We turned to look at the two new boys who avoided eye contact with everyone.

Now let me get started. My name's Mrs. Wu, as I'm sure you already know. I'm the strictest teacher in this school, as I'm sure you also know. All your friends have told you stories about me. Some of it is true, some of it not so much. When I was growing up, parents and teachers believed in spanking. When I was in school, the teachers would walk around with long rulers (she took one out of a drawer) and if we even *looked* away from the blackboard, FTHWOPK (she hit her palm), you'd go home with welts...and if we were caught daydreaming, FTHWOPK FTHWOPK (she hit her palm twice)...not like here, where students can argue with teachers, it's a total disgrace. I believe in discipline and in punishment for disobedience because that's how you learn. So what I'm saying is that I expect your best behavior. You're all here for one reason— your parents can testify to this—and that is the chance to live comfortably. That's why you're all here.

The discordant wail of a siren was heard through the open window; it got louder before it got softer...and with it came the memories, the fodder for escapism...

...if your floor evacuation signal sounds after this message, walk to the nearest stairway and leave the floor, broadcasted over the loudspeaker...I remembered an aerial view of the street and a small group of people gathered at the door. May was asleep—what I would have given to trade places with her, to hide from that oscillatory alarm behind a thick curtain of sleep! I wrung my fists, watching the clock, only half an hour, half an hour before Ma was due back. Two fire engines arrived, followed by a thumping of boots up the stairs. I prayed that Ma would come home soon; perhaps she was excused from work early and was heading back that very moment. I pictured her walking down the street, seeing the fire trucks, running the rest of the way, racing up the stairs, and at any moment she would come through the door. No such luck. I rewound the reel in my mind, trying to map out my projections onto real time. Again I saw her leaving work, traversing the familiar path home, walking, walking, and then she sees spinning dabs of red—her pace quickens—now she sees the fire trucks, and...the doorbell rang. It couldn't be her, I thought. There was no way. Don't open the door unless you know who it is, she had always said. The doorbell rang again. I asked who it was. To my relief, it was the neighbor. I let her in, and she picked up my sister who was still sleeping and brought us both downstairs to join the other residents. As the red and silver lights twirled on in perpetuity, I imagined the firemen raising ladders skyward and unraveling loops of hose for a daring rescue. They did no such thing. The firefighters entered the building for some time, and then they came back out and drove off. Back in the apartment, I

305

sat by the window and kept a lookout for Ma who, at her usual time, rounded the corner, crossed the street, and disappeared into the main door...

...most of your mothers are probably waitresses or maids and most of your fathers are cooks, am I right? Raise your hand if that's true. They work very hard and earn very little. When I was growing up, both my parents worked all day and night. They had four jobs total, two each. I know how difficult it is for them to put you through school. I want you to behave for me as you would for your parents. That way, you won't bring out my bad side. I can tell by the looks on some of your faces that you're thinking, How mean could she get? You don't want to know. I've seen some of you in the hallways and at the bus stops so I know who the mischievous ones are. Other teachers have told me stories as well but I like to give everyone a clean slate. Sometimes troublemakers decide to adopt good behavior, and by that same reasoning, those who've been good decide they want to be cool and popular and start rebelling. Let me get to my main point—I know how important jobs are to your parents...it's so important that they can't make a single mistake, not even a slight one. If you act up, here's what will happen: You each get one warning for a misdemeanor—talking out of turn, being disrespectful, not passing in homework, things like that—if you get a second warning, I call up your parents at work, I keep calling them again and again, I'll be a nuisance, and then I'll call the manager, and every time you misbehave, I'll keep making those calls. Some managers get very annoyed by the disturbance. Believe me, I've done it before. They get so irritated that they might fire your parents. So, when there's no food at home, you'll know exactly why. It sounds outrageous, but trust me, it's happened before. Remember, only one warning, just one...does anyone smell that?...

...cola or ice cream? Ma asked, and I opted for the latter, so the man behind the cart picked his scooper out of a small pail of warm water and stacked two round scoops of vanilla ice cream on a crispy wafer cone wrapped in paper. We got home, and Ma opened the padlock on our door; I sauntered over to the couch but not before stepping over something that elevated me an inch off the ground. What is that? What's that on the floor? she exclaimed, bending down for a closer look at the rubbery sausage crawling along at a miniscule pace. Did you see this? she asked, but I was too busy crunching away on the wafer cone and licking the ice cream running down my hand to answer. She hurried into the kitchen for a pair of metal tongs with which she clamped the enormous worm, its black skin thick and tough as leather, and placed it onto the stove that was subsequently lit. It shriveled into ash, filling the house with a bitter, fetid smell...

...a cringe of nostrils, a jolt of stomachs; we eyed each other suspiciously. I turned around and looked at Jia Ming who pinched his nose shut.

Where is that coming from? Does anyone else smell it? Mrs. Wu walked to the back of the first row, her nose in the air, sniffing like a dog. Do you smell it? she asked one of the new boys who vigorously shook his head.

I smell it, said Jia Ming. It's awful.

Good, I thought I was going crazy here. Now it's gone, how strange...what was I about to do?...now I remember. She headed over to the stack of textbooks and began to distribute them. I expect these books to be covered tomorrow. I have extra paper bags if anyone needs them. I'll pass around...that smell is back.

We looked around trying to identify the culprit. The odor spiked in intensity; the lot of us in the back covered our noses.

Mrs. Wu, I think I'm going to die from the stench, said Jia Ming.

We all wondered whether he would get his first warning, whether Mrs. Wu would unleash the fury she so promised.

You're right, Mrs. Wu said. It's suffocating me.

I feel like I'm being strangled, Jia Ming shouted. For the first time that day, there was class-wide laughter. Perhaps her tough exterior was a mask after all.

She perused the rows, trying to find the source. It's coming in waves. Does anyone know where it's coming from? She stopped again beside one of the new students and stooped down to sniff, a sight of such hilarity that we cupped our hands over our mouths and snorted tiny jets of air through the cracks between our fingers. The boy remained perfectly still, staring straight ahead with a straight face. She leaned over him and asked in a tone of genuine inquiry, Is it you?

Jia Ming could not resist and shouted, I think it's him! It smells like the farm animals he left behind!

Mrs. Wu laughed. It smells worse than farm animals. It smells like their droppings!

The new boy blushed crimson.

It's going away now. This is very strange. Okay, let's get back to business...you've all received your textbooks, right? Let me talk about homework policy. There will be homework every day that's due the next morning unless I say differently. If you don't pass it in on time, you'll be given an extra assignment for each day that it's late. Remember that the work ethic you develop now will affect the rest of your life. Tests are given at the end of the week and they will be graded over the weekend. You have to redo all the wrong questions and pass them in...that smell is back! She walked over to one of the new boys and told him to stand up. Are you sure it's not you?

He shook his head.

Why don't you step out of the room for a moment? She turned back to the class and asked, Is it him? I think it's him. The smell isn't as strong when he's gone. She pointed to the other new student, a boy in a red shirt, and said, You, accompany him to the bathroom and see if he's the problem.

A few girls snickered.

When he's gone, the smell is fainter, said Mrs. Wu. I swear he's lying. He's lying to me on the first day of school...

...tell Ma we just went to the park, okay? We were on our way home from the fountain where lights were embedded in the stone steps and gurgling ribbons of water spewed from the mouths of stone turtles and frogs. With my jeans rolled up, I waded through the pool. Each step made slurping waves that splashed onto someone else's shins. The granite steps were flat and cold under my soles. There were twenty other children in the large rectangular fountain—I had been there one winter after the water had drained; the pennies, nickels, dimes, and quarters that had been thrown in had lain exposed and unclaimed, so Ba and I had picked up all the coins and spent it on two hamburgers and a soda—and we were all walking laps past the turtles and frogs spitting out liquid arcs flecked with the reflections of streetlamps and traffic lights. The sun, having set, stained the sky the color of eggplants. I waded through the water cold and numbing, so cold that I did not feel the thing I stepped on, so cold that the break of skin went unnoticed, the pain slow in onset, and I walked two more laps in the pool before I stepped out. Ba lifted me up because I was limping, his hands under my knees made my legs splay; my bloody foot waved in the air—I was reminded of the hallway that retracted and the doorway that enlarged while Ma was trying to stand herself up after the earthquake in her womb—dripping a trail of blood over grass and asphalt. He brought me to the nearest unoccupied bench. Tell Ma we just went to the park, okay? I nodded. Tell her a sharp rock got stuck in your sandal. We won't hear the end of it if she finds out what really happened. When the bleeding stopped, he carried me home the rest of the way and told me the story of his fondest memory: I took your sister to daycare on her first day. It was raining that morning. I held her in one arm, and we crossed the bridge over the turnpike. The wind was so strong it kept flipping my umbrella, and the cars that rushed past kept spraying up rainwater. We got to the building, and I took your sister inside. You should've seen her! She was so eager to play with the others—no anxiety, no crying, nothing. I was so proud of her. There she goes, I thought. I said goodbye and crouched down to kiss her on the cheek, and you know what she did? She pulled the hood over my head and said, Make sure you don't get wet, and then she kissed me on the cheek. My heart literally melted. It was cold that morning but I didn't shiver one bit on the way home....

The boy in the red shirt returned by himself a few minutes later and said, He...he...he—

Stop stuttering. What happened? Was it him?

He pooped himself.

What an awful way to start the school year! Who's ever

heard of such a thing? Soiling yourself in the fourth grade...where is he now?

He's still in the bathroom.

Was it a lot?

I don't know. He said his pants are clean. It's just on his underwear.

She found an empty plastic bag and handed it to the boy in the red shirt. Bring this back to him, tell him to put his underwear in, and tie up the bag. Make sure he cleans himself thoroughly. I don't want him stinking up the classroom.

The boy came back with the bag in hand and sheepishly placed it by the foot of his desk.

Why didn't you just ask for permission to use the bathroom? Mrs. Wu asked.

He averted his eyes and shook his head.

At lunch, out of our collective laughter was born a new rumor: Mrs. Wu's sphincter-weakening orations, and this one we knew to be true.

♦

—Hello?...what?...again?...when did this happen?...what did the doctor say?...you never said...why didn't you tell me earlier?...you should've told me earlier...I can't do anything about it here, but I'd rather know than not know...he's been hospitalized for a week?!...you should've called me the day...I know I can't...all I can do is worry, but I still need to know, it's better to know than not know...

The call was unexpected, sudden, like a hiccup in time; the telephone felt limp as if it were melting in her fingers. She stared at her blurred reflection in the rain-battered

311

window, the reality of each moment heavy as the silence between each clockwork tick.

*　*　*

—How long was he there last time?...what have they told you?...did you see him today?...what did they say?...I'd give anything right now to be there with him...it puts things into perspective, I take for granted our health...the medical technology here is so advanced, people in this country live through multiple heart attacks and strokes...is he still smoking?

*　*　*

—When is that scheduled?...you need to be more assertive, this is no time for...there's no reason to feel uncomfortable about asking questions...did the doctor tell you the diagnosis?...I already have enough to worry about here...the nurse? The nurse told you that? Where the hell is he getting cigarettes from? They don't sell them in the hospital, so it must be from his friends, they're always bringing him imports, I know he likes that brand with the red and white box...go through his room and if you find any, throw them away...yell at him! Get some sense into his head, it's his health we're talking about, he can be stubborn about other things but not his health...

*　*　*

—I don't have a moment of peace, I can't sleep...when I do fall asleep, I can't stay asleep, I keep waking up in the middle of the night...there's a band of tightness across my head and it never goes away...I worry about everything, even the littlest things, I always worry, it's as if I *need* to worry...I haven't had a full night's sleep since you told me...sometimes I feel a pressure on my chest or a gnawing ache in my stomach...I can't bear the uncertainty, I don't know what to expect, maybe I'll wake up one morning and you'll tell me he's dead...if the doctors can't tell you what's wrong, then what are we supposed to do?

* * *

—Intensive care unit?...what are they treating if they don't know the diagnosis? It makes no sense...I wish he could be here, the medical care in the States is unmatched...I'm doing my best to hold on to my sanity...does he take the medicine they prescribe?...what are the side effects?...has he gotten any better?...I can't stop worrying no matter how much I tell myself not to...

* * *

—Every morning I wake up and there's this empty feeling, the feeling of nothing to look forward to...I feel like I'm evading responsibility, like I'm avoiding something...I'm his daughter, too, but I'm not there for him...instead, I'm here pushing my dim sum cart around so I can help stuff more money into the pocket of some selfish bastard and hope that he throws me a few cents before I go home to have a screaming contest with another bastard...

* * *

—What am I supposed to do? Sit here and wait?...these past few weeks have been hell for me, I don't know what to think anymore, I feel like I've abandoned you, I've abandoned him, and for what?...I've flown halfway across the world for a better life but at what cost?...let's be honest, I've no one here, I've no one close, and that's a sad thing for a married woman to say...I need to come back, I need to come back, I don't care, I'll talk with the boss and figure something out...the boy has to stay, I can't take him out of school, his vacation isn't until

313

the summer, he'll be kept back a grade for an absence like that...the girl I can bring back with me...I don't know, I'll have to figure something out, what would you do if you were me?

* * *

I'm going back.

Ba said nothing.

Did you hear me?

What?

I know you heard me. I said I'm going back. The Old Man is sick. He's in the hospital again, the intensive care unit this time.

How are you getting back?

What do you mean?

Airfare costs money.

I know that. But I can't bear to sit here knowing how poorly he's doing and how he's deteriorating and how the doctors can't figure out what's going on...you've no idea the stress I feel—

Do you know the financial stress you'd cause by going back to China? Do you have any idea how much a plane ticket costs?

I see where this is going. You think I'm asking you for money. Tell me, what have I asked you for? What have I *ever* asked you for? Let me ease your mind right now. Don't give it a moment's thought, you selfish bastard. I'm going to pay for it myself. Don't you worry about it.

Have you thought about this at all?

Do you think I'm overreacting? Do you think I'm going back for fun? For a vacation?

All I'm saying is—

I know what you're saying. You're too predictable. You're thinking, It's your father, not mine, so don't involve me. You're thinking, She's talking about money, she wants me to pay for her trip. You're thinking, She ought to save herself the trouble. That's because you can't think of anyone but yourself!

He was in the hospital before. Why didn't you go back last time?

He wasn't as sick. Why do you keep talking like he's a stranger? Have you forgotten how much he's done for us?

Am I indebted to him for the rest of my life because—

I won't let anyone talk about him like that, especially not you. Don't forget where you came from. We told everyone that you paid for the wedding so you wouldn't look bad in front of your brothers. You told me you had no money but obviously that was a lie. I said, Old Man, he's struggling, he's just out of culinary school, his wages will go up soon, but we need a little help at the moment. He paid for the wedding and he bought all the furniture in the house. The only thing you contributed, the only thing you could afford, was the bed!

What's past is past. It doesn't matter now. Don't bring up—

Why not? Don't want to be reminded of your humble roots? My father is sick, and I can't believe you're trying to stop me from seeing him.

Do you ever take time to think? Your decisions are always spontaneous and based completely on emotion. You *feel* you ought to do something so you do it...on a whim. You never think about the consequences—

Why do you care whether I go or not? It's like you said, you shouldn't be affected one bit, he's not *your* father.

I don't think you understand how big of an expense your trip would be.

I don't spend money impulsively. When was the last time I went shopping for myself? I'm not like Ah San. I don't buy clothes to wear just once, I don't sit at home all day with no job, and I don't cover my face with expensive makeup. Let me tell you something: I buy all the groceries, I cook all the meals for the kids, I buy their clothes, I have a budget to work with...I know what it means to live frugally!

I—

You have no reverence for anything besides money!

It's because of me that you're even here. If not for me, you'd still be in China begging.

You're a bastard.

If not for me, you'd be on the street waving around a bowl. Go the hell back to China. See if I care. Leave if you're so unhappy. Buy that ticket—in fact, buy three, and make them all one-way. Go find a lawyer, and I'll sign the papers. We'd both be better off.

If only that were true. Ma turned to me and continued, How many times has your father asked for a divorce? Do you remember the first time? Probably not, you were too young. Back in China, after we paid Hu back for the motorcycle, do you know what your father did? He admitted that he had money all along, that he had been keeping his money with Lone Eye for years! He trusted him more than he trusted me...so why did he confess? She turned back to Ba. Tell me, why *did* you confess? Were you conflicted? Couldn't ignore your conscience? Did you feel shame? Who am I kidding? You can't feel shame! You said with a shy tongue that you had money stowed away even before you married me...and all that time, I was struggling to make ends meet. I turned to the Old Man again and again for help. I even sold off my pearl necklace to buy you that motorcycle. It was a gift from my father on our wedding day! I sold it because I thought, You're my husband, you're family now, you're the most important man in my life. How stupid of me! After that confession, the arguments started. We fought every night. Do you remember the first time you shouted for a divorce? You cursed at me with all your breath, you wanted all the neighbors to hear it, and you said you'd go with me the next day to a lawyer and draw up the papers, do you remember? I woke up the next morning and cleaned the entire house, top to bottom, I dusted every corner, I swept and mopped the whole floor, I took out the trash and organized the cabinets and drawers, I packed two suitcases, one for me, one for the boy, and we sat by the door waiting. He wasn't even two years old then, but I told him the truth. I said to him, Your father doesn't want us around so we're going to live at Grandfather's for a while. He got very excited. I was so stupid then, I was an idiot, what the hell was I thinking? I should've packed the suitcases for you, not me. Why did I have to leave my own house? And why the fuck did I clean it? I wasn't thinking at all. I should've sent you crawling to Lone Eye's. You trusted him so much so why not go live with him? I sat there waiting all morning and afternoon, and finally you came back with a stomach full of dim sum as if nothing had happened. I thought we were going to find a lawyer, I said, and you looked at me and laughed, do you remember that? You looked at me and laughed like it was all a joke—

I don't know how you digressed. All I'm saying is I'm not paying for your plane ticket.

I'm not expecting you to.

And his medical bills?

Is *that* what you're worried about? You think I want

317

you to pay his hospital fees?

You're not looking for conversation. You just want me to say, Yes, that's good, that's right, go do that—

The Old Man's in the hospital. All I want is a little support!

What's the point of asking me to agree when I don't? You've already made up your mind, so go ahead and do whatever you want.

She turned to me and said, Learn from your father, this is what selfishness does to a family—

Don't ever think like your mother...or, in her case, *not* think. Don't base your actions on emotion, because you'll end up making bad decisions, Ba said to me.

Ma's voice escalated: I can tell you all about bad decisions! Do you know what the *worst* decision of my life has been? Marrying someone I can't love!

9

A THOUSAND THANKS for taking him in on such short notice, Ma said. I can't leave him home. And as you know, my husband gets back too late from work. My father is sick and I have to go back to see him.

I'm sorry to hear that, Shorty replied. I'm sure your father will be fine...and don't worry about your son, we'll take good care of him.

I said goodbye to Ma and accompanied Shorty downstairs with a small suitcase of my belongings to where Wei Jian was idling the car. The prospect of being away from Ma, of being free from her strict discipline for the next eighteen days left me giddy. I remembered that Mei Lan had unabashedly boasted about her new house, yet despite her verbose descriptions, I had never formed a clear mental picture of it. Would it be like Uncle Hu's house with ample rooms and multiple floors and adventures around every corner, the perfect setting for the world's greatest hide-and-seek game? As we drove out of Chinatown, I imagined all the escapades we would have in the coming weeks and could not refrain from smiling. I was reminded of the inevitable discord between anticipation and reality when I noticed that we were driving through seemingly endless blocks of public housing poured in dismal concrete where the only distinguishing feature between one building and any other was the number above the main doors.

Wei Jian and Shorty, having moved out of Chinatown about a year ago, now resided in a neighborhood on the western part of town. They lived in a complex that encircled a parking lot demarcated with faded white lines where seagulls circled at dawn and swooped into the communal dumpsters to rip apart plastic bags in search of food amidst broken chairs and busted televisions and cracked cabinets and extinguished desk lamps, things once sought now discarded to be lifted in a crescent moon arc and crushed in the rear-end jaws of the machine at dawn and transported to the landfill, the stench of which was so putrid we could smell it on hot days even with the windows closed when the yellow bus sped across the iron bridge to school; our fingers would pinch our noses, our guts would jerk, and our sphincters would collapse shut to hold down the morning's breakfast from rushing up and staining clothes washed by mothers who wanted their children to look clean for all judging eyes. The door to their unit on the fifth story was russet in tone, and the knocker, a hinged wishbone on a small shield, was nailed several inches below the round lens to be peered through from the other side.

Aside from the floor plan, the only significant difference between Mei Lan's new home and the unit that we had all shared upon arrival, was just the location. Otherwise, it was like any other generic urban apartment with its plastered walls and beige linoleum tiles, an emergency sprinkler embedded in the ceiling, and an intercommunication system connected to the main lobby. In Mei Lan's room, which she shared with her brother, there was a bunk bed, two small desks each with three drawers, a tall floor lamp, a two-tiered bookshelf, purple curtains, and a clicking radiator that emitted columns of warm air faintly smelling of paint and metal. There was also a calendar tacked on the wall, the kind mass-printed by Asian supermarkets and given away around Chinese New Year, featuring pages of colorful dragons, proverbs for luck and health and happiness, peach trees, gold coins, and laughing Buddhas. The mattress on the ground where I would sleep was already fitted with clean sheets. A faint smell of tobacco filled the house even though no one in her family smoked. The window in her room overlooked the dreary parking lot.

I was also meeting Mei Lan's brother possibly for the first time. I did not remember if I had ever seen him before, and if I had, I clearly did not recognize any of his features. He appeared as a perfect stranger, like an abstract idea of a younger sibling, as if he had been picked out of an orphanage to fill the role. Perhaps I felt that way because there was no resemblance between him and his family members—his swollen eyelids concealed all but a sliver of his chocolate brown irises and black pupils that were perpetually shifting about, his nose resembled the convex underside of a spoon, and his lips were thin and wiry as if drawn on with a colored pencil—in short, this stranger, her brother, whose name I had forgotten despite being told by Mei Lan several times, was an ugly creature. I did not speak to him directly, and he did not speak to me. Whether he possessed a quiet nature or whether I chose to ignore him, I did not know. At times, it felt like he was not there at all, only making cameo appearances at dinner and other gatherings.

The first few days of my stay felt awkward and uneasy. I was exceedingly cautious of how I conducted myself. All I could think about was what Ma drilled into me before she left: Remember to be polite...show them good manners...don't leave a mess...say good morning and good night...eat the food even if you don't like it...always clean up after yourself...keep your clothes folded...don't ask for anything if they take you shopping...help Mei Lan with her chores...don't shout or scream in the house...make yourself

321

presentable each morning...don't be late for school...pay attention in class...if they ask questions about our family, don't be shy, but don't say things you shouldn't say...leave a good impression...be polite, remember to always be polite. We were allowed to watch television only after our homework was done, we washed our hands before every meal, and we brushed our teeth after each meal and before bed. I made sure that my blanket was folded each morning, my dirty clothes collected in the laundry basket, and my shoes neatly placed on the rack by the door.

* * *

The plane descends and gently kisses the runway. A rumbling jolt wakes the passengers. Ma removes the luggage from the overhead compartment, grabs May's hand with a tight grip (perhaps she has forgotten the pink leash?), and leads her down the queue to step across the gap between plane and elevated walkway two stories above the ground. Once they are inside the terminal, May gets a nosebleed; the blood pools in a tiny puddle in her cupped palm. Ma hands her a tissue as they navigate through the airport—no, she has not forgotten the leash; they are attached by the wrists, but it is not pink; it is, this time, a morning sky blue—toward baggage claim where May is hypnotized by the snaking conveyor belt, its whirring surface of rectangular scales that turn trapezoidal at the corners.

Aunt in a yellow blouse, caramel-colored pants, and once-white sneakers now grayed in the turbulence of miniature dust storms kicked up by aimless feet, shouts, This way, over here!

There's your aunt! Ma says excitedly. Wave hello.

Aunt runs up to them and lifts May into the air. Look at that smile! Did you cry a lot on the plane?

May shakes her head.

This is for you. Aunt hands my sister a red envelope stuffed with money and a pair of earrings.

Amidst hundreds of striding legs clothed in slick black pants, concealed by swishing dresses, wrapped in tight stockings, adorned with torn sandals, polished leather shoes, or old sneakers, standing still in a crisscrossing network of erratically synchronized movement, they smile and embrace. Ma is almost crying. Moisture seeps over her eyes wrung from the bliss of being home after having been away for so long. They flag down a red taxi; the seat inside is wrapped in a white plastic sheath. The driver opens the trunk but does not come out to help with the luggage. No need because Ma has packed lightly. He turns on the meter by tapping a button with the knuckle of his middle finger. A digital number appears on the screen. The driver is aggressive, alternating between gas and brake pedals with sporadic suddenness, constantly switching lanes on the freeway with no signal as they drive through land that Ma does not recognize, land once barren but now populated with giant embryonic buildings in a cocoon of green mesh and bamboo scaffolding. A light drizzle begins to fall, studding the glass with slivers of rain. The driver lights a cigarette, filling the car with the smell of tobacco and burnt paper.

There's a child in the car. Her lungs can't handle the smoke, so please be considerate, Ma says.

The man scowls, rolls down his window, and flicks the cigarette out. The cigarette curves over the car and hits the windshield of the taxi behind, leaving a faint circle of ash that is immediately erased by the wind. The driver behind curses and flashes a profane gesture with his hand.

You must be hungry and tired, but probably more hungry, says Aunt.

Airplane food is terrible. In fact, American food is

downright awful. The meat is either undercooked or overcooked, the bread is rock hard, and the worst is salad—it's just a bunch of raw leaves. I don't understand it.

Then let's get something to eat.

The taxi drops them off, and they walk into a restaurant and sit down at a table under an elaborate wood carving of a peach tree hanging with plump peaches and upside-down bats. Aunt names a roster of dishes which the waiter jots down on a small notepad.

Do we need so much food for three people?

It's cheap, we'll pack up what we can't finish.

The server returns with a tub of prickly-clawed, raisin-eyed crustaceans having just come fresh out of the sea and into a boiling pot of water. They crack the shells and break the legs at the joints and suck out the juices and dip the stringy white flesh into a saucer of soy sauce flecked with ginger, scallion, and garlic. Another tub arrives, then another, and another, each tub of a different species; shells pile up in the middle of the table, eventually spilling onto the floor. The waiters are standing by with brooms and dustpans, but they have been instructed by the manager not to clean anything until the meal is over.

Look, she must be so tired, says Aunt, pointing to May who has fallen asleep on a bed of crab shells and bundled herself up with a corner of the tablecloth, her hair sticky with crab meat.

I don't think she slept at all on the plane.

How's the boy doing?

He's fine. He's getting high marks in school, so I'm happy. I wish I could've brought him back to see the Old Man. It's been four years. Wei Jian and Shorty were willing to look after him. It's not optimal, I really didn't want to turn to them for help but I had no choice.

After a dessert of sweet red bean soup, Aunt reaches

for her wallet but does not find it. I must have left it at home. Do you have any money on you?

Just American money.

Let me think...okay...when it's time to go, we go.

What? I don't understand.

Just follow my lead, Aunt says. She walks over to the cash register, picks up the machine, and hurls it to the top of the mound of crab shells. The waiters panic and run after it, but the shells give out under their weight and the heap collapses, burying them all.

My daughter!

Aunt grabs Ma by the arm. She's outside waiting for us already, let's go...we sure won't be going back there for a while, she says, cackling madly.

On the way home, they pass a truck unloading crates of bananas. At the opportune moment when no one is looking, they stuff a few bunches into their sweaters and down their pants until they assume the shape of morbidly obese women. After a clap of thunder, the light drizzle becomes a downpour and drenches them as they rush home, hands over their heads. The bananas rub against their skin, and the warmth of their bodies dots the peels with black moles. The rain accumulates in the cupped leaves of the banana trees that line the street until the leaves overflow and invert, dumping their burden of rainwater onto the road in loud, roaring cascades.

* * *

Wei Jian came home, his jeans streaked with white paint, his boots caked with mud. I left work early so we can all go out to dinner, he said.

That's a good idea, said Mei Lan. But isn't Jia Ming coming over tonight?

We'll go pick him up.

Jia Ming knew I was staying with Mei Lan, so he

wanted to come over for the weekend. They'll have fun together, Ah San had said on the phone. It'll get some of his energy out. He's always so bored at home.

We'll head out two hours from now...no, let's make it one-and-a-half hours. How does that sound?

Mei Lan beamed a big smile. While her father was in the shower, she and her mother tidied up the house. When it was time, we left the apartment with jackets zipped, hoods and hats over our heads, and fingers concealed in mittens. The snow had partially melted and refrozen overnight, leaving a thick layer of uneven ice over the parking lot. Mei Lan skidded three times on the way to the car; her outstretched arms struggled to find balance. The third time, I extended my arm, and she caught onto me, and we flailed together trying to stay upright. Her brother laughed, and her father smiled, and we looked at each other with relief that neither had fallen. With a turn of the key, the engine started with a VVREEOULVVVVVVVV and the air, gradually heating up, rushed out of the vents smelling of fuel and stale bread. The windows were fogged; the world outside became a collage of blurry illuminations.

Where are we taking them? Shorty asked.

I thought maybe a steakhouse. It'll be a new experience for our guests.

We drove through the crowded streets of Chinatown, rounded the familiar corner bakery, and pulled up to the apartment building where we once lived together for several months in a unit on the third floor. Jia Ming was standing with his mother on the sidewalk in almost the exact spot where we stood that first day playing rock-paper-scissors. Mei Lan wiped away the fog on the window and waved at him. He sneered and stuck out his tongue.

Move over, you bums! The master is here!

A rush of frigid wind accompanied him into the car. His cheeks were red from the sting of winter. His hair was gelled, strands thickened, hardened, and smelling of mango. He threw his whole body against Mei Lan, knocking her into her brother, who slammed his head against my jaw. Ah San tapped the trunk, and Wei Jian opened it for her to deposit a backpack of her son's belongings. Mei Lan shouted goodbye as the car pulled away. Jia Ming flashed his middle finger at his mother who, not having seen the vulgar gesture, kept on waving.

Jia Ming, how are you doing? Shorty asked.

Better than ever.

That's good to hear...guess what we're having for dinner.

I don't want to guess, just tell me.

We're going to eat steak. Have you ever been to a steakhouse before?

No.

Do you like beef?

Maybe.

I'm sure you'll like it. Steak is very tasty.

My mom's right, said Mei Lan. You'll like it.

Her parents talked softly amongst themselves, and we kept to ourselves. After his initial burst of energy, Jia Ming became somewhat subdued, though there remained a restlessness in his eyes which darted about like spastic pendulums and fixated on the yellow starbursts of highway lights reeling past behind the fogged glass. It became so quiet in the car that we could almost hear our own heartbeats.

At the restaurant, we were led to a booth by a woman whose name tag was partly hidden by a lapel or some other loose flap of cloth. She gave us menus and returned later with a pitcher of water and a basket of bread. Jia Ming

327

picked up one of the rolls and tore off a piece with his teeth, growling like a dog, sending a shower of bread crumbs onto his lap. He was chomping wildly, face contorted, snorting and grunting. Mei Lan and I tried to suppress our laughs. Wei Jian shot a quick glance at his wife, who gently reminded Jia Ming that we were in a public place. When the waitress returned, Jia Ming and I ordered the same plate off the junior menu at the recommendation of Mei Lan, as we both had no idea what distinguished one cut of meat from another.

How would you like it cooked? the waitress asked.

Mei Lan quickly assumed the role of precocious child and began explaining the different ways to cook a steak. Her parents did not interfere and allowed her to finish her lengthy explanation while the waitress stood by awkwardly looking at us and looking away. We settled on medium rare. Jia Ming requested a soda and, after the first sip, complained that it was too flat and watered down. After twenty minutes, the waitress returned with our steaks and fries and pointed out the bottles of ketchup and steak sauce on the table. The slab of meat, crisscrossed with charcoal lines, shone in its coat of grease. The fries, a soft pale yellow, were still giving off thin fluffs of steam. Mei Lan gave us another tutorial on the proper way to use a fork and knife—which one belonged in which hand, where to pierce the meat, and where to cut so that the piece would be bite-size. She then demonstrated by cutting up her brother's steak.

Forget all that, said Jia Ming, who stabbed his fork through the meat in the center, lifted it off his plate, and tore a chunk off with bared teeth like he had done with the bread. Red juice smeared on his cheeks, stained his chin, and spurted onto his shirt, prompting another more serious reminder that we were in a public place. Over the course of dinner, he entertained us with impersonations of our classmates and at one point stuck some fries into his ears and nose and imitated a monkey. This prompted one final reminder from Shorty, who exchanged a few glances with her husband, waved the waitress over for the check, and packed the rest of our food to go.

Where will I be sleeping? he asked when we got home.

You'll be in this room which I normally share with my brother. He'll be sleeping with my parents so you can have the bottom bunk.

A bunk bed? I don't remember this when I was here last time.

We got some new furniture since.

He jumped onto the ladder and shook the entire frame with his arms. Can I have the top?

Be careful!

Don't worry, I won't break it. With two big strides, he hopped to the top and reclined on Mei Lan's pillow.

Get down from there!

It's comfortable up here. I can touch the ceiling. Can we trade?

No, Jia Ming, please come down.

He leapt off, landing with a room-shaking thud onto my mattress.

My room isn't a playground!

What's all the noise? Is everything okay? Wei Jian asked.

Yes, we're fine...Jia Ming's just unpacking, Mei Lan replied.

Jia Ming turned to me and asked, Have you been here before?

No.

I came here with my parents once but I didn't get to really enjoy the place, you know what I mean? he said, snickering.

We watched television for the rest of the night, browsing through fifty-two channels of cartoons, dramas, sporting events, documentaries, old movies, and game shows, all interspersed with advertisements for board games, kitchen utensils, motor vehicles, diamond rings, living room sets, detergents, breakfast cereals, dog food, vacation packages, flavored potato chips, chain restaurant promotions, home insurance, designer eyeglasses....

*   *   *

The door is shut and locked. They walk down the single flight of stairs past the nameless mailboxes and out into the courtyard surrounded on three sides by the looming apartment complex. Aunt says it might rain. People are visible on multiple stories holding out long sticks with a Y at the end to retrieve clothes hung out to dry on clotheslines straddling across the buildings tied to pipes, hung out to flap in muggy winds and release their billions of squares of invisible moisture snared between fibers into the vast atmosphere. Some garments are still dripping wet. There is a boom of thunder, the flash of lightning is not seen, and a small drizzle promises to become another relentless downpour. A man and his wife emerge out of the same window on the top story to withdraw their clothes from the oncoming deluge, he in an undershirt, his chin lathered in shaving cream, finishing a long-craved cigarette that he drops from the grip of his lips after the last puff, she with her hair just washed and wrapped in a bundled towel, her face thick with a mask of cleansing mud.

Ma and Aunt exit the main gate, it slams behind them, and they walk by the low-rise tarp-covered storage shacks that surround the apartment building on the outside.

Children throw garbage, banana peels especially, on top of the shacks, and because of the incline, the garbage rolls down into the meter-wide crevice accessible only by stepping through windows on the first floor. The space has become a breeding ground for geckos. Grandfather does not mind because they eat all the mosquitoes in the summer. They pass the cola cart where the seller is standing under the red parasol as a second roll of thunder is heard. Everyone scrambles for the nearest awning, people cover their heads with newspapers and plastic bags, mothers are screaming at their children to stay together, fathers rush to flag down taxis, and cyclists pedal quickly on home. Ma and Aunt are waiting at the bus station. The ink is running off the money in their hands. The bus pulls up, and they get on; it is crammed with a hundred sweating bodies. Someone stuck in the middle shouts for the driver to keep the door open, but it is too late—the bus is already on the move with its large windshield wipers swaying awkwardly back and forth. They get off near the hospital which is across town. The rain has stopped. The roads leading to the main entrance are confusing, seemingly circular.

You think they'd put up signs somewhere, Aunt says.

No matter which turn they take, the shining block of white concrete remains in the distance straight ahead, partly obscured by trees.

Haven't you been here before?

I get lost every time.

Ma sighs, holding back frustrations, and waves down a passing car. Excuse me, what's the quickest way to the main entrance?

Just go straight, the stranger replies.

They pass a small courtyard with patients sitting catatonic on benches, patients dragging intravenous poles

331

on paved paths, and patients in wheelchairs pushed by nurses in uniform. Various groups of children are playing tag without supervision, hiding behind and running around the mentally unstable. There are rows of ambulances, some with whirling red and blue lights, some silent, some idling, and others with their rear doors open and stretchers being transported in and out. An old man is receiving chest compressions, but he already looks dead, his face is green like phlegm that has been trapped in the lungs for too long. Taxis drop off visitors carrying bouquets of flowers and canteens of homemade soup. The front door of the hospital is automatic; one step and they are inside. The air smells of bleach, nurses' shoes squeak on the spotless white tiles, food carts are being wheeled by maids in aprons, janitors on their knees are scrubbing the walls, and sounds from distant wards are heard: repetitive coughs, asthmatic wheezes, projectile vomiting, profuse diarrhea, the screech of surgical knives being sharpened....

* * *

Wake up! shouted Jia Ming.

I struggled to open my eyes and found myself stuck for a few seconds in an impossible place between dreaming and waking. The next thing I felt was a warm, pungent breath in my face.

How does it smell? I didn't brush my teeth before bed.

Mei Lan groaned and peered down from her bunk. You guys are awake already? What time is it?

Time for an adventure.

What?

Just come down.

What time is it?

Just get down here.

She descended from the top bunk, her feet tapping

lightly on the rungs, sending minute vibrations over the frame of the bed. Now what?

I have a prank we can pull on your parents.

No, go back to sleep.

Don't worry, it'll be funny. You'll laugh when you see the look on their faces.

I won't let you. She lunged forth and held out one arm to bar his way. I don't care what you do at home, but you can't do it here.

Relax, it'll be funny.

What are you going to do?

You'll see, he said, reaching for the door. I did this to my parents once, and it was hilarious. Do you know what adults do at night?

What?

They fuck.

Mei Lan threw her hands over her mouth and gasped. You can't say that word!

They take off all their clothes and have sex. Sometimes they get so tired afterwards they just fall asleep. My friend told me this once, so I went—

I'm not listening to you.

Too bad because I'm going to keep talking. He continued in a lowered voice, What you do is you go in and yank the covers off...I did that once, and my dad was naked. He jumped up and smacked me, but I saw his privates, and his face turned red. Come on, let's go.

Mei Lan resorted first to reason. My brother is sleeping in their room tonight...so they wouldn't do such a thing. The hesitation in her voice gave away her lack of confidence.

How would you know? asked Jia Ming.

Mei Lan, panicking, blocked the door. I won't let you out, she declared.

I looked on, unsure if I wanted to help Mei Lan restrain him or just let Jia Ming have his fun. I looked on and did nothing.

Move aside, he said, wrestling his way through her.

Stop! she screamed, but he pushed her out of the way and headed for the master bedroom. Mei Lan grabbed onto his arm and shrieked, No, stop it!

At the sound of footsteps, they both stood still.

You stupid girl, you just messed it up, whispered Jia Ming.

The door cracked open, and Mei Lan's father came out. What's all that noise in the middle of the night?

Jia Ming...he wanted...he wanted...to make breakfast for us, Mei Lan said.

It's two in the morning...are you guys hungry already?

They shook their heads.

You both better get back to sleep.

Back in our room, Mei Lan sat up in bed, quiet and tense. I looked at Jia Ming until he slowly went out of focus, until he became a silhouette, a silhouette of two different people—he was the familiar class clown who respected no authority, the boy I pinned on the couch and whose forehead I bit into, the one who walked into the city on a sunny afternoon taking big proud bites of his first slice of pizza...but he also appeared as a stranger, a stranger whose path diverged so far from us that, looking back, he was perhaps the truly precocious one. It was the first time I had seen Jia Ming so vicious over his pursuit of laughter and the first time I had seen Mei Lan so weak and powerless and needing to succumb to the use of physical force.

Well, *that* was perfectly ruined. He wasn't having sex anyway. Maybe your dad can't get it up.

* * *

The cab driver takes them on several circuitous routes before stopping at the spitting fountain of dual intertwined dragons outside the hospital. The water is sparkling, but the sun is blanketed by an overcast sky. The automatic doors part as the vehicle drives off, leaving a trace of exhaust that wafts into the lobby and makes the receptionist cough politely with her hands over her mouth. While waiting in line, Ma and Aunt have a conversation: Aunt says that the past is mere memory of the past, that the past has no objective basis and exists only in one's mind for as long as one is alive, that the past has the ability to live and die and reincarnate because memories can be forgotten or remembered or distorted, memories can be influenced, tainted, or embellished by dreams, public opinion, or the narrative of another party involved, and since all events are multifaceted and there is no such thing as a cumulative Memory, no such thing as a universal Memory of the human race, all individual perceptions of the past are incomplete and subject to change, and thus memory is nothing but an amalgam of truths and lies, a hybrid, a chimera of reality and fiction that over time is vainly assumed to be an absolute reality. Ma does not agree at all. There may be no universal Memory, but have you ever had someone lie to you consistently? she asks. You want to murder the bastard!

Nurses are walking about in triangular hats and uniforms of white canvas (if one were to splatter paint on them with a paintbrush, it would not seem inappropriate); their heels click on disinfected tiles while their leather shoes shimmer with reflections of the phosphorescent tubes hanging from the ceiling. Someone pushing a two-shelved cart across the lobby shouts, Excuse me! Watch out! Please stand aside! On the top shelf: boxes of alcohol pads, bottles of iodine with crusted bottle caps, syringes, bags of intravenous fluid, disposable stethoscopes, spools of bandages, surgical knives, a portable ultrasound machine, sterilized needles of a single caliber, empty bio-hazard containers, a tower of bedpans, a pile of fresh linens, a pile of soiled linens, and a pail of screws, nuts, and bolts from dissembled stretchers. On the bottom shelf: sacks of carrots, cauliflower, cabbage, spinach, bok choy, corn, watercress, tomatoes, bitter squash, and scallions, as well as butchered meat from the neighboring slaughterhouse, padded crates of chicken, duck, and quail eggs, jugs of corn oil, and jars of spices and dried herbs.

May observes her own reflection in the spotless tiles while they are waiting for the receptionist to direct them to the Old Man's room. She sees her own sparkling eyes and her cheeks like doughy buns on the rise. Aunt repeats Grandfather's name to the receptionist who turns the pages of a thick volume, running her finger down the list of all the patients in the hospital organized in no particular order. Aunt sneezes and accidentally propels a drop of saliva that lands on Grandfather's name. Bless you, says the receptionist, closing the directory. She hands them a slip of paper with written instructions to his room. As they make their way through the wards, they hear a symphony of raspy breaths, labored coughs, cries, whines, moans, unheard prayers, and wails so puny as to be totally insignificant. Sunlight is streaming in from the windows, the courtyard outside is emerald green, the banana leaves are swaying and rustling in the breeze, and birds are chirping so happily the only conclusion to draw is that they are entirely unaware of death or that it is mating season.

All the patients are out for exercise, says a nurse walking past the empty ward. You can't visit anyone at the moment, you need to leave.

Ma explains that she traveled all the way from America to see her father, that it was a long trip, and that it would be appreciated if they could wait for his return. The nurse refuses, so Aunt hands her a folded wad of money.

In that case, please make yourselves comfortable, the nurse says before leaving.

I can't believe bribes work in a place like this.

Bribes will always work, Aunt says. It all depends on the sum.

The walls must be thin—paper thin, mosquito net thin, spider web thin—because they can hear all the happenings in the adjacent ward: wheezing asthmatics, honking ventilators, musical stridor, and an argument between the nurse who just took their money and a chain-smoking patient. The nurse wants the patient to put out his cigarette, but he blows a purple haze of smoke in her face, insults her, and curses her family. In fact, he adds, I'd be drinking whiskey too if my pancreas didn't flare up every time!

You can't smoke in here sir, the nurse repeats. It's a fire hazard. You'll have to go outside.

Fine, he says. Help me screw on my prosthetic leg. He drags his oxygen tank behind him and puffs away, hacking up bits of charred and bloodied lung, which he spits into the palm of his left hand and wipes onto the lap of his pants.

The cushions on the chairs are worn and torn and smell of disinfectant, but they pay no attention to it because their noses are more bothered by the faint odor of formaldehyde in the air. They are right above the morgue. The floor too must be thin—paper thin, mosquito net thin, spider web thin—for such faint odors to penetrate so strongly. Aunt removes her shoe and sock and touches the ground with her bare toe. It's warm...the heat generated by the body freezers must keep this place above room temperature, she says.

The patients file back in. The silence of the pulmonary ward is replaced by a chaotic orchestra of coughs. Aunt watches as an old woman struggles to expel a globule of phlegm stuck to her bottom lip, and imagines for a moment the contents of every spittoon in China collected and emptied into the abdomens of cement trucks to be churned and dumped into Pearl River.

* * *

What are we having for breakfast?

Mei Lan, still sour over Jia Ming's antics, did not answer him.

Hello? Anybody home? I just asked you what we're going to eat. Hello?

Wei Jian was in the kitchen surrounded by colanders and sieves of meatballs, cilantro, baby bok choy, and white mushrooms, stirring a large pot. I hope you boys like noodles, he said.

I remembered that Ba once took me to a noodle shop on the second floor of an old building where naked bulbs hung from the ceiling and columns of blue smoke rose from ashtrays to coalesce into one hovering shroud swirled about by ceiling fans. As we ate, he told me how he used to hunt birds when he was my age, how he would find a suitable fork of branch, strip off the bark, smooth it down with sandpaper, then cut a square of soft leather from an old shoe and incise two slits for a link of four rubber bands to be tied to each prong. A stone propelled with the elastic bands fully stretched could shatter any avian skull on contact. He would sit beside a tree by Pearl River, having scattered rice to attract a feeding throng; upon release of the rock, there would be a flash of red in the levitating bird-storm of panic—a bludgeoned belly, a bloodied wing, a mangled head—and he would snatch up the bird, unconscious or wobbling flightless, stuff it into a paper bag, bring it home, chop off its head, pluck off its feathers, and toss its eviscerated carcass into a boiling pot of scallions, ginger, garlic, and egg noodles.

After seasoning the broth to an ideal saltiness, Wei Jian ladled it into the noodles which had already been cooked and were resting in bowls. The snaky yellow strands floated in the brown liquid flecked with circles of oil on the surface. Jia Ming stirred the bowl with his chopsticks, creating a miniature whirlpool, the edge of which swirled dangerously close to the rim until several drops spilled over onto the placemat. Mei Lan watched him with a frown on her face until her parents and brother joined us at the table.

I waited for the food to cool and watched the pale clumps of steam billow up from my bowl. I remembered something Ma said some time ago: I wore noodles for a wig once—did I ever tell you that story? Your grandfather was so strict. Kids nowadays have the audacity to talk back to their parents. It wasn't like that when I was growing up. You think I'm strict, but your grandfather was worse. One time I was out with some friends, and I told him that I'd be back for dinner. He made soup noodles, but I came home late, and they had gotten cold. He got annoyed and started asking where I had been and what I had been doing, and I got so irritated that he was prying into my business that I purposely told him I had already eaten and that I didn't want the noodles anymore. Do you know what he did? He picked up the bowl and turned it upside down over my head.

Shorty started to ask about school, and Mei Lan

339

wasted no time telling her about the fundraiser we were having. We're selling chocolate bars again. The class that sells the most will get a pizza party, and the top three students school-wide will get special prizes. Mrs. Wu said the top seller in her class will get a prize as well. A boy in our class sold one to her within the first five minutes.

How?

A group of us approached Mrs. Wu before the dismissal bell rang and asked if she wanted to buy one. She said it wasn't realistic to buy one from each of us, and that it would also be unfair to buy from just one of us. This boy offered to sell a bar for eighty-five cents instead of a dollar and paid the fifteen cents himself. Mrs. Wu shook his hand, patted him on the back, and said, Class, this is how good business is done. His parents are both very successful in finance, so it's no surprise that he came up with such a tactic.

* * *

He lies in bed covered with a white blanket. It seems like he has aged decades in the last few years. The hairs on his head are gray, brittle, and coarse. There is a mask over his face with two holes like a dragon's snout through which plumes of mist escape with each breath. The wrinkles on his forehead are like the wind-battered, sand-blasted sides of mountains, the mole on his cheek has grown, his lips are chapped, his eyebrows are flecked with moisture, the lines on his skin appear fluid as if affected by the pull of the moon, but his eyes remain bright and lively. He looks different, like something that had been there is missing, or something that should not be there is present; Ma cannot tell which. Each beat of his heart is echoed by a mechanical tone of the monitor and accompanied by a spike in the colored line. They draw the privacy curtain.

How are you doing, Old Man?

He nods, an affirmative nod that could mean anything.

It's been four years, Ma says.

He starts to speak, but his words are muddled. She recognizes the sound of his voice now, free of distortion over international wires, the voice whose gentle warnings and wise advice and poetic proverbs she had defied, the voice that had once asked what she was doing out so late and she had replied that she was watching someone on the street corner make a pair of pants from scratch, the voice that had offered to pay for the wedding and the furniture and the motorcycle and had asked, Is there any reason to go so far? You'll be there alone, and if things don't go well, you've no family to turn to. Is there any reason to go so far?

Say hello to your grandfather, Ma tells May.

May looks at him and looks away. She does not know what to say or when to say it or what to do or when to do it.

Say hello to your grandfather.

Hello.

Look at those plump cheeks and bright eyes. I bet that hypnotic smile of yours makes your mother think that all her hard work is worth it. He turns to my mother and says, In some ways, she looks just like her brother, but in other ways, totally unlike him.

Ma nods, remembering his voice that had once asked, Do you need to go all the way there?

In her mind now, the answer is clear. I don't need to go, I don't really want to go, but I have to go, I have to go, she had said.

The Old Man had replied, I want you to think hard about it. I don't want someone else making your decision. If it's for the sake of your son, know that there are schools here and there are futures here. Consider what you're giving up...I'm biased of course, I want you to stay, I want my daughters close by me, but I know that's not realistic...I won't stop you from going, no, but I want you to understand what it means to leave and whether or not you're ready for such solitude.

She could have stayed—she knows that now, but it did not feel that way back then. Now it is useless knowledge; it only leads to more regret.

You don't have to do this. It may seem that way but that's not true. You don't have to go. There is nothing there for you except schooling for your son, and though that may be enough of a reason, I don't think you'll be happy, the Old Man had said.

I will be, I will, Old Man—don't you worry, Ma remembers herself saying.

My concern is not him, not the boy, the Old Man had said. He'll be fine, he'll speak the language and talk circles around you, he'll adapt to the food and make American friends, he'll listen to American music and watch American television and read American books, he'll grow up and think you're too traditional in your ways, he'll lament that you're too old-fashioned, he'll find himself an American girlfriend, so it's not him that I worry about, no, it's you...you've been home your whole life, you're set in your ways, and like me, you're stubborn...you won't let old habits die, you value family perhaps too much, and now you're flying across the world with a man whose commitment to family is questionable...

Why are you so quiet? Aren't you happy to see me? What are you thinking about? the Old Man asks suddenly.

Ma is thinking about the day when we all stood on the platform with our luggage and how Grandfather did not utter a single word. They're going to step all over you, Aunt had said. What are you going all the way there for? It's not because of your husband, that's for sure—even a halfwit can see there's no love between you two. You were a little skeptical before the marriage, and that was five years ago. Five whole years, and nothing has changed. In fact, you're more skeptical now, so why follow him all the way there?

I can't back down now, Ma had said. His brother's gone through all the trouble to sponsor us over, and I've already agreed. If I back out now, what a mess that will make of things!

And Aunt had responded in a scolding tone, Stop right there! Again with the selfless thinking...it's not always good to put other people's interests before your own. There are times when you should listen to others, and then there are times when you should listen to your own heart. Ask yourself: Can you really be happy there? Can you?

* * *

How does the food compare? Shorty asked.

I said it was good, that it tasted just like the food Ma made at home.

That's good...and how's your mom doing?

She's okay.

Just okay?

I nodded.

How about your grandfather?

I don't know.

You don't know? You talk to your mom on the phone every night...doesn't she tell you about him?

I shook my head.

Your grandfather is ill, isn't he?

I nodded.

Illness is never a good thing, even a little of it. It was so sudden. How long has he been in the hospital?

I don't know, I said. I felt like I was being interrogated; the tone of the conversation did not feel like that of past

343

nights.

Don't say anything stupid, Ma had said. If they ask questions about our family, just say you don't know. I don't want them prying into our business. Don't answer them, but don't be rude. I don't want them to think that my son has no manners. If they ask about our family and you think they're prying into our private lives, just politely say you don't know. Make sure you keep eye contact and don't be shy...if you're shy, or if you look away or say your words sheepishly, they'll think you're hiding something or they'll think you know the answer but you're ashamed to say it, understand? (I had nodded.) I'd have you stay with someone else but I couldn't find anyone. So don't say anything stupid...they've no business getting into our affairs. They want to hear about our problems so they can go and tell their friends. I don't want to give them that privilege, do you understand? (I had nodded again.) She had been silent for a while before continuing, They're good for nothing but gossip and looking down on others...especially Ah San. If she comes over and starts asking you questions, just say: If you're so interested, why don't you ask my mom yourself? If they ask about Grandfather, say you don't know anything. You'll understand when you get older. Some people just like to see others suffer. They hide behind fake gestures, they snicker behind your back, and they're always rooting against you. That's why you need to prove them wrong, that's why you need to graduate at the top of your class and go to the best college and be successful at what you do so you can shove everything back into their faces. They'll have nothing to scoff at because you'll be better than all of them, you'll make them all envious one day.

It was so unexpected. I got a call from your mom and she told me that she needed to go back to China and asked if you could stay with us. I don't know how your mother puts up with so much. If you think about it, it's not fair. If you take all the suffering in the world and look at who gets what, you'd realize how unevenly it's distributed. Some people are born into rich families, and they never have to work a single day for anything, and then there are those who sacrifice everything and get nothing in return. Your mom is one of the nicest people I know. She has a tough exterior but she's soft inside...she really is a—

The door opened and Wei Jian walked in, shivering. You won't believe how cold it is outside! He put down his toolbox and took off his boots.

Shorty, having stopped mid-sentence, took a deep breath and coughed a gentle, palm-covered faux cough, abruptly ending the conversation.

* * *

I want to know the truth: How long have you been sick?

The Old Man does not answer. Instead he recites the names of all the pills the doctors have given him so far.

Why didn't you tell me earlier? Why didn't you tell me you were sick again?

The silence feels scripted.

How long have you been sick? Ma asks again.

I'm fine actually, I'm doing well.

No, you're not. How long have you been feeling so miserable?

Grandfather runs the tip of his tongue across his teeth, making a high-pitched sucking sound and says, The better question is: How long have *you* been feeling so miserable?

Tears begin to flow down Ma's cheeks. I don't know what to think anymore, she says. What does it matter? In the end, there's no difference between joy and misery.

345

Yes, that's what unhappy people think.

How would you know? Ma asks. Are you unhappy?

Another long silence that feels premeditated. May remains seated on a chair with a coloring book in her lap, sketching bloated airplanes with oversized wheels along the margins. The Old Man looks at his granddaughter and asks, Where did she get that scar?

Her careless father dropped the telephone on her forehead.

Grandfather lets out a good, long guffaw, a laugh of such force it makes him cough until he is purple in the face and a plug of phlegm the same color is propelled into his hand. Nurse! Bring me a new spittoon! Now, what was I saying? He thinks for a moment and asks, Wasn't it obvious that your marriage would never culminate to a point of mutual respect? Few things are truly irreconcilable, but you two...you two are beyond all hope.

Ma has no choice but to agree, and she does so by flattening her lips until they are almost colorless. A clap of thunder shakes the whole hospital, sending some patients into fits of hysteria: an old woman babbles about *fengshui* and the unfortunate placement of the windows, a young girl starts a mesmerizing dance, a pair of old men, war veterans, suddenly seize, their arms and legs stiffen and start jerking, one clamps his tongue between his teeth, the other wets himself and leaves a pool of urine on the floor that, by any standard, is too much for a single bladder to hold, no matter how much it is stretched, stroke patients in the neurology ward temporarily regain the ability to speak, babies in the neonatal ward howl like lone wolves, and patients on the psychiatric floor howl back. There is a typhoon outside. Rain is splashing against the windows. Aunt draws the curtains so as not to get distracted by the weather. The lights flicker. May is sitting on Ma's lap. Ma's thoughts are too vertiginous to comprehend; all of her questions are rhetorical and her regrets are infinite.

Go on, bring her closer, Grandfather says. I'm not contagious. Let me get a good look at my granddaughter. Let me hold her. You're heavy! It must be all that fresh cow milk.

May is fascinated by his oversized, line-ridden palms, rough and brown, and his stubby fingers crowned with deformed nails.

I can't believe it's been four years. It feels like I just left yesterday. I still remember waiting at the train station...Ma stops mid-sentence. Her throat is tense, her jaw clenches, and her neck strains as if she is trying to hold something back.

* * *

We were dismissed early the day the blizzard, in the span of hours, transformed the city into a primordial soup of zero visibility. With radar and color-coded legends, the newscasters had mapped out the storm but it arrived earlier than expected. Earth-grazing clouds dropped snowflakes the size of bottle caps, quail eggs, newborn fists, and unripe kumquats. The snowplows awoke from slumber and scurried like mechanical hounds over the streets, creating mounds that turned street-crossing into a hike. Trucks with rear-end propellers scattered sand and salt over the roads. It was all over the news: severe wintry conditions across the state, speed limits halved, and aerial shots of accidents that created massive jams.

On the way home from school, the fog was so thick it felt like we were breathing it in, tens of thousands of little droplets dampening the insides of our nostrils. Mei Lan, who had been quiet since the weekend, was walking swiftly ahead of me. I was tailing her and watching the snow swirl aimlessly at the mercy of the wind, the various up-drafts and down-currents that blended the flakes into furious flurries of indecision like bloated moths hovering around a porch lamp on a summer night. When we got to the crosswalk, I took a step into the street.

It's red! she snapped.

But the road's empty.

Rules are rules. If you want to get hit by a car, go right ahead.

As we waited for the light to turn green, I noticed an exposed grated gutter by the curb and began to kick snow down into it, watching the white flakes fall into the blackness, repeating the motion, faster and faster until my thigh burned...I wanted to shovel all the snow in the city down that gutter so that it would dissolve in the warm, flowing sewage and flush into the ocean where snow-water, sewage-water, and salt-water could not be distinguished from one another.

Mei Lan was already across the street when I looked up. I ran to catch her. Then I heard a faint voice in the distance calling my name. It was one of our classmates, bundled up like a large ball of laundry. Wait up! Wait up! he shouted, stumbling toward me, his galloping legs trying to support the forward lunge of his body but falling more behind with each step until he collapsed into the unmarred whiteness of a flowerbed. His boot laces were untied, the straps of his heavy schoolbag were unequal in length, and his orange knit hat fell off his head.

What a slob, Mei Lan muttered, turning away.

What are you doing here? Do you live here now? he asked.

I'm just staying with my cousin.

Mei Lan's your cousin?

I nodded.

Didn't know that...where does she live?

Over there, I said, pointing vaguely, not wanting to tell him exactly where because I knew Mei Lan would get upset if she found out.

I live over there, he pointed, reciting his address. You can come by anytime. We're having a snowball fight later this afternoon in our courtyard. All the kids in my building will be there. You should come.

Maybe.

I need to go home and change into my battle gear. I even have a face shield! He sprinted off, his backpack bouncing awkwardly on his shoulders, his hat left behind in the snow.

When I turned around, Mei Lan was gone. Though we walked the same path every day, I had passively followed her and paid no attention to the surroundings. Now, in the confusion of the snow, I could not recognize any of the streets. I suppressed the first wave of panic and called after her but there was no answer. I darted toward the next intersection, looking left and right, but the sidewalks were empty. I made out the names on the street signs but they did not seem familiar. I called out her name again, and again no answer. Instinct told me to go straight. Then I took a left because it felt right. I ran full speed, not caring if I were to fall or twist an ankle, and caught up to a hooded figure turning into a parking lot. Why did you leave me back there? I asked. In my mind, the words were condemning and full of anger, but they came out, lacking volume, lacking force, in between desperate breaths like a broken whimper.

I didn't know how long you were going to talk for. I wasn't going to wait forever.

She retrieved her keys and opened the door wide enough for herself to go through. I shot out my arm to prevent its closing. There was a strong gust of wind. I felt, for a brief instant, the force of the door against my fingers. My eyes closed in anticipation of disaster, but I was able to hold it open with my other hand. After I went inside, the door slammed shut and the walls shook with a shotgun explosion.

Did you just try to lock me out?

No, but I'm not here to hold doors for you either.

What are you so mad about?

I'm not mad.

I decided then that I would stay silent on the subject. She would hold onto her grudge until she decided it was time to let go. We shook the snow from the soles of our shoes and took them off before entering the living room. The wind seeped in through the windows and chilled the house to frigid temperatures. The cars in the parking lot huddled motionless like abandoned orphans. I reclined on the mattress, the ceiling a screen for the cinema of my mind: I imagined all the kids in town running in a vast field, hurling snowballs at each other, building fortresses, and laughing so hard that they cried and the tears froze on their cheeks...I saw them go home and sit by clicking radiators to warm frostbitten hands....

* * *

May is wearing a dress of white and pink flowers with stamens protruding like corncobs. We are waiting in line to get into the amusement park. With two tickets in hand, we enter through the turnstiles. The air is filled with the joyous screams of children and the continual pleading of their parents to leave for other engagements, but the children do not obey. They pretend not to hear, they focus on something else, and some even verbalize an adamant refusal.

350

Such lax discipline, I say to myself. Ma would've climbed over the fence and dragged me off the ride with her own two hands. She'd have straddled the train tracks at the end of the tunnel like a giant, and when the train passed through her legs, she'd have hunched over and plucked me up from the seat. Then she'd have smacked me on the cheeks for making her resort to a manner so physical in a place so public.

Is this the park you always think about? May asks.

Yes, I say. Are you thrilled?

I've never been here before.

That's why it's so exciting for you...it's your first time.

No, she disagrees. It's actually more exciting for you because you know what to expect and you've been waiting years with much anticipation to come back, whereas it's only my first time, so I've no expectations...not to mention you could just be excited over the memory of this place, and if you see it now for yourself again, you might wonder why you thought it so special in the first place...so, in essence, you are more prone to disappointment than I am.

Who taught you to say such things?

Nobody, some things are just intuitive.

The park is overflowing with people, and I lose her in the crowd. I stroll past the swinging dragon boat that, with the advance of technology, now spits fire from its nostrils. A wave of nausea overcomes me. A group of kids are strapped onto a wooden board suspended in midair near the tip of the dragon's flame. They gasp and giggle each time the flame approaches, they come down scorched red, giddy, asking to go again, but the man at the ticket counter allows only one go per child per day. I make my way to the anti-gravity bumper cars, the stiff cables sparking on the floor, the neon beetle cars running smoothly along the ceiling; the drivers are wearing safety helmets and shock-retardant suits in case they fall out. May is nowhere to be found. I shout for her but get no answer. I begin to run. There is no end to the crowds; the deeper I go, the more people there seem to be, all floating about like puppets controlled by celestial hands. I head to the holy house for help, the red-faced temple with doors open like a mocking mouth, its laughter tickling the surrounding trees until they shiver and shake off excess leaves. I grab a handful of incense and imagine that the sticks are lit; a thin wisp of smoke rises from their tips, the ends begin to glow, dully at first and then with intensity until a full-fledged flame is formed. I hold them up high and run through the temple to the giant urn where I plant the torch of incense into the ash. I fall on my knees to pray, to pray that my sister is safe and that I will soon find her.

Please let me find her, please, I will give anything to find her, I keep muttering, but it is useless. There are no answers, no signs; there is no change in the weather, no whispering voice, no guiding hand; there is no indication that the prayer has had any effect. I get up and walk out of the temple, now green-faced and echoing sobs of heartbreak like those heard at funerals and around deathbeds, cries that make everyone weep and draw butterflies to settle on their cheeks and lick up the salt of their tears.

I know where you can find your sister.

I spin around. Sitting on the ground is a shirtless old man with a bent back and black-rimmed glasses who is stroking his beard and drinking something out of a cup. His white pants are gray with dust, and his gray hair is white with age.

Where is she?

He takes a sip and smacks his lips.

At the sound of his delight, I forget about May. I

forget about the temple, now blue-faced and sleeping, its snores rumbling through the sky shaking loose sprinkles of rain from the clouds. I forget about Ma and Aunt, both at home chewing on sugar canes, grinding the stems into a mashed ball of fiber to be spat out. I forget about the park and all of its amusements. Can I have a sip of your drink?

He laughs a big thunderous laugh, a laugh brewed from the dark cavern of his soul, a place of such purity that no words and hence no distinctions exist. His gaunt chest flails; the notches of skin between his ribs, tight like that of a leather drum, pulsate in unison. He coughs and takes a big swig from his cup and holds it before me upside down, and I watch with anxiety as the last drop clinging to the rim of the cup falls to the ground with a hiss.

There you are! I've been looking all over for you.

I recognize the voice at once—it is my sister. She is tugging at my shirt with her left hand, an ice cream cone in her right.

Where did you get that? I ask.

Someone gave it to me, that lady right there.

I follow the imaginary line traced by her index finger and see Ah San in the distance who, upon seeing me, quickly averts her eyes and dives into a hedge. No! I scream, knocking the ice cream from her hand.

Why did you do that? she yells, punching me repeatedly in the stomach. Why? Why? Why?

Get a hold of yourself! It's poisoned. That was Jia Ming's mother, she's trying to kill you, she's an evil woman. Tell me the truth, the absolute truth: Did you eat any of it? Any at all? Even a lick? And don't you lie to me. Don't you dare lie like your bastard father!

May shakes her head.

We better go. I don't know what else that bitch is planning.

We follow the signs out of the park and find ourselves along Pearl River where farmers are harvesting watermelons, digging them out of the earth with trowels and piling them into pyramids between two magnolia trees.

A strange man has been following us since we left, May whispers into my ear.

I turn around and see the shirtless man from the temple.

Would you still like a drink? he asks.

He hands me the cup now filled to the brim. I let go of my sister and reach for it but neither of my arms will move. They remain motionless hanging from my shoulders; they feel heavy, almost foreign, as if they no longer belonged to me.

* * *

We drove out to pick up Jia Ming who was coming to stay for another weekend. Ah San had called Shorty and told her how much fun he had had and asked whether he could come by again. Shorty could not refuse. When we arrived back at the house, Mei Lan took Jia Ming into her room, closed the door, and said, I need to tell you some basic rules of the house.

What rules?

You can't do whatever you want here. You need to follow our rules.

You're no fun.

I'm serious. I purposely closed the door so we could have this talk in private.

Fine, I'll follow your dumb rules.

Do you promise?

Whatever.

First, you can't jump on the furniture in the house. I don't want anything to break—

What else? What else?

Second, you can't pull pranks on anyone, especially not my parents. Third, you have to—

He put his hand in front of her face and told her to shut up. I've heard enough, he said, and walked out of the room.

At dinner, Jia Ming was unusually well-mannered. He engaged Shorty in conversation, asked how she was doing, and gave sincere answers in response to her questions. He flashed Mei Lan looks that said he could put on a mask just as easily as she could. As if to reaffirm her superior behavior, she announced that she would start her homework right after dinner and get it all done before the weekend. She sat at her desk with a pencil in hand and a stack of workbooks. An eraser, a ruler, a portable pencil sharpener, and other gadgets were all laid out in a row for easy access. Jia Ming sprawled out on the bottom bunk with his legs propped up against the wall.

Mei Lan, do you remember how we had to make mobiles in the first grade for a project? Do you remember how your mobile got destroyed on the bus? That was so funny. You almost cried...no, wait, you did cry! Do you remember? Those boys were wrestling and they crashed into you and crushed all the paper cranes you had folded...and you said afterwards they had all flown up to heaven! Getting no response from her, he turned to me and began talking about his recent forays into mischief with escalating animation: how he kept a cockroach in an empty soda bottle and freed it onto his sleeping mother one afternoon and watched it crawl down her shirt, how he amassed a small fortune by stealing a few dollars from her wallet whenever she came back from shopping, and how he took her dirty underpants and brassieres from the laundry basket and swapped them out with clean ones

355

from her dresser.

When he left the room, Mei Lan asked me, Why do you encourage him?

What?

You laugh at all his stories so he keeps telling them. You have to ignore him. You're in my house so you need to obey the rules, too.

* * *

Where is my father? Why does he keep getting moved? Aunt asks the nurse who is replacing all the bedpans, some heaped high with feces.

Don't talk to me in such a chastising tone. It's not my decision to move him. I didn't want him moved because now I have to walk up five flights of stairs every time he rings his bell, which is quite often, usually asking for a cigarette—

No need to tell us your life story, just tell us where he is.

Before I do that, you need to sign these papers. She puts down the bedpans, putrid and swarming with flies, and pulls out a thick, stapled packet from her pocket. Sign on all the lines.

What for?

I will explain this only once, so listen carefully. This paragraph states that you're here to visit one designated patient, that you will not visit anyone else, not because you're not allowed to but because you have no such intention. This paragraph says you have not brought anything from home such as flowers or soup for fear of contamination. This paragraph says you have read the above two paragraphs and that you understand what they generally say but that you're not expected to understand all the nuances of the wording or the circumstances in which those statements do not apply. The next paragraph states that you're financially responsible for breaking any medical equipment in the room including those for decorative purposes. The next three paragraphs summarize the visitor policy—that is, the hours, frequency, attire, noise level, conduct, and the need to show respect toward all medical staff. The last paragraph says that I have personally reviewed all these terms with you. Finally, the addendum states that the hospital is not responsible for any diseases that you may contract while on its premises.

We've never had to sign anything like this before.

Your father has been moved to a different floor which entails more paperwork for us so, by definition, more paperwork for you as well. Let me also tell you that the addendum was put there by our lawyers in case you get ill, which is unlikely, statistically speaking, because that's happened to only one person since this hospital was built, but as you already know, statistics are just numbers that can be changed with an eraser or a backspace key or using multiplication instead of addition.

This is preposterous. Who's ever heard of such nonsense?

The nurse leans over and whispers, It's not polite to badmouth the institution that's taking care of your father. Now, follow me.

After wandering through labyrinthine hallways and staircases, they arrive at the same ward in a different place, or maybe it is a different ward in the same place. The Old Man is in bed, his hands gripping the guardrails as he heaves and heaves, trying to expel a clump of bloody phlegm rooted in his lungs with snakelike tendrils.

Are you okay? The concern in Ma's voice is not apparent, but it is certainly there. One look at her face would convince any doubter of any degree.

He is fatigued. The muscles in his neck are taut, his

nostrils flare, and the skin over his chest retracts into the grooves of his ribs with each breath. Ma throws her arms around his shoulders while Aunt violently beats his back trying to hasten his expectorations.

* * *

Get whatever you want because the next meal won't be until dinner. If you want any specific kind of dim sum, just wave it down, Shorty said. This is your last weekend with us. Your mom will be back in a few days...are you excited to see her again?

I nodded.

You don't look too excited if you ask me. Staying with us is fun, isn't it? Wei Jian said.

I nodded again.

It's more carefree at our house, isn't it? When your mom comes back, tell her you want to live with us instead, tell her you like us better and see what she says.

Don't kid around with him like that, said Shorty. What if he doesn't understand? She turned to me and continued, Don't listen to him, he's just fooling with you.

I know, I replied.

You never know, said Shorty. Kids sometimes take the silliest things seriously, and the serious things they ignore. We're very strict with Mei Lan. Good parents need to make sure their children make the most of everything and let no opportunities slip by...

I watched Jia Ming move the small dish of chili oil closer to him. He winked at me and touched his index finger to his puckered lips.

...if you kids don't take full advantage, it'd be a waste. When we were growing up, we were rushed through primary school with fake test scores so we could go labor out in the countryside...

Jia Ming had moved the saucer of chili oil behind his

plate and hid it from view. He winked at me again, a smirk on his face, the face of the joker, the goal of whose actions was laughter at any expense. A waitress circled past. Wei Jian waved her down for two plates of tripe. Jia Ming took advantage of the opportune timing.

...remember to impress your teachers so the school knows who its star pupils are. I'm so envious of you guys. Think about it. The three of you are better off than millions of kids in China. When you look at it that way, you know you can't slack off and be lazy.

I shifted my gaze onto Shorty and nodded along with feigned interest. Mei Lan stared dreamily at her mother, mesmerized by her speech about the promise of education.

AHRECGHK! AHERHK! AHHKARRGH!

Jia Ming immediately hunched under the table and pretended to tie his shoes; his arched back shook with spasms of laughter.

What's the matter? Mei Lan asked, rushing over to her brother.

His face was scrunched up and flushed red. One look at him and I felt like I would lose all composure. Mei Lan frantically patted and rubbed his back, Are you all right?

He continued to cough and gag; a layer of perspiration beaded on his nose. He started to cry, alternating between fits of hacking and sobbing, and was seized with another coughing spell that left a puddle of half-digested dim sum and stomach acid seeping through the tablecloth. When he finally calmed down, still wet-eyed, he said, The tea is spicy!

All eyes fell on Jia Ming.

How could you do this?! Shorty screamed.

It's okay. Wei Jian extended his hand. We're in public—

No, it's *not* okay. Jia Ming, what did you do?

I didn't do anything, Jia Ming said.

Then why were you hiding under the table? You're always up to mischief...I don't even know why I thought it was a good idea for you to stay with us.

Do you really feel that way? I thought you liked me, Jia Ming replied, pretending to be hurt by her comment.

Just let it go, people are watching, said Wei Jian.

Two busboys came by and offered to clean up the table. No need, Shorty said, and handed them the card. Get someone to tally it up, we're done here.

But I'm still hungry. I didn't eat enough. How can you starve me like this?

We're not starving you! shouted Mei Lan in defense.

Then we should get more food, I'm still very hungry.

It's time to go, said Wei Jian.

We donned our coats and hats and left the restaurant. The argument continued outside.

How could you do that to my brother?

What are you talking about?

You know what you did.

Don't accuse me like your mom. Nobody witnessed anything.

I know how you are, I know you love pranks...and you're an even worse person if you can't admit to it.

We got into the car and drove back in silence. When we got to the apartment, Jia Ming started to pack his things at Shorty's request. Wei Jian took his wife into the bedroom to talk behind a closed door. He's just a boy. We'll surely antagonize Ah San if we send him back now.

Out in the living room, Mei Lan said, I know you were responsible, just admit it.

You're a stupid girl.

Don't call me stupid!

But you *are* stupid, that's a fact.

360

Stop staying that!

Your parents are stupid, too. Your house is an asylum, and you're all a bunch of retards.

Mei Lan began to cry. Against the erratic rhythm of her sobs, I thought about the long way we had come, about how different we all turned out since that first day of arrival when we flushed bits of packing foam down a gurgling toilet.

* * *

Did I ever tell you how I felt when you left? Do you remember the watermelon man by Pearl River? Probably not, you were too young. He died after a heart attack. He used to sell watermelons by the dock. It was a popular place for boys to congregate. On hot days, we'd jump into the river for a swim—the water was so dirty you were sure to get an ear infection or a bout of diarrhea, and that irritated our parents to no end. There was nothing more refreshing after a swim than a cut of sweet watermelon; there was nothing special about his watermelons except that they were always what you wanted...I can still recall those bites bursting with warm juices that would run down our cheeks and drip onto our toes and make our elbows sticky. Then one day, he wasn't there anymore; he was gone. We didn't show it then, but each of us grieved for him. Our throats were parched, and we dreamt of watermelon—not just any watermelon, but his in particular...that cavernous craving, that was what I felt when you left...

...your son loved cola...I still remember I used to take him to the vendor under the red parasol. I'd lead him by the hand, and we'd buy two. Sometimes the man was smoking a cigarette or playing poker with his buddies, but whenever he saw us, he would slide open the fridge, dig his hands into the ice, and pull out two bottles. He'd crack off the caps, and we'd always drink it right then and there. The fizz stung our tongues and quenched our thirst more than the freshest, purest water in the world. He loved it, that sugary elixir, and he was fascinated with the bottle—more often than not, it was old and scratched up, parts of the glass were faded or smudged, but that didn't matter—he was fascinated by it, the feel of it, the look of it...I could tell he wanted to keep the bottles, so I explained to him that they get shipped back to the factory to be reused. Wouldn't it be nice if life was like that? If whenever you ran out of something that brought you so much joy, you could just send it back in a crate and have it refilled?...

...do you remember breakfast from the congee stand? I'd wait in line to fill up my canteen and bring it home and pour out equal portions. When you woke up, you'd sit at the table and take in deep breaths, savoring the smell of fried dough. You loved that fried dough so much I always bought an extra stick even though it made your throat sore. It is the most delicious breakfast in the world, you used to say. You said you'd never trade anything for it, and sometimes on rainy days, the stand would be closed. During the typhoon season when the streets were flooded, you'd wake up expecting that familiar aromatic greeting, but all you could smell was the rain. Sometimes you'd tell me on those rainy days you wanted the congee so much, your yearning was so deep that you could feel pangs in your heart, sharp pains the exact path of which you could trace. After you left, it was like that for me...

...I remember bringing him apples in the summers when the tropical winds rolled in from the balcony and moistened the wallpaper until it was nearly peeling off. I'm no braggart, but I was unmatched at mahjong. I could've played competitively, but I wanted to keep it a pastime.

362

Every time you're close to winning, there's a rush you feel; your sweat smells a little different, your heart beats a little different...whenever it came time to draw for a win, I would rub my thumb on the tile, and I could always tell what it was by touch without looking at it. Every once in a while, maybe one in a thousand draws, I'd make a mistake. I would need a certain tile to win, and I'd actually trick myself into thinking that I had drawn it. Then when I'd look at the tile and realize that my sense of touch, clouded by desire, had misled me, that I had in reality drawn a different tile, I'd be overtaken by disappointment. That rare discrepancy between sight and touch was like a glitch on a record etched with a timeless tune—after you left, everything I touched was different than what I saw...I still felt as if you were around but my eyes refused to tell the lie I was telling myself...

...I'm sure you know how irrational children can be...it's their irrationality that makes them immune to the burdens of life for they always desire what is not possible, they dream and wish with a persistence that adults would deem foolish, and they transport themselves to imaginary worlds for hours, days, months, sometimes years. I was brought to such a state when you left...I'd walk through the market for fruits and vegetables, I'd watch the fishermen display their daily catch on beds of ice, I'd pick out meats hanging from hooks at the butcher shop, and I'd mentally concoct recipes for soups depending on what the freshest ingredients were. Surely you remember that one time I made soup with snake and you didn't want to drink it because you thought it might be poisonous. Every time I passed the snakes at the market, I'd think about that. I'd come home and put all my groceries on the kitchen counter and realize I'd purchased one serving more of everything. I'd sit with your sister at the dinner table and she'd say to me, The food's getting cold, why aren't we eating yet? Then I'd say, We're waiting for...and I'd catch myself before finishing the sentence...

...there was no deity more fitting than Guan Yu to look over my grandson; he is the ultimate symbol of honor, and he could vanquish anything with his *guandao*. You were right to choose him. The boy got sick so frequently no one could fault you for turning to religion. I knew when you brewed those herbal broths for him because he'd show me the welts on his butt. That medicine tastes like shit, like a fresh feculent mound dropped by a squatting vagrant—you think I'm exaggerating, but I'm not. Have you thought about the mental trauma you've inflicted with those beatings? He'll remember them for the rest of his life, he'll associate sickness with bitter brews being forced down his throat, but maybe, I suppose, he'll come to understand suffering at a young age and know what it feels like to have something forced upon him, something that is ultimately good for him but forced upon him nonetheless. You had to leave us. There was really no other choice—there's no doubt about that—but the pain you caused...it felt like my ass was being perpetually whipped with the wooden end of a feathered duster...

...was it true, or did I dream it and assign it truth? Your husband brought home a white rabbit in a cardboard box—white as the sun behind a cloud on a clear afternoon, white as untrammeled snow—and the boy was elated. He thought it was a new pet and was allowed to feed it bok choy. What kind of a father does that to his son when he knows he's going to kill it? My grandson described to me how it nibbled away at bok choy leaves with its little incisors. There was such unrestrained excitement in his voice. Then one day, it was gone; the cardboard box was empty. What did you do? he screamed. His father said, I gave it a bath. But your son understood; he knew that it meant a bath in boiling water. So you mean it's dead? Why did you do that? Why would you do that? Why?! His father sat at the table picking the meat out of his teeth, and said, That's how life is, it starts and it ends...you can't change that. Where am I going with this story? What emotion am I trying to wrench out of you? I don't know...I don't know anything anymore...

...I was in the kitchen making noodles. The smell of broth filled the house, the kind of smell that clung to clothes and stuck to hair. I worked so meticulously, I cooked everything to perfection, I timed everything so that when you got back, the temperature would be just right. Your sister and I sat around and waited, watching clumps of steam rise to the ceiling. Do you remember what happened? You were out with friends, and you came home very late. It was the only time you'd ever done such a thing and the only time I'd ever gotten so angry. When you walked in, I asked where you'd been, and you thought I was trying to pry into your personal life. You had such a temper then. You said you'd already eaten and that you didn't want the food I'd made—just to annoy me—so I picked up the bowl and turned it upside down over your head. You got drenched in broth and you wore those noodles like a wig. It was irrational, I know, but I was so upset. They say that all things equal out in the end. When you left, it felt like someone flipped the world over my head and I had to bear all of its weight. Why are you smirking? Do you think I'm talking like a fool? Like a movie star? Do you think my absurd metaphor is an exaggeration crafted to tug at your heartstrings?...

...do you know what I have? I have his book of poems, the book of four hundred verses that you made him memorize. I swiped it from your house, and now it's on a shelf in my bedroom. I let no one touch it. The pages are yellowed, almost brittle, and I'm sure there's mold growing on the back cover slowly eating away at the binding, but I don't care. Whenever I look at it, I'm reminded of how he chose the calligraphy brush on his first birthday. Despite how much modern folk like to ridicule our traditions, they hold some iota of truth. He's a smart boy and he's got a bright future—I knew then, and I know now that the decision to leave had to be made, it was the right choice. What I've left are memories, memories of him memorizing poetry, especially *Jing Ye Si*. He used to recite it without understanding what it meant. I could tell he loved the rhythm of its words and the musical beat of its four simple lines. Poetry appeals to our inherent desire for order and predictability...but predictability can be quite unsettling. I knew you'd leave. On the night of your wedding, I had predicted that you'd leave. I knew...and much like a poet seeking truth and beauty, nothing could have altered your course...

...I also have the first dress you made. I never told you, but I kept it all along. I still remember how you came home one day and asked me for money to buy a sheet of gray fabric patterned with lime green flowers. Your sister did the measurements, and you traced out all the different parts with blue chalk and cut them out and sewed them together. It was so beautiful and so simple—it was better than anything you could buy in a store. Then you wore it one night and came back crying because one of your friends had spilled something on it. No matter how hard you scrubbed, you couldn't wash off the stain. I kept telling you it was fine, that clothes were meant to be worn, but you wouldn't listen. You were so upset you refused to eat for a whole week. I got so angry I wanted to hit you for making such a big deal out of nothing. I told you the stain wasn't noticeable and that you were smart in choosing a dark fabric. Then one day, you balled it up and threw it away. I picked it out of the trash...it's in my closet now...on the day you left...I wanted to...I wanted...I...

Grandfather's sentences become more fragmented; his voice becomes weaker until he is no longer speaking.

What? Finish your story!

The Old Man does not respond.

What are you trying to say? Ma's voice becomes desperate, almost pleading. She looks at him, and he is looking straight ahead, looking right through her with a piercing stare.

There is a sound like the bellow of an animal rising from the cavern of his lungs.

Ma answers with a wail of her own, scaling octaves before the fade.

The nurse runs in with an oxygen mask as the entire wall of the hospital disappears. They are exposed to the clouds, the birds, the sun, the trees, and the sky. The alarm of a truck in reverse is heard; its rear door is lifted. Plug it in! Plug it in! yells the driver. The nurse pushes the crates aside, spilling the cargo of bananas, and uncovers a small hole into which she attaches the plastic tubing of the nasal cannula. It is not oxygen that comes out but strawberry-flavored anesthetic gases. The Old Man struggles in vain to keep his eyes open. In one concentrated effort, his eyelids flare open with the vitality of a rushing mountain river; he looks at his two daughters and his granddaughter one last time before the anchors of slumber drag his eyelids back down.

Old Man, take care of yourself wherever you're going, Ma says.

They unplug all the wires from the monitors; the cords are left dangling with rounded stickers on their ends stuck with stray chest hairs. Upon loss of contact with his skin, the spikes slump over and fall amorphously on top of one another; the rhythm degenerates, and the representation of beats, no longer registered, collapse into exhausted piles. Grandfather is driven away, sleeping soundly, snoring lightly, cushioned on a bed of ripe bananas. Ma asks where he is being driven to, but there is no answer. She is the only one left.

There is a silence that consumes the moment and condenses the tragedies of the world into a solitary room. Tears quench her desert-dry face cracked with rifts that run immeasurably deep down into the very heart of regret, a place of discarded prayers for what could have been but simply is not. It is unfathomable, the primal silence that bears our eternal fears and submerges us, heads bowed, into the void.

10

ON THE LAST DAY of my stay, Mei Lan avoided eye contact and maintained a physical distance from me. After my things were packed, she gathered up the sheets I had slept on and threw them into the laundry basket with an assertive force. She tried to move the mattress out of her room by herself and, realizing that it was too heavy, asked for help from her mother, who told her to wait until her father got back home. We went downstairs to the car, Shorty turned the key to switch on the ignition with a purring rumble, a step on the gas pedal led to a brief immobile spinning of the wheels over a patch of thick ice, and then onto the street we turned, the hood dipping slightly over the inclined curb. For the next forty minutes, we navigated through the lunging-halting mass of rush-hour traffic. The sky darkened as the incandescent hues of the half-submerged sun dispersed and the facades of skyscrapers glittered with the mirrored myriad of star-crested waves.

We burrowed into the tunnel where ceiling lights reeled past like a detached neon line, a barred-off crowd of construction men were working on some leaking pipes, and two police cars had stopped on the side with another vehicle, the hazard lights of which were blinking. Shorty stared intently at the road ahead and kept the car within the boundaries of the lane with her gloved hands gripping the steering wheel. The pressure of her foot on the gas pedal varied inversely with the degree of traffic congestion.

Be sure to tell your mom how much fun you had. You can always come and stay with us.

Ba, having taken off from work early, was waiting for me behind the main doors of our apartment building. He came out when the car pulled up and took my bags out from the trunk. Shorty greeted Ba and repeated her invitation for me to stay with them anytime. When we got upstairs, Ba went into the kitchen and started to prepare dinner. During the meal, he was unusually talkative. I heard Jia Ming was also there on the weekends, so you must've had a lot of company, he said. But it's good to be back home, isn't it? He then asked if I had fun at Mei Lan's house, whether I enjoyed the food they made, whether I watched a lot of television, he asked about my schoolwork and grades and upcoming tests, and he asked if I was having any problems in class and if I had made any new friends. I responded to all of his questions with a simple nod or shake of the head.

After dinner, we took the subway to the airport and waited for Ma at baggage claim. I felt like I could hear the planes landing, the whir of their propellers, the seismic contact of their wheels on the runway, the jolt to wake all who had slept through the descent, the creaky deployment of flaps and slats, and the rumble of shifting luggage. Passengers exhibited hugs, handshakes, and kisses, those comforting signs of reunion, and swarmed around the conveyor belt waiting for their belongings. I spotted Ma in the crowd. She flashed a big smile, came up to me, and rubbed her hand vigorously through my hair. She was thinner, much thinner, her hair was noticeably longer, down to her shoulders, and her clothes smelled as if they were being worn for the first time. She was holding May's hand. I felt a sudden joy at seeing my sister again and touched the tip of her nose with the tip of my index finger. May let go of Ma's hand and gave me a big hug.

How was the flight? Ba asked.

She ignored him; she did not even look at him. She kept her eyes on me and asked, Was everything okay at Mei Lan's?

I nodded.

Were you respectful and polite?

I nodded again.

The luggage circled about, having slid down the chute onto the conveyor belt. We were on the lookout for her bags, one black suitcase and two red-blue-white plastic-woven bags, durable and spacious, overstuffed with clothes she had purchased, the handles tied with a white cloth upon which was written in permanent marker her name and home address and telephone number. They tumbled out together like fat, limbless slobs. I'll get it, let me get it, said Ba, but she stepped forward and yanked them off the belt onto a cart by herself. We headed outside for a cab home, May's hand in mine, Ba trailing several steps behind.

What did you buy? I asked.

A lot of clothes, she said. Shirts and sweaters and pants and socks and underwear—everything is so cheap in China.

When the automatic doors parted, we were greeted by a rush of chilling wind. Ma shivered and said, I forgot how cold it gets here.

Do you want my jacket? Ba asked.

She ignored him again. She turned to me and asked, Do you remember our old house?

Of course, I said. Did you go back to see it? Who's living there now?

No one. Your aunt and I passed by our old street

many times. It's completely fenced off now. You can't walk onto it. They're going to do some major construction there. Do you remember how all the people used to sit by their front doors in the summer fanning themselves? That whole area is walled off now. They're going to knock everything down and build new apartments...to think it's been only four years, can you believe it?

What about the family beneath us? Where are they now?

I don't know.

We waited in the taxi queue while Ma told me all about her trip, about the disappearance of familiar streets and the appearance of new ones, about the new skyscrapers being built on the other side of Pearl River, about the amusement parks that still operated, about the cola and congee stands....

Where to? asked the driver.

I gave him our address. He tapped some buttons on the meter, and with an aggressive compression of the gas pedal, we were off, weaving in and out of lanes on the roads beneath the colossal strips of elevated highways, their undersides illuminated by yellow lights revealing the complex crisscrossing lattice of steel beams dripping with melting snow. After some more twists and turns, we passed through a tollbooth and began our ascent onto the motorway. Ma was telling me what she and May did back in China, all the places she took her to visit and how each of those places had changed or stayed the same. She said she forgot how smoggy the air was, how fresh the food was, how sweet the fruits tasted, how beautiful the dresses looked, how many shopping centers there were, how professional the newscasters sounded, how hectic it was to navigate through the city, how many hilarious sitcoms were on television each night, how many famous singers gave performances on the weekends....She told me how much Aunt and Grandfather had missed us, and then all of a sudden, she stopped talking; the flow of her words ceased as if a heavy gate had come down to bar their expression.

Stagnant wisps of cloud floated like plucked fibers of a cosmic cotton in the staggeringly immense sky...to think Ma was just up there, that we were all up there at some point, in a metallic cylinder with wings....

The cabbie fumbled with the radio dial and settled on a station where a man delivered broken rhymes to a thumping beat on repeat.

How's Grandfather doing? I asked.

He's doing well...you don't need to worry about him...he'll be all right, she answered.

Distorted bright circles and shiny surfaces rushed past us, an ever-moving, ever-glittering collage of sparks and starbursts in a grand hypnotic dance accompanied by impatient horns blaring like discordant jazz. It was night, the sun had set, the day had ended, and this hour, this moment, was no different than any other that could be spent listening to a teacher, running in a playground, lying sick in an infirmary, crying for home, or lost in the dream of a luxurious future.

Ma remained quiet, but for how long, I did not remember. She spoke no more of old memories. We all sat in the car heading into the heart of the city toward the speckled assortment of lighted windows, a pointillist mural of neon pixels, tiny gems studded in earthbound structures soaring skyward, the collective glow of which drowned out distant stars. We sped toward the glimmer of manmade fires, toward our stars within reach and tangible, hundreds of thousands of electrified rectangles that defied the impenetrable blackness of night.

Tears welled up in Ma's eyes. May was asleep. Ba was in the passenger seat, his face out of view. And I—I was there. We were all there, the four of us, being driven by a stranger bobbing his head to music, unaware that he was retracing for us the same route of our very first arrival when we were one of three families traveling, having just left a country of rampant poverty for one with unheard-of abundance, one of three families that could never have foreseen how far apart they would drift in so short a time...when Ba was awestruck by the reality of arrival and thought back to the night before the flight when he could neither sleep nor stop smiling, enamored by the glamour of the West...when Ma reflected with a tender sadness on the selling of their furniture and the motorcycle and the cat, wondered why his suit was nowhere to be found, and realized that what the Old Man felt standing on the platform at the station and what she felt looking at him through the window as the train lurched ahead were one and the same...when I was breath-taken by the initial shimmer of urban immensity and futilely wished for the privilege of the window seat...

...here we were again, four years later, cruising along the same road into the slumbering metropolis, beckoned still by the silent promise of transoceanic lights....

S. Li was born in Guangzhou, China in 1984 and moved to the US in 1989. He graduated with an A.B. from Harvard in 2006, and an M.D. from the University of Massachusetts in 2010. He lives near Boston with his Pembroke Welsh Corgi. This is his debut novel.

More books from Harvard Square Editions

People and Peppers, Kelvin Christopher James
Dark Lady of Hollywood, Diane Haithman
Gates of Eden, Charles Degelman
Living Treasures, Yang Huang
Close, Erika Raskin
Anomie, Jeff Lockwood
Nature's Confession, J.L. Morin
Love's Affliction, Dr. Fidelis O. Mkparu
Fugue for the Right Hand, Michele Tolela Myers
A Little Something, Richard Haddaway
Growing Up White, James P. Stobaugh
Calling the Dead, R.K. Marfurt
Parallel, Sharon Erby

CPSIA information can be obtained
at www.ICGtesting.com
Printed in the USA
LVOW13s1131260217
525458LV00010B/779/P